DEPARTMENT OF PUBLIC INFORMATION

The United Nations Today

United Nations
New York, 2008

Preamble to the Charter of the United Nations

We the peoples of the United Nations
  determined

> *to save succeeding generations from the scourge of war,*
> *which twice in our lifetime has brought untold sorrow*
> *to mankind, and*

> *to reaffirm faith in fundamental human rights,*
> *in the dignity and worth of the human person,*
> *in the equal rights of men and women*
> *and of nations large and small, and*

> *to establish conditions under which justice and respect*
> *for the obligations arising from treaties and other*
> *sources of international law can be maintained,*

> *and to promote social progress and better standards*
> *of life in larger freedom,*

and for these ends

> *to practice tolerance and live together in peace*
> *with one another as good neighbours, and*

> *to unite our strength to maintain international*
> *peace and security, and*

> *to ensure, by the acceptance of principles and the*
> *institution of methods, that armed force shall*
> *not be used, save in the common interest,*

> *and to employ international machinery for the promotion*
> *of the economic and social advancement of all peoples,*

have resolved to combine our efforts
to accomplish these aims.

Accordingly, our respective Governments ...
have agreed to the present
Charter of the United Nations
and do hereby establish an international
organization to be known as
the United Nations

CONTENTS

PART THREE

Boxes

Charts and maps

United Nations Specialized Agencies:

Food and Agriculture Organization of the United Nations (FAO): *www.fao.org*

International Civil Aviation Organization (ICAO): *www.icao.org*

International Fund for Agricultural Development (IFAD): *www.ifad.org*

International Labour Organization (ILO): *www.ilo.org*

International Maritime Organization (IMO): *www.imo.org*

International Monetary Fund (IMF): *www.imf.org*

International Telecommunication Union (ITU): *www.itu.int*

United Nations Educational, Scientific and Cultural Organization (UNESCO): *www.unesco.org*

United Nations Industrial Development Organization (UNIDO): *www.unido.org*

Universal Postal Union (UPU): *www.upu.int*

The World Bank Group: *www.worldbank.org*

World Health Organization (WHO): *www.who.int*

World Intellectual Property Organization (WIPO): *www.wipo.int*

World Meteorological Organization (WMO): *www.wmo.ch*

World Tourism Organization (UNWTO): *www.world-tourism.org*

Related Organizations:

International Atomic Energy Agency (IAEA): *www.iaea.org*

Organization for the Prohibition of Chemical Weapons (OPCW): *www.opcw.org*

Preparatory Committee for the Nuclear-Test-Ban Treaty Organization (CTBTO): *www.ctbto.org*

World Trade Organization (WTO): *www.wto.org*

IMO	International Maritime Organization
ITC	International Trade Centre UNCTAD/WTO
ITU	International Telecommunication Union
MIGA	Multilateral Investment Guarantee Agency (World Bank Group)
NGLS	United Nations Non-Governmental Liaison Service
NGOs	Non-Governmental Organizations
OCHA	Office for the Coordination of Humanitarian Affairs
OHCHR	Office of the United Nations High Commissioner for Human Rights
OIOS	Office of Internal Oversight Services
OLA	Office of Legal Affairs
OPCW	Organization for the Prohibition of Chemical Weapons
PFII	Permanent Forum on Indigenous
UNAIDS	Joint United Nations Programme on HIV/AIDS
UNCTAD	United Nations Conference on Trade and Development
UNDP	United Nations Development Programme
UNEP	United Nations Environment Programme
UNESCO	United Nations Educational, Scientific and Cultural Organization
UNFIP	United Nations Fund for International Partnerships
UNFPA	United Nations Population Fund
UN-HABITAT	United Nations Human Settlements Programme
UNHCR	Office of the United Nations High Commissioner for Refugees
UNICEF	United Nations Children's Fund
UNICRI	United Nations Interregional Crime and Justice Research Institute
UNIDIR	United Nations Institute for Disarmament Research
UNIDO	United Nations Industrial Development Organization
UNIFEM	United Nations Development Fund for women
UN-INSTRAW	International Research and Training Institute for the Advancement of Women
UNITAR	United Nations Institute for Training and Research
UNMOVIC	United Nations Monitoring, Verification and Inspection Commission
UNODA	Office for Disarmament Affairs
UNODC	United Nations Office on Drugs and Crime
UNOG	United Nations Office at Geneva

FOREWORD

The world is changing in the United Nations favour, as more people and governments understand that multilateralism is the only path in our interdependent and globalizing world. The United Nations advocates values that are the cornerstone of this emerging era: freedom, justice and the peaceful resolution of disputes; better standards of living; equality and tolerance and human rights. Globalization can work only if these values are paramount.

In fact, a world of complex and global challenges is exactly the environment in which the United Nations should thrive, because these are challenges that no country can resolve on its own. Terrorism and organized crime transcend state borders. Diseases such as AIDS are spreading globally, destroying human lives and disrupting economic activities. Climate change and environmental degradation pose major challenges and not only to future generations. Inequality and poverty can lead to instability and conflict that can quickly engulf entire regions.

The UN is the only Organization that has the worldwide membership, the global reach and universal legitimacy needed to successfully address these trends. The UN stage enables political leaders to reach out to one another in ways they may be unwilling or unable to otherwise. The UN's impartiality allows it to negotiate and operate in some of the toughest places in the world. When a disaster strikes, like the tsunami in south-east Asia, our workers are already on the ground ready to respond. And more than 100,000 UN peacekeepers on four continents perform their duties more effectively and with far less money than what any government can do on its own.

Today, the United Nations is doing more to translate its ideals into real, measurable change than ever before. That is why, as the world looks to the United Nations for solutions, we must, in turn, find new and better ways of working. We must find ways to deliver more fully on our promises. We must be open to new approaches and ideas, and have the courage to question our traditional way of doing things. And, above all, we must get ordinary people everywhere to trust our Organization, and to become more engaged in its work.

The United Nations Today seeks to promote understanding of the UN's worldwide activities, and it invites you, the reader, to participate in them. It is meant as a concise yet invaluable reference tool for the seasoned diplomat as well as the interested lay-person. It is designed to demystify the many acronyms that populate the UN system, and to associate them with the daily work performed by UN agencies and entities. It seeks to describe reforms to the Organization, from changes to our peacekeeping operations to rethinking our human rights machinery, while also supplying insights into the forces driving these changes.

THE UNITED NATIONS ORGANIZATION

The name "United Nations", coined by United States President Franklin D. Roosevelt, was first used in the "Declaration by United Nations" of 1 January 1942, during the Second World War, when representatives of 26 nations pledged their governments to continue fighting together against the Axis powers.

States first established international organizations to cooperate on specific matters. The International Telecommunication Union was founded in 1865 as the International Telegraph Union, and the Universal Postal Union was established in 1874. Both are now United Nations specialized agencies.

In 1899, the first International Peace Conference was held in The Hague to elaborate instruments for settling crises peacefully, preventing wars and codifying rules of warfare. It adopted the Convention for the Pacific Settlement of International Disputes and established the Permanent Court of Arbitration, which began work in 1902.

The forerunner of the United Nations was the League of Nations, an organization conceived in similar circumstances during the First World War, and established in 1919 under the Treaty of Versailles "to promote international cooperation and to achieve peace and security."

The International Labour Organization was also created under the Treaty of Versailles as an affiliated agency of the League. The League of Nations ceased its activities after failing to prevent the Second World War.

In 1945, representatives of 50 countries met in San Francisco at the United Nations Conference on International Organization to draw up the United Nations Charter. Those delegates deliberated on the basis of proposals worked out by the representatives of China, the Soviet Union, the United Kingdom and the United States at Dumbarton Oaks, United States, from August to October 1944. The Charter was signed on 26 June 1945 by the representatives of the 50 countries. Poland, which was not represented at the Conference, signed it later and became one of the original 51 member states.

The United Nations officially came into existence on 24 October 1945, when the Charter had been ratified by China, France, the Soviet Union, the United Kingdom, the United States and a majority of other signatories. **United Nations Day** is celebrated on 24 October each year.

United Nations Charter
(www.un.org/aboutun/charter)

The Charter is the constituting instrument of the Organization, setting out the rights and obligations of member states, and establishing the United Nations organs and procedures. An international treaty, the Charter codifies the major principles of international relations — from the sovereign equality of states to prohibition of the use of force in international relations in any manner inconsistent with the purposes of the United Nations.

Francisco, who have exhibited their full powers found to be in good and due form, have agreed to the present Charter of the United Nations and do hereby establish an international organization to be known as the United Nations."

Purposes and principles

The *purposes* of the United Nations, as set forth in the Charter, are:

- to maintain international peace and security;
- to develop friendly relations among nations based on respect for the principle of equal rights and self-determination of peoples;
- to cooperate in solving international economic, social, cultural and humanitarian problems and in promoting respect for human rights and fundamental freedoms;
- to be a centre for harmonizing the actions of nations in attaining these common ends.

The United Nations acts in accordance with the following *principles:*

- it is based on the sovereign equality of all its members;
- all members are to fulfil in good faith their Charter obligations;
- they are to settle their international disputes by peaceful means and without endangering international peace and security and justice;
- they are to refrain from the threat or use of force against any other state;
- they are to give the United Nations every assistance in any action it takes in accordance with the Charter;
- nothing in the Charter is to authorize the United Nations to intervene in matters which are essentially within the domestic jurisdiction of any state.

Membership

Membership of the United Nations is open to all peace-loving nations which accept the obligations of the Charter and are willing and able to carry out these obligations.

The General Assembly admits new member states on the recommendation of the Security Council. The Charter provide\s for the suspension or expulsion of a member for violation of the principles of the Charter, but no such action has ever been taken.

Official languages

Under the Charter, the official languages of the United Nations are Chinese, English, French, Russian and Spanish. Arabic was later added as an official language of the General Assembly, the Security Council and the Economic and Social Council.

- to consider and approve the United Nations budget and to apportion the contributions among members;

- to elect the non-permanent members of the Security Council, the members of the Economic and Social Council and additional members of the Trusteeship Council (when necessary); to elect jointly with the Security Council the Judges of the International Court of Justice; and, on the recommendation of the Security Council, to appoint the Secretary-General.

Sessions

The General Assembly's regular session begins each year on Tuesday in the third week of September, counting from the first week that contains at least one working day. The election of the President of the Assembly, as well as its 21 Vice-Presidents and the Chairpersons of its six main committees, takes place at least three months before the start of the regular session. To ensure equitable geographical representation, the presidency of the Assembly rotates each year among five groups of states: African, Asian, Eastern European, Latin American and the Caribbean, and Western European and other states.

In addition, the Assembly may meet in special sessions at the request of the Security Council, of a majority of member states, or of one member if the majority of members concur. Emergency special sessions may be called within 24 hours of a request by the Security Council on the vote of any nine Council members, or by a majority of the United Nations members, or by one member if the majority of members concur.

At the beginning of each regular session, the Assembly holds a general debate, often addressed by heads of state and government, in which member states express their views on the most pressing international issues. Most questions are then discussed in its six Main Committees:

- **First Committee** (Disarmament and International Security);

- **Second Committee** (Economic and Financial);

- **Third Committee** (Social, Humanitarian and Cultural);

- **Fourth Committee** (Special Political and Decolonization);

- **Fifth Committee** (Administrative and Budgetary);

- **Sixth Committee** (Legal).

Some issues are considered directly in plenary meetings while others are allocated to one of the six Main Committees. Resolutions and decisions, including those recommended by the committees, are adopted in plenary meetings — usually before the recess of the regular session in December. They may be adopted with or without a vote.

The Assembly generally adopts its resolutions and decisions by a majority of members present and voting. Important questions, including recommendations on international peace and security, the election of members to some principal organs and budgetary matters, are

- to call upon the parties to a dispute to settle it by peaceful means;
- to investigate any dispute or situation which might lead to international friction, and to recommend methods of adjusting such disputes or the terms of settlement;
- to determine the existence of a threat to the peace or act of aggression and to recommend what action should be taken;
- to call upon the parties concerned to comply with such provisional measures as it deems necessary or desirable to prevent an aggravation of the situation;
- to call on members of the United Nations to take measures not involving the use of armed force — such as sanctions — to give effect to the Council's decisions;
- to resort to or authorize the use of force to maintain or restore international peace and security;
- to encourage the peaceful settlement of local disputes through regional arrangements and to use such regional arrangements for enforcement action under its authority;
- to recommend to the General Assembly the appointment of the Secretary-General and, together with the Assembly, to elect the Judges of the International Court of Justice;
- to request the International Court of Justice to give an advisory opinion on any legal question;
- to recommend to the General Assembly the admission of new members to the United Nations.

The Security Council is so organized as to be able to function continuously, and a representative of each of its members must be present at all times at United Nations Headquarters. The Council may meet elsewhere: in 1972 it held a session in Addis Ababa, Ethiopia; in 1973 it met in Panama City, Panama; and in 1990 it met in Geneva, Switzerland.

When a complaint concerning a threat to peace is brought before it, the Council's first action is usually to recommend that the parties try to reach agreement by peaceful means. The Council may set forth principles for a peaceful settlement. In some cases, the Council itself undertakes investigation and mediation. It may dispatch a mission, appoint special envoys or request the Secretary-General to use his good offices.

When a dispute leads to hostilities, the Council's first concern is to bring them to an end as soon as possible. The Council may issue ceasefire directives that can be instrumental in preventing an escalation of the conflict.

The Council may also dispatch military observers or a peacekeeping force to help reduce tensions, keep opposing forces apart, and create conditions of calm in which peaceful settlements may be sought. Under Chapter VII of the Charter, the Council may decide on enforcement measures, including economic sanctions, arms embargoes, financial sanctions, travel bans or collective military action.

Sessions

The Council generally holds several short sessions and many preparatory meetings, roundtables and panel discussions with the members of civil society throughout the year, to deal with the organization of its work. It also holds a four-week substantive session in July, alternating between New York and Geneva. That session includes a high-level segment, attended by Ministers and other high officials, to discuss major economic, social and humanitarian issues. The year-round work of the Council is carried out in its subsidiary and related bodies.

Subsidiary and related bodies

The Council's subsidiary machinery includes:

- eight functional commissions, which are deliberative bodies whose role is to consider and make recommendations on issues in their areas of responsibility and expertise: Statistical Commission, Commission on Population and Development, Commission for Social Development, Commission on the Status of Women, Commission on Narcotic Drugs, Commission on Crime Prevention and Criminal Justice, Commission on Science and Technology for Development, Commission on Sustainable Development;

- five Regional Commissions: Economic Commission for Africa (Addis Ababa, Ethiopia), Economic and Social Commission for Asia and the Pacific (Bangkok, Thailand), Economic Commission for Europe (Geneva, Switzerland), Economic Commission for Latin America and the Caribbean (Santiago, Chile), and Economic and Social Commission for Western Asia (Beirut, Lebanon);

- three standing committees: Committee for Programme and Coordination, Committee on Non-Governmental Organizations, Committee on Negotiations with Intergovernmental Agencies;

- a number of expert bodies on subjects such as development policy; public administration; international cooperation in tax matters; economic, social and cultural rights; energy and sustainable development;

- other bodies, including the Permanent Forum on Indigenous Issues and the United Nations Forum on Forests.

The Council also cooperates with and to a certain extent coordinates the work of United Nations programmes (such as UNDP, UNEP, UNFPA, UN-HABITAT, and UNICEF) and the specialized agencies (such as FAO, ILO, UNESCO and WHO), all of which report to the Council and make recommendations for its substantive sessions.

Relations with non-governmental organizations

Under the Charter, the Economic and Social Council consults with non-governmental organizations (NGOs) concerned with matters within its competence. Over 2,870 NGOs have consultative status with the Council. The Council recognizes that these organizations submit disputes to it. The Court is not open to private persons and entities or international organizations.

The General Assembly and the Security Council can ask the Court for an advisory opinion on any legal question. Other organs of the United Nations and the specialized agencies, when authorized by the Assembly, can ask for advisory opinions on legal questions within the scope of their activities.

Jurisdiction

The Court's jurisdiction covers all questions that states refer to it, and all matters provided for in the United Nations Charter, or in international treaties and conventions. States may bind themselves in advance to accept the jurisdiction of the Court, either by signing a treaty or convention that provides for referral to the Court or by making a declaration to that effect. Such declarations accepting compulsory jurisdiction often contain reservations excluding certain classes of disputes.

In accordance with its Statute, the Court decides disputes by applying:

- international conventions establishing rules expressly recognized by the contesting states;
- international custom as evidence of a general practice accepted as law;
- the general principles of law recognized by nations; and
- judicial decisions and the teachings of the most qualified scholars of the various nations.

Membership

The Court is composed of 15 Judges elected by the General Assembly and the Security Council, voting independently. They are chosen on the basis of their qualifications, and care is taken to ensure that the principal legal systems of the world are represented in the Court. No two Judges may be from the same country. The Judges serve a nine-year term and may be re-elected. They cannot engage in any other occupation during their term of office.

The Court normally sits in plenary session, but may form smaller units called chambers if the parties so request. Judgments given by chambers are considered as rendered by the full Court. The Court also has a Chamber for Environmental Matters and forms annually a Chamber of Summary Procedure.

Secretariat
(www.un.org/documents/st)

The Secretariat — consisting of international staff working in duty stations around the world — carries out the diverse day-to-day work of the Organization. It services the other principal organs of the United Nations and administers the programmes and policies laid

---

Previous Secretaries-General

Under the Charter, the Secretary-General is appointed by the General Assembly upon the recommendation of the Security Council. Mr. Ban Ki-moon's predecessors were: Kofi Annan (Ghana), who served from January 1997 to December 2006; Boutros Boutros-Ghali (Egypt), who held office from January 1992 to December 1996; Javier Pérez de Cuéllar (Peru), who served from January 1982 to December 1991; Kurt Waldheim (Austria), who held office from January 1972 to December 1981; U Thant (Burma, now Myanmar), who served from November 1961, when he was appointed acting Secretary-General (he was formally appointed Secretary-General in November 1962) to December 1971; Dag Hammarskjöld (Sweden), who served from April 1953 until his death in a plane crash in Africa in September 1961; and Trygve Lie (Norway), who held office from February 1946 to his resignation in November 1952.

This creative tension accompanies the Secretary-General through day-to-day work, which includes attendance at sessions of United Nations bodies; consultations with world leaders, government officials, representatives of civil society groups, the private sector and individuals; and worldwide travel intended to keep him in touch with the peoples of member states and informed about the vast array of issues of international concern that are on the Organization's agenda. Each year, the Secretary-General issues a report on the work of the Organization that appraises its activities and outlines future priorities.

One of the most vital roles played by the Secretary-General is the use of his "good offices" — steps taken publicly and in private, drawing upon his independence, impartiality and integrity, to prevent international disputes from arising, escalating or spreading. The good offices of the Secretary-General have been used in a wide range of situations, including Cyprus, East Timor, Iraq, Libya, the Middle East, Nigeria and Western Sahara. *(For a list of the Secretary-General's special and personal representatives and envoys, see www.un.org/Depts/dpko/SRSG)*

Each Secretary-General defines his role within the context of his particular time in office. Demands for UN peacekeeping have grown at an unprecedented rate in recent years, leading Secretary-General Ban Ki-moon to propose basic structural reforms to enable the Organization to keep pace.

As a result, the General Assembly, in June 2007, approved the creation of a **Department of Field Support (DFS)** to take over the day-to-day management of peacekeeping operations, leaving the **Department of Peacekeeping Operations (DPKO)** free to focus on overall strategy, planning and deployment. (See *box*, "Reform and Revitalization: Peacekeeping and Disarmament")

- *Environment.* Recognizing the serious challenge of climate change; acting through the UN Framework Convention on Climate Change; assisting the most vulnerable, such as small island developing states; creating a global early warning system for all natural hazards.

- *International Health.* Scaling up response to HIV/AIDS, TB and malaria, through prevention, care, treatment and support, and mobilizing additional resources; fighting infectious diseases, including full implementation of the new International Health Regulations, and support for the Global Outbreak Alert and Response Network of the WHO.

- *Humanitarian Assistance.* Improving the Central Emergency Revolving Fund, so that relief arrives reliably and immediately when disasters occur; recognizing the Guiding Principles on Internal Displacement as an important framework for protecting the internally displaced.

- *Updating the UN Charter.* Updating the Charter by winding up the Trusteeship Council, marking completion of UN's historic decolonization role, and deleting the Charter's anachronistic references to "enemy states".

Many of these commitments have already been accomplished, and many others are well under way. (For the full text of the 2005 World Summit Outcome, see *www.un.org/summit2005*)

Secretary-General Ban has been particularly outspoken on climate change, describing it as "a defining issue of our time". He has also promoted establishment of the new, hybrid peacekeeping mission in the Sudan (see *box* on **UNAMID** in chapter 2), and taken steps to bring the UN disarmament machinery into closer relationship with his office — as the new **United Nations Office for Disarmament Affairs**.

Mr. Ban's priorities for action include: Africa, particularly the situation in the Sudan and the tragedy in Darfur; the situation in the Middle East; non-proliferation and disarmament; achievement of the development goals that emerged from the 2000 Millennium Summit; climate change; human rights; and UN reform. (See "My priorities as Secretary-General, at *www.un.org/sg/priority.shtml*)

Mr. Ban Ki-moon's actions follow and build on those of his predecessor, Mr. Kofi Annan, whose efforts focused on wide-ranging reforms aimed at helping the UN adapt to a new era in global affairs. Innovations during Mr. Annan's 10-year tenure included the establishment of such internal bodies as the UN Ethics Office and the Office of the UN Ombudsman; and such major UN bodies as the Human Rights Council and the UN Peacebuilding Commission. He also established the office of Deputy Secretary-General, to assist in the array of responsibilities assigned to his office.

The Office of the Special Adviser on Africa, established by Mr. Annan in 2003, coordinates the UN systems efforts for Africa's development. The UN Democracy Fund finances projects that build and strengthen democratic institutions and processes and promote human rights.

The United Nations and the Nobel Peace Prize

Throughout the years, the United Nations and its far-flung family of agencies, organizations and supporters have frequently been awarded the annual Nobel Peace Prize, in recognition of their contribution to the cause of world peace, in all its aspects. A list of UN-related Nobel Peace Prize laureates since the establishment of the Organization includes:

- Cordell Hull — United States Secretary of State instrumental in establishing the UN (1945)

- Lord John Boyd Orr — founding director-general of the UN Food and Agricultural Organization (1949)

- Ralph Bunche — UN Trusteeship Director and principal secretary of the UN Palestine Commission, also led efforts for mediation in the Middle East (1950)

- Léon Jouhaux — one of the ILO founders (1951)

- Office of the United Nations High Commissioner for Refugees (1954)

- Lester Bowles Pearson — honoured for his role in trying to end the Suez conflict and to solve the Middle East question through the UN, also served as General Assembly President in 1952 (1957)

- UN Secretary-General Dag Hammarskjöld — one of only two posthumous awards (1961)

- United Nations Children's Fund (1965)

- International Labour Organization (1969)

- Sean MacBride — UN Commissioner for Namibia and human rights promoter (1974)

- Office of the High Commissioner for Refugees (1981)

- United Nations Peacekeeping Forces (1988)

- United Nations and its Secretary-General, Kofi Annan (2001)

- International Atomic Energy Agency, and its Director-General, Mohamed ElBaradei (2005)

- Intergovernmental Panel on Climate Change (IPCC) and Albert Arnold (Al) Gore Jr., former Vice President of the United States (2007)

This list does not include the many Nobel laureates who have worked closely with the United Nations or at common purpose with it, in pursuance of their particular contribution to the human family.

A World of Support for the United Nations

The entire UN family benefits from the energy and enthusiasm of grassroots organizations and movements to bring the high ideals of the United Nations Charter into practical form. The UN also benefits from its partnership with various members of civil society, including the business and labour communities and international charitable organizations, as well as the support of prominent figures in all fields of endeavour.

From the children who "Trick-or-Treat for UNICEF", to the educational activities of some 5,000 UNESCO Clubs in more than 120 countries, to thousands of NGOs on the ground, people all around the world are engaged in helping the UN make this world a better place.

United Nations Associations. Inspired by the opening words of the UN Charter, "We the Peoples", a self-described "people's movement for the United Nations" was born in 1946, one year after the UN itself. UN Associations in over 100 member states bring the power and energy of hundreds of thousands of people to bear in a global network of support for the aims and purposes of the United Nations Charter (see *www.wfuna.org*)

Non-governmental organizations. The World Federation of UN Associations is but one of thousands of non-governmental organization (NGOs) which have enlisted in the cause of the UN — including some 2,870 NGOs in consultative status with the Economic and Social Council (www.un.org/esa/coordination/ngo), and more than 1,660 NGOs with strong information programmes that work in partnership with the UN Department of Public Information (*www.un.org/dpi/ngosection/index.asp*).

NGOs are active across the broad spectrum of UN issues, including peacebuilding, disarmament, outer space affairs, AIDS, malaria prevention, agriculture, food aid, sustainable development, information and communication technologies, disaster reduction, desertification, humanitarian operations, the global drug problem, and the environment — to name but a few (see specific references in subsequent chapters).

The Global Compact. Over 3,800 participants, including more than 2,900 businesses, as well as international and national labour groups and hundreds of civil society organizations in 100 countries, work with the UN to advance universally recognized principles in the areas of human rights, labour and the environment. (See *www.unglobalcompact.org*)

UN Messengers of Peace and Goodwill Ambassadors. From the earliest days of the United Nations, world famous actors, sports figures and other prominent world citizens have lent their names and public recognition in support of the United Nations work for a better world. Today, there are 9 UN Messengers of Peace appointed by the Secretary-General, and 156 Goodwill Ambassadors of the UN System (see *www.un.org/sg/mop*).

Public Charities. The United Nations Foundation is among a number of public charities which support the work of the UN. It was created in 1998 with entrepreneur/philanthropist Ted Turner's historic $1 billion gift in support of UN causes and activities (see *www.unfoundation.org*). The UN Fund for International Partnerships (UNFIP) was subsequently established within the UN to coordinate, channel and monitor the Foundation's contributions (*www.un.org/unfip*).

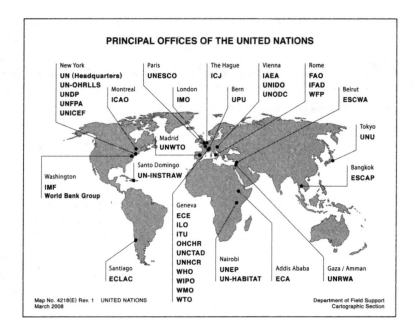

PRINCIPAL OFFICES OF THE UNITED NATIONS

human rights (*www.unog.ch*). The **United Nations Office at Vienna (UNOV)**, headed by Director-General Antonio Maria Costa (Italy), is the headquarters for activities in the fields of international drug-abuse control, crime prevention and criminal justice, peaceful uses of outer space and international trade law (*www.unvienna.org*). The **United Nations Office at Nairobi (UNON)**, headed by Director-General Anna Kajumulo Tibaijuka (Tanzania), is the headquarters for activities in the fields of environment and human settlements (*www.unon.org*).

Office of Internal Oversight Services (OIOS)

(www.un.org/Depts/oios)

Under-Secretary-General   **Ms. Inga-Britt Ahlenius (Sweden)**

The Office of Internal Oversight Services provides independent, professional and timely internal audit, monitoring, inspection, evaluation and investigation services. It aims to be an agent of change that promotes responsible administration of resources, a culture of accountability and transparency, and improved programme performance. The Office:

- conducts comprehensive internal audits;

- conducts inspections of programmes and organizational units;

- monitors and evaluates the efficiency and effectiveness of the implementation of programmes and mandates;

- investigates reports of mismanagement and misconduct;

- monitors the implementation of recommendations emanating from audits, evaluations, inspections and investigations.

Economic and Social Council

Functional Commissions

Commissions on:
  Narcotic Drugs
  Crime Prevention and Criminal Justice
  Science and Technology for
    Development
  Sustainable Development
  Status of Women
  Population and Development
Commission for Social Development
Statistical Commission

Regional Commissions

Economic Commission for Africa (ECA)

Economic Commission for Europe (ECE)

Economic Commission for Latin
  America and the Caribbean (ECLAC)

Economic and Social Commission for
  Asia and the Pacific (ESCAP)

Economic and Social Commission for
  Western Asia (ESCWA)

Other Bodies

Permanent Forum on Indigenous Issues

United Nations Forum on Forests

Sessional and standing committees

Expert, ad hoc and related bodies

Related Organizations

WTO World Trade Organization

IAEA[5] International Atomic Energy
Agency

CTBTO Prep.Com[6] PrepCom for the
Nuclear-Test-Ban Treaty Organization

OPCW[6] Organization for the
Prohibition of Chemical Weapons

International Court of Justice

Specialized Agencies[7]

ILO International Labour
Organization

FAO Food and Agriculture
Organization of the United Nations

UNESCO United Nations
Educational, Scientific and Cultural
Organization

WHO World Health Organization

World Bank Group

  IBRD International Bank
    for Reconstruction and
    Development

  IDA International Development
    Association

  IFC International Finance
    Corporation

  MIGA Multilateral Investment
    Guarantee Agency

  ICSID International Centre for
    Settlement of Investment
    Disputes

IMF International Monetary Fund

ICAO International Civil Aviation
Organization

IMO International Maritime
Organization

ITU International Telecommunication
Union

UPU Universal Postal Union

WMO World Meteorological
Organization

WIPO World Intellectual Property
Organization

IFAD International Fund for
Agricultural Development

UNIDO United Nations Industrial
Development Organization

UNWTO World Tourism
Organization

Secretariat

Departments and Offices

OSG[3] Office of the Secretary-
General

OIOS Office of Internal Oversight
Services

OLA Office of Legal Affairs

DPA Department of Political Affairs

UNODA Office for Disarmament
Affairs

DPKO Department of Peacekeeping
Operations

DFS[4] Department of Field Support

OCHA Office for the Coordination
of Humanitarian Affairs

DESA Department of Economic and
Social Affairs

DGACM Department for General
Assembly and Conference
Management

DPI Department of Public Information

DM Department of Management

UN-OHRLLS Office of the High
Representative for the Least
Developed Countries, Landlocked
Developing Countries and Small
Island Developing States

OHCHR Office of the United
Nations High Commissioner for
Human Rights

UNODC United Nations Office on
Drugs and Crime

DSS Department of Safety and
Security

೦೮೮೦

UNOG UN Office at Geneva

UNOV UN Office at Vienna

UNON UN Office at Nairobi

Published by the United Nations
Department of Public Information

DPI/2470—07-49950—December 2007—3M

The head of the Office — the Legal Counsel — represents the Secretary-General at meetings and conferences of a legal nature, as well as in judicial and arbitral proceedings. The Legal Counsel also certifies legal instruments issued on behalf of the United Nations, convenes meetings of the Legal Advisers of the United Nations System, and represents the United Nations at such meetings.

Department of Political Affairs (DPA)
(www.un.org/Depts/dpa)

Under-Secretary-General   **Mr. B. Lynn Pascoe (United States)**

The Department of Political Affairs plays a central role in United Nations efforts to prevent and resolve deadly conflict around the world and to consolidate peace in the aftermath of war. To that end, DPA:

- monitors, analyses and assesses political developments throughout the world;
- identifies potential or actual conflicts in whose control and resolution the United Nations could play a useful role;
- recommends to the Secretary-General appropriate action in such cases and executes the approved policy;
- assists the Secretary-General in carrying out political activities decided by him, the General Assembly and the Security Council, in the areas of preventive diplomacy, peacemaking, peacekeeping and peacebuilding;
- advises the Secretary-General on requests for electoral assistance received from member states and coordinates programmes established in response to such requests;
- advises and supports the Secretary-General in the political aspects of his relations with member states;
- services the Security Council and its subsidiary bodies, as well as the Committee on the Exercise of the Inalienable Rights of the Palestinian People and the Special Committee of 24 on decolonization.

The head of the Department — the Under-Secretary-General for Political Affairs — among other things undertakes consultations and negotiations relating to peaceful settlement of disputes, and is the focal point for United Nations electoral assistance activities.

Office for Disarmament Affairs (UNODA)
(http://disarmament.un.org)

High Representative for Disarmament   **Mr. Sergio de Queiroz Duarte (Brazil)**

The Office for Disarmament Affairs promotes the goal of nuclear disarmament and non-proliferation, as well as the strengthening of the disarmament regimes with respect to other weapons of mass destruction, including chemical and biological weapons. It promotes disarmament in the

---

Reform and Revitalization: Peacekeeping and Disarmament

During the first months of his tenure, Secretary-General Ban Ki-moon proposed a number of basic reforms aimed at strengthening the capacity of the UN to carry out its mission in the world. Among these was the restructuring of the United Nations peacekeeping and disarmament machinery.

In a letter to the General Assembly, the Secretary-General noted that "the number of peace operations is at an all-time high, with almost 100,000 personnel in the field". Reforms in 2000 had aimed to enable DPKO to launch one new multidisciplinary mission per year, but "the past 36 months alone have seen the start-up or expansion of nine field missions, with three additional missions currently in active start-up".

"Over the course of the next year, the number of personnel in UN peace operations could increase by as much as 40 per cent", the Secretary-General said. He therefore proposed the creation of a new Department of Field Support to handle the planning, deployment and support of peacekeeping operations, leaving the Department of Peacekeeping Operations to focus on such matters of strategic oversight and operational policy guidance.

On 15 March 2007, the General Assembly endorsed this proposal, and on 29 June 2007 it formally established the new **Department of Field Support (DFS)** to ensure more effective, coherent and responsive support to field operations and more efficient management of resources. The Under-Secretary-General heading DFS reports to and receives direction from the Under-Secretary-General for Peacekeeping Operations, to ensure unity of command and clear lines of responsibility. This reform is to be phased in over a period of 12 months.

Also on 15 March, the Assembly endorsed the Secretary-General's proposal to transform the Department of Disarmament Affairs into a **United Nations Office for Disarmament Affairs (UNODA)**, to be led by a High Representative for Disarmament, who would report directly to the Secretary-General. The reform is intended to promote fresh progress on the disarmament agenda, including efforts towards entry into force of the *Comprehensive Nuclear-Test-Ban Treaty*, which was adopted by the General Assembly in September 1996.

- Analyses emerging policy questions and best practices related to peacekeeping, and formulates policies, procedures and general peacekeeping doctrine;

- Coordinates all UN activities related to landmines, and develops and supports mine-action programmes in peacekeeping and emergency situations.

The head of the Department — the Under-Secretary-General for Peacekeeping Operations — directs peacekeeping operations on behalf of the Secretary-General; formulates policies and guidelines for operations; and advises the Secretary-General on all matters relating to peacekeeping and mine action.

(For information on changes currently under way in DPKO, see "Department of Field Support", and the box on "Reform and Revitalization: Peacekeeping and Disarmament".)

The Emergency Relief Coordinator also chairs the Inter-Agency Standing Committee (IASC), an umbrella organization that comprises all major humanitarian actors — including the Red Cross Movement and three consortia of non-governmental organizations. By developing common policies, guidelines and standards, the Committee ensures a coherent interagency response to complex emergencies and natural and environmental disasters.

OCHA has a staff of 1,064 worldwide. Its budget for 2007 was $159 million, 92 per cent of which came from extrabudgetary resources.

Department of Economic and Social Affairs (DESA)
(www. un. org/esa/desa)

Under-Secretary-General   **Mr. Sha Zukang (China)**

The Department of Economic and Social Affairs has three broad, interlinked areas of work:

- It compiles and analyses a broad range of social, economic and environmental data and information on relevant issues and trends. This analytical information serves to inform the United Nations policy-making processes, as well as a wider audience.

- DESA facilitates negotiations in the General Assembly and in the Economic and Social Council and its subsidiary bodies, providing support to member states and other participants as they build consensus on matters of global concern in the economic, social and related areas.

- It also advises governments, at their request, on ways and means of addressing their development challenges — including the development of national programmes and activities to carry out actions agreed to at the Millennium Summit, the Monterrey International Conference on Financing for Development, the World Summit on Sustainable Development, and other global economic, social and environmental conferences and summits.

DESA works in the areas of sustainable development, gender issues and the advancement of women, development policy analysis, population, statistics, public administration and e-government, and social policy and development. Its work includes support for the Permanent Forum on Indigenous Issues, the United Nations Information and Communications Technologies Task Force, and the United Nations Forum on Forests. DESA collaborates closely with NGOs, as well as other representatives of civil society.

Department for General Assembly and Conference Management (DGACM)
(www.un.org/Depts/DGACM)

Under-Secretary-General   **Mr. S. Muhammad Shaaban (Egypt)**

The Department for General Assembly and Conference Management provides technical and secretariat support services to the General Assembly, the Security Council, the Economic and Social Council, their committees and other subsidiary bodies, and to conferences held and produces and distributes radio and video documentary and news programmes about the United Nations.

It also covers the daily press briefings and statements by the Office of the Spokesperson for the Secretary-General (*www.un.org/News/ossg*), which is administered by the Department. The Office is responsible for planning the Secretary-General's media-related activities and explaining the policies and work of the United Nations to the world's media. The Spokesperson briefs journalists on a daily and continuous basis on the work of the Secretary-General and on developments throughout the UN system, including the Security Council and other principal organs, along with the tribunals, agencies, funds and programmes. The Spokesperson reports directly to the Secretary-General.

The main United Nations library — the Dag Hammarskjöld Library (*www.un.org/Depts/dhl*) — is part of the Outreach Division, as are the sections of the Department that work with non-governmental organizations (*www.un.org/dpi/ngosection*) and educational institutions and those that market United Nations information products and services (*www.un.org/Pubs*). The Outreach Division organizes special events and exhibitions on priority issues, as well as an annual training programme for journalists from developing countries. It also develops partnerships with private and public sector organizations to further the aims of the United Nations. Other responsibilities of this Division include conducting guided tours of UN Headquarters (*www.un.org/tours*), responding to public inquiries (*www.un.org/geninfo/faq*), and providing public speakers on UN issues. It also produces the *Yearbook of the United Nations*, the quarterly *UN Chronicle* magazine, and *The United Nations Today*.

Department of Management (DM)
(www.un.org/Depts/DGACM)

Under-Secretary-General   **Ms. Angela Kane (Germany)**

The Department of Management provides strategic policy guidance and management support to all entities of the Secretariat in three management areas: finance, human resources and support services. These fall under the purview of the Offices of Programme Planning, Budget and Accounts; Human Resources Management; and Central Support Services.

The Department is responsible for formulating and implementing improved management policies in the Secretariat; the management and training of staff; programme planning, budgetary, financial and human resources management; and technological innovations. It also provides technical servicing for the General Assembly's Fifth Committee (Administrative and Budgetary), as well as servicing for the Committee for Programme and Coordination.

As head of the Department, the Under-Secretary-General for Management provides policy guidance, coordination and direction for preparation of the Organization's medium-term plan and biennial budgets. She represents the Secretary-General on matters relating to management and monitors emerging management issues throughout the Secretariat. With authority delegated by the Secretary-General, the Under-Secretary-General also ensures the efficient implementation of the Organization's internal system of justice.

UN-OHRLLS assists the Secretary-General in ensuring the full mobilization and coordination of international support for the effective implementation of the *Brussels Programme of Action* and a number of related international commitments — including the *Almaty Declaration* and its Programme of Action, *"Addressing the Special Needs of Landlocked Developing Countries within a New Global Framework for Transit Transport Cooperation for Landlocked and Transit Developing Countries"*. That Programme emerged from the first global conference to address the specific needs of landlocked developing countries, held at Almaty, Kazakhstan, in August 2003.

The Office also works to ensure implementation of the *Barbados Programme of Action for the Sustainable Development of Small Island Developing States*, adopted at the 1994 Global Conference on the Sustainable Development of Small Island Developing States, and the *Mauritius Strategy* for implementation of the Barbados Programme, adopted at an international conference held in Mauritius in January 2005.

UN-OHRLLS facilitates coordination within the UN system in implementing these programmes, and support the Economic and Social Council and the General Assembly in assessing progress made. It also engages in advocacy and promotion of global awareness of these issues, in partnership with the relevant UN bodies, civil society, the media, academia and foundations.

The Office also prepared and coordinated the General Assembly's High-Level Mid-term Review of the Implementation of the *Programme of Action for the Least Developed Countries*, held on 18 and 19 September 2006.

Regional commissions

The United Nations regional commissions report to ECOSOC and their secretariats are under the authority of the Secretary-General. Their mandate is to initiate measures that promote the economic development of each region and strengthen the economic relations of the countries in that region, both among themselves and with other countries of the world. They are funded under the regular UN budget.

Economic Commission for Africa (ECA)
(www.uneca.org)

Set up in 1958, ECA carries out activities encouraging the growth of the economic and social sectors of the continent. It promotes policies and strategies to increase economic cooperation and integration among its 53 member countries, particularly in the production, trade, monetary, infrastructure and institutional fields. ECA focuses on producing information and analysis on economic and social issues; promoting food security and sustainable development; strengthening development management; harnessing the information revolution for development; and promoting regional cooperation and integration. Special attention is paid to improving the condition of women, enhancing their involvement and decision-making in development, and ensuring that women and gender equity are key elements in national development.

Executive Secretary: Mr. Abdoulie Janneh (Gambia)
Address: PO Box 3001, Addis Ababa, Ethiopia
Tel: (251-11) 551-7200; Fax: (251-11) 551-0365; Email: *ecainfo@uneca.org*

Economic and Social Commission for Asia and the Pacific (ESCAP)
(www.unescap.org)

ESCAP, established in 1947, has a mandate to address the economic and social issues of the region. It plays a unique role as the only comprehensive intergovernmental forum for all the countries of Asia and the Pacific. Its 53 member states and 9 associate member states represent some 60 per cent of the world's population. ESCAP gives technical support to governments for social and economic development. The assistance comes through direct advisory services to governments, training and sharing of regional experience, and information through meetings, publications and inter-country networks.

ESCAP executes programmes and projects to stimulate growth, improve socio-economic conditions and help build the foundations of modern society. Four regional research and training institutions — for agricultural development, agricultural machinery and engineering, statistics, and technology transfer — operate under its auspices. ESCAP also has a Pacific Operation Centre. Current priority areas are poverty reduction, managing globalization and addressing emerging social issues.

Executive Secretary: Ms. Noeleen Heyzer (Singapore)
Address: United Nations Building, Rajadamnern Nok Avenue, Bangkok 10200 Thailand
Tel: (66-2) 288-1234; Fax: (66-2) 288-1000; Email: *escap-registry@un.org*

Economic and Social Commission for Western Asia (ESCWA)
(www.escwa.un.org)

Established in 1973, ESCWA facilitates concerted action for the economic and social development of the countries of Western Asia by promoting economic cooperation and integration in the region. Comprised of 13 member states, ESCWA serves as the main general economic and social development forum for the region within the United Nations system. Its programmes address such areas as economic development, social development, agriculture, industry, natural resources, the environment, transport, communications and statistics.

Executive Secretary: Mr. Bader Al-Dafa (Qatar)
Address: PO Box 11-8575, Riad el-Solh Square, Beirut, Lebanon
Tel: (961-1) 98-1301, or 1-212-963-9731, 9732 (Satellite, via New York);
Fax: (961-1) 98-1510; Email: Click "Contact Us" form on website.

International tribunals

International Criminal Tribunal for the Former Yugoslavia (ICTY)
(www.un.org/icty)

Established by the Security Council in 1993, the Tribunal is mandated to prosecute persons responsible for serious violations of international humanitarian law committed in the former Yugoslavia since 1991. It has 16 permanent judges, 27 ad litem judges, of whom it can use up to 12 at any given time, and a staff of more than 1,140 from 81 countries. Its 2006-2007 budget was $276.5 million.

UNCTAD's main goal is to help developing countries and transition economies use trade and investment as an engine for development, poverty reduction and integration into the world economy. In pursuing these objectives, UNCTAD conducts research, analysis and technical cooperation activities; organizes intergovernmental deliberations; and promotes interaction with other key development stakeholders, including civil society and the private sector.

UNCTAD's highest decision-making body is its quadrennial ministerial conference, at which the organization's 193 member states (including the Holy See) debate issues on the international economic agenda and set UNCTAD's mandate. The next conference, UNCTAD XII, will take place in Accra, Ghana, in April 2008. UNCTAD's executive body, the Trade and Development Board, meets annually in regular session to review the work of the secretariat.

The annual operating budget is about $61 million, drawn from the UN regular budget. UNCTAD's technical cooperation activities, financed from extrabudgetary resources, amount to some $31 million. Currently there are more than 280 such activities under way in about 100 countries — all of them demand-driven. Based in Geneva, UNCTAD has a staff of about 400. Its main publications are: the *Trade and Development Report, World Investment Report, Economic Development in Africa Report, Least Developed Countries Report, UNCTAD Handbook of Statistics, Information Economy Report,* and *Review of Maritime Transport.*

Secretary-General: Dr. Supachai Panitchpakdi (Thailand)
Headquarters: Palais des Nations, CH-1211 Geneva 10, Switzerland
Tel: (41-22) 917-5809; Fax: (41-22) 917-0051; Email: *info@unctad.org*

International Trade Centre (ITC)
(www.intracen.org)

The International Trade Centre (ITC) is the technical cooperation agency of the United Nations Conference on Trade and Development (UNCTAD) and the World Trade Organization (WTO) for operational, enterprise-oriented aspects of trade development. It supports developing and transition economies — and particularly their business sector — in their efforts to realize their full potential for developing exports and improving import operations.

ITC's goals are: to facilitate the integration of developing and transition economy enterprises into the multilateral trading system; to support national efforts to design and implement trade development strategies; to strengthen key trade support services, both public and private; to improve export performance in sectors of critical importance and opportunity; and to foster international competitiveness within the business community as a whole, and the small and medium-sized enterprise (SME) sector in particular.

The Centre's technical programmes include: strategic and operational market research; business advisory services; trade information management; export training capacity

United Nations Environment Programme (UNEP)
(www.unep.org)

The United Nations Environment Programme was founded in 1972. Its mission is to provide leadership and encourage partnerships in caring for the environment by enabling nations and peoples to improve their quality of life without compromising that of future generations.

As the principal United Nations body in the field of the environment, UNEP sets the global environmental agenda, promotes implementation of the environmental dimension of sustainable development in the United Nations system, and serves as an authoritative advocate of the global environment.

UNEP's governing body — the Governing Council — made up of 58 countries, meets annually. Programmes are financed by the Environment Fund, made up of voluntary contributions from governments and supplemented by trust funds and a small allocation from the United Nations regular budget. The Fund's budget for 2006-2007 was $144 million. UNEP has a staff of approximately 800.

Executive Director: Mr. Achim Steiner (Germany)
Headquarters: United Nations Avenue, Gigiri, PO Box 30552, 00100, Nairobi, Kenya
Tel: (254-20) 762-1234; Fax: (254-20) 762-4489, 4490; Email: *unepinfo@unep.org*

United Nations Development Programme (UNDP)
(www.undp.org)

The United Nations Development Programme (UNDP) is the UN's global development network. It advocates for change and connects countries to knowledge, experience and resources, to help their people build a better life. UNDP is on the ground in 166 countries, working with them on their own solutions to global and national development challenges. As they develop local capacity, they draw on the expertise of UNDP and its wide range of partners.

World leaders have pledged to achieve the Millennium Development Goals, which include the overarching goal of cutting poverty in half by 2015. UNDP's network links and coordinates global and national efforts to reach these goals. Its focus is on helping countries build and share solutions to the challenges of poverty reduction, crisis prevention and recovery, environment and sustainable development, and democratic governance, including the governance of HIV/AIDS responses.

UNDP also administers the UN Capital Development Fund (UNCDF), the UN Development Fund for Women (UNIFEM) and the UN Volunteers (UNV). It is governed by a 36-member Executive Board, representing both developing and developed countries. Among its major publications is the annual *Human Development Report.*

Administrator: Mr. Kemal Derviş (Turkey)
Headquarters: 1 UN Plaza, New York, NY 10017, USA
Tel: (1-212) 906-5000; Fax: (1-212) 906-5364; Email: *www.undp.org/comments/form.shmtl*

Executive Coordinator: Mr. Ad de Raad (Netherlands)
Headquarters: Postfach 260 111, D-53153 Bonn, Germany
Tel: (49-228) 815-2000; Fax: (49-228) 815-2001; Email: *information@unv.org*

United Nations Population Fund
(UNFPA)
(www.unfpa.org)

Established operationally in 1969 at the initiative of the General Assembly, the United Nations Population Fund is the largest internationally funded source of population assistance to developing countries and those with economies in transition. It assists countries, at their request, to improve reproductive health and family planning services on the basis of individual choice, and to formulate population policies in support of efforts towards sustainable development. It is a subsidiary organ of the General Assembly and has the same Executive Board as UNDP.

UNFPA is wholly funded by voluntary contributions, which totalled $389.3 million from 180 countries in 2006, plus $216.2 million earmarked for specific activities, for a record-breaking grand total of $605.5 million. Some 61.5 per cent of this assistance was used for reproductive health, including safe motherhood, family planning and sexual health, to refine approaches to adolescent reproductive health, reduce maternal disabilities such as obstetric fistula, address HIV/AIDS, and provide assistance in emergencies.

Another 21.3 per cent of this assistance related to population and development strategies. UNFPA aims to ensure a balance between development and population dynamics by providing information, influencing policy, and building national capacity in population programming. The rest is used for advocacy. UNFPA seeks to mobilize resources and political commitment for population activities relating to agreed international development goals, including those in the *Millennium Declaration*. Some 77 per cent of the Fund's 1,031 staff members work in the field, in 154 countries, areas and territories.

Executive Director: Ms. Thoraya Ahmed Obaid (Saudi Arabia)
Headquarters: 220 East 42nd Street, New York, NY 10017, USA
Tel: (1-212) 297-5000; see also *www.unfpa.org/help/contact.htm*

Office of the United Nations High Commissioner for Refugees
(UNHCR)
(www.unhcr.org)

Created by the General Assembly in 1950, the Office of the United Nations High Commissioner for Refugees is mandated to lead and coordinate international action for the worldwide protection of refugees and the resolution of refugee problems. Since its creation, UNHCR has helped around 50 million refugees, earning two Nobel Peace Prizes in 1954 and in 1981.

exploitation and abuse. In all its work, UNICEF encourages young people to speak out and participate in the decisions that affect their lives.

The United Nations Children's Fund is governed by an Executive Board comprising delegates from 36 countries who govern its policies, programmes and finances. There are 8,200 UNICEF employees working in 157 countries and territories around the world. UNICEF is funded entirely by voluntary contributions; its total programme expenditures in 2006 totalled $2.34 billion. While its strongest support comes from governments (58 per cent in 2006), UNICEF also receives considerable aid from the private sector — $799 million — and from some 6 million individuals who give through 37 National Committees in the industrialized world.

In 1965, UNICEF was awarded the Nobel Peace Prize. Its major publication, *The State of the World's Children*, is released annually.

Executive Director: Ms. Ann M. Veneman (United States)
Headquarters: UNICEF House, 3 United Nations Plaza, New York, NY 10017, USA
Tel: (1-212) 326-7000; Fax: (1-212) 888-7465; Email: *www.unicef.org/about/contact.html*

World Food Programme (WFP)
(www.wfp.org)

Established in 1963, the World Food Programme is the world's largest humanitarian organization. Funded entirely by voluntary contributions, WFP leads the global fight against hunger by providing emergency food assistance to the most vulnerable victims of calamity, whether natural or man-made. It also uses food aid, coupled with technical and logistical expertise and its significant presence in the field, to help eradicate the root causes of hunger. Together with its partners, WFP is doing its utmost to reach the first Millennium Development Goal — cutting the proportion of those hungry in half by 2015.

WFP provides food assistance, expertise and resources to build self-sustaining communities in the most impoverished and disadvantaged corners of the world, where most of the planet's 854 million undernourished people live. Through its global school feeding campaign, for example, WFP supplies daily meals to close to 20 million school children a year. In emergencies, WFP delivers fast, life-sustaining relief to victims of wars and civil strife, as well as to people hit by drought, flood, hurricanes, earthquakes.

In 2006, 27 per cent of WFP's resources were directed to emergency relief and 46 per cent to post-emergency protracted relief and recovery efforts. In all, WFP provided nearly 70 per cent of the world's emergency food aid.

WFP has a staff of 10,587, 92 per cent of whom work in the field. By land, sea and air, WFP delivered 4 million tonnes of food to 87.8 million people in 78 countries during 2006, at a cost of $2.7 billion.

WFP is governed by a 36-member Executive Board which meets three times a year.

Executive Director: Ms. Josette Sheeran (United States)
Headquarters: Via C.G. Viola 68, Parco dei Medici, 00148 Rome, Italy
Tel: (39-06) 6513-1; Fax: (39-06) 6513-2840; Email: *wfpinfo@wfp.org*

Office of the United Nations High Commissioner for Human Rights (OHCHR)

(www.ohchr.org)

The General Assembly in 1993 established the post of United Nations High Commissioner for Human Rights as the official with principal responsibility for United Nations human rights activities. The High Commissioner is charged with promoting and protecting the enjoyment by all of civil, cultural, economic, political and social rights. The mandate is carried out through the Office of the High Commissioner for Human Rights.

OHCHR acts as the focal point for all human rights activities of the United Nations. It prepares reports and undertakes research at the request of the General Assembly and other policy-making bodies. It cooperates with governments and international, regional and non-governmental organizations for the promotion and protection of human rights. It acts as the secretariat for the meetings of United Nations human rights bodies. OHCHR, which has some 576 staff, is organized into four branches:

- The Treaties and Council Branch services the human rights treaty bodies, the Human Rights Council, and the United Nations Voluntary Fund for Victims of Torture. It prepares and submits the documents for the various treaty bodies, processes communications submitted to them under optional procedures, follows up on recommendations and decisions taken at treaty-body meetings, and helps to build national capacities to implement treaty-body recommendations.

- The Special Procedures Branch provides support to the fact-finding and investigatory mechanisms of the Human Rights Council — including such thematic mechanisms as special rapporteurs, special representatives and thematic working groups — with a view to documenting human rights violations worldwide, enhancing the protection of victims, and promoting their rights.

- The Research and Right to Development Branch is responsible for promoting and protecting the right to development. To that end, it conducts research, provides support for the Working Group on the Right to Development, and seeks to mainstream human rights in development activities. It also services the UN Voluntary Trust Fund on Contemporary Forms of Slavery, as well as the UN Voluntary Fund for Indigenous Populations.

- The Capacity Building and Field Operations Branch develops, implements, monitors and evaluates advisory services and other technical-assistance projects relating to human rights, at the request of governments. It also provides support to human rights fact-finding missions and investigations.

OHCHR's budgetary requirement for 2006-2007 came to $245.6 million, of which $85.6 million was provided by the United Nations regular budget, with the balance of $160 million being sought through voluntary contributions.

At the request of its clients, UNOPS provides the people, tools, and operational know-how needed to launch and implement large-scale, complex projects in a variety of settings. UNOPS has particular proficiency in construction, census and elections support, environmental rehabilitation, fund supervision, and mine action. It is the designated UN lead office for physical infrastructure projects in post-conflict settings.

UNOPS income for 2006 totalled $53.4 million, with project delivery valued at $706 million.

Executive Director: Mr. Jan Mattsson (Sweden)
Headquarters: Midtermolen 3, P.O. Box 2695, DK-2100 Copenhagen, Denmark
Tel: (45-3) 546-7511; Fax: (45-3) 546-7501; Email: *hq@unops.org*

United Nations University (UNU)
(www.unu.edu)

The United Nations University is an international community of scholars engaged in research, policy study, institutional and individual capacity development, and the dissemination of knowledge to further the United Nations aims of peace and progress. The Charter of the University was adopted in 1973, and UNU commenced operations in Tokyo in 1975. The University has 13 Research and Training Centres and Programmes around the world, and is supported by 14 UNU Associated Institutions, as well as hundreds of cooperating institutions and individuals worldwide.

UNU is financed entirely by voluntary contributions from governments, agencies, foundations and individual donors. It receives no funds from the United Nations budget: its basic annual income for operating expenses comes from investment income derived from its Endowment Fund. UNU's budget for the biennium 2006-2007 was $88.0 million. At the end of 2006, it had 356 staff members from 68 countries, 24 per cent of whom were nationals of developing countries.

UNU is directed by a 24-member Governing Council that meets annually.

Rector: Prof. Dr. Konrad Osterwalder (Switzerland)
Headquarters: 53-70 Jingumae 5-chome, Shibuya-ku, Tokyo 150-8925, Japan
Tel: (81-3) 3499-2811; Fax: (81-3) 3499-2828; Email: *mbox@hq.unu.edu*

United Nations International Research and Training Institute for the Advancement of Women (UN-INSTRAW)
(www. un-instraw. org)

The United Nations International Research and Training Institute for the Advancement of Women was established in 1976 on the recommendation of the first World Conference on Women. It has the unique mandate to promote and undertake policy research and training programmes at the international level to contribute to the advancement of women; to enhance their active and equal participation in the development process; to raise awareness of gender issues; and to create networks worldwide for the attainment of gender equality.

United Nations Institute for Training and Research (UNITAR)
(www.unitar.org)

An autonomous United Nations body established in 1965, the United Nations Institute for Training and Research has the mandate to enhance the effectiveness of the United Nations through training and research. UNITAR provides training and capacity development to assist countries in meeting the challenges of the 21st century; conducts research on innovative training and capacity-development methodologies; and forms partnerships with other UN agencies, governments and NGOs to develop and organize training and capacity-development activities that meet countries' needs.

In 2006, UNITAR offered over 300 courses, seminars and workshops, benefiting over 10,000 participants — mainly from developing countries and countries in transition. Some 30,000 trainees also benefited from its e-learning courses.

UNITAR is governed by a Board of Trustees *(ad personam)*. Currently, the Institute is fully self-funded and is sponsored by voluntary contributions from governments, intergovernmental organizations, foundations and other non-governmental sources. UNITAR's activities are conducted from its headquarters in Geneva, as well as through its New York and Hiroshima offices. It has a total staff of some 50 permanent professionals.

Executive Director: Mr. Carlos Lopes (Guinea-Bissau)
Headquarters: International Environment House, Chemin des Anémones 11-13, CH-1219 Châtelaine, Geneva, Switzerland
By mail: UNITAR, Palais des Nations, CH-1211 Geneva 10, Switzerland
Tel: (41-22) 917-8455; Fax: (41-22) 917-8047

United Nations Research Institute for Social Development (UNRISD)
(www.unrisd.org)

An autonomous United Nations body created in 1963, the United Nations Research Institute for Social Development engages in research on the social dimensions of contemporary development issues. UNRISD provides governments, development agencies, civil society organizations and scholars with a better understanding of how development policies and processes of economic and social change affect different social groups.

UNRISD relies wholly on voluntary contributions for financing its activities and has an annual operating budget of approximately $4 million. In 2006, it received more than $2.8 million in contributions, as well as $1.3 million for specific projects. An 11-member Board approves its annual budget and research programme.

Director: Mr. Thandika Mkandawire (Sweden)
Headquarters: Palais des Nations, CH-1211 Geneva 10, Switzerland
Tel: (41-0-22) 917-3020; Fax: (41-0-22) 917-0650;
Email: *info@unrisd.org*

- The International Labour Conference brings together governmental, employer and worker delegates from member countries every year. It sets international labour standards and acts as a forum where social and labour questions of importance to the entire world are discussed.

- The Governing Body meets twice a year and directs ILO operations, prepares the programme and budget and examines cases of non-observance of ILO standards.

- The International Labour Office is the permanent secretariat of the Organization.

Opportunities for study and training are offered at the International Training Centre in Turin, Italy. ILO's International Institute for Labour Studies' means of action include: research networks; social policy forums; courses and seminars; visiting scholar and internship programmes; and publications.

On its fiftieth anniversary, in 1969, ILO was awarded the Nobel Peace Prize.

ILO employs 2,500 officials and experts of more than 110 nationalities at its Geneva headquarters and in 40 field offices around the world. It adopted a programme and budget for 2006-2007 of $594.3 million.

Director-General: Mr. Juan Somavía (Chile)
Headquarters: 4, route des Morillons, CH-1211 Geneva 22, Switzerland
Tel: (41-22) 799-6111; Fax: (41-22) 798-8685; Email: *ilo@ilo.org*

Food and Agriculture Organization of the United Nations (FAO)
(www. fao.org)

The Food and Agriculture Organization of the United Nations is the lead agency for agriculture, forestry, fisheries and rural development in the UN system. It works to alleviate poverty and hunger by promoting agricultural development, improved nutrition and the pursuit of food security. Such security exists when all people at all times have physical and economic access to sufficient, safe and nutritious food to meet their dietary needs and food preferences for an active and healthy life.

FAO offers development assistance, provides policy and planning advice to governments, collects, analyses and disseminates information, and acts as an international forum for debate on food and agriculture issues. Special programmes help countries prepare for emergency food crisis and provide relief assistance.

During 2006, FAO had over 1,600 field projects, totalling more than $410 million. Of these, 444 were emergency operations amounting to more than $180 million and accounting for nearly 45 per cent of total programme delivery.

FAO is governed by the Conference of member nations, which meets biennially. The Conference elects a 49-member Council that serves as the governing body between sessions of the Conference. FAO has a staff of 3,600, working at headquarters and in the field. Its regular programme budget for 2006-2007 was $765.7 million.

WHO's strategic direction for the decade 2006-2015 includes: investing in health to reduce poverty; building individual and global health security; promoting universal coverage, gender equality and health-related human rights; tackling the determinants of health; strengthening health systems and equitable access; harnessing knowledge, science and technology; strengthening governance, leadership and accountability.

Its governing body, the World Health Assembly, is composed of 192 member states (including the Cook Islands) and meets annually. Its decisions and policies are given effect by the Executive Board, composed of 34 government-appointed health experts, which it meets twice a year.

WHO has Regional Offices in Brazzaville, Congo; Washington, D.C., USA; Cairo, Egypt; Copenhagen, Denmark; New Delhi, India; and Manila, Philippines. With a staff of some 3,500 health experts and other experts and support staff, WHO's regular budget for 2006-2007 was $3.3 billion.

Director-General: Dr. Margaret Chan (China)
Headquarters: 20 Avenue Appia, CH-1211 Geneva 27, Switzerland
Tel: (41-22) 791-2111; Fax: (41-22) 791-3111; Email: *inf@who.int*

International Monetary Fund (IMF)
(www.imf.org)

Established at the Bretton Woods Conference in 1944, the International Monetary Fund:

- facilitates international monetary cooperation;

- promotes exchange rate stability and orderly exchange arrangements;

- assists in the establishment of a multilateral system of payments and the elimination of foreign exchange restrictions;

- assists members by temporarily providing financial resources to correct maladjustments in their balance of payments.

The IMF has authority to create and allocate to its members international financial reserves in the form of "Special Drawing Rights (SDRs)". The Fund's financial resources consist primarily of the subscriptions ("quotas") of its 185 member countries, which totalled SDR 216.7 billion as of end-March 2007, or about $327 billion. Quotas are determined by a formula based upon the relative economic size of the members.

A core responsibility of the IMF is to provide loans to countries experiencing balance-of-payments problems. This financial assistance enables them to rebuild their international reserves, stabilize their currencies, continue paying for imports, and restore conditions for strong economic growth. In return, members borrowing from the Fund agree to undertake policy reforms to correct the problems that underlie these difficulties. The amounts that

International Bank for Reconstruction and Development (IBRD)
(www.worldbank.org)

The articles of IBRD were drawn up in 1944 at the Bretton Woods Conference, and the Bank began operations in 1946. IBRD aims to reduce poverty in middle-income and creditworthy poorer countries by promoting sustainable development through loans, guarantees and non-lending — including analytical and advisory services. IBRD does not maximize profit but has earned a net income each year since 1948.

The Bank, which has 185 members, raises almost all its money through the sale of AAA-rated bonds and other securities in international capital markets. The amount paid in by countries when they join the Bank constitutes less than 5 per cent of IBRD's funds, but it has been leveraged into some $433 billion in loans since the Bank was established.

In fiscal 2007, the Bank's new loan commitments amounted to $12.8 billion, covering 112 new operations in 34 countries.

International Development Association (IDA)
(www.worldbank.org)

IDA helps the world's poorest countries reduce poverty by providing credits — loans at zero interest with a 10-year grace period and maturities of 35 to 40 years. Since its establishment in 1960, IDA has provided $181 billion in interest-free credits to the world's 82 poorest countries, home to some 2.5 billion people. IDA commitments in fiscal 2007 reached $11.9 billion, 25 per cent higher than the previous year, and the highest in IDA's history. The largest share, around 50 per cent, went to Africa, which has 39 of the world's poorest countries.

The bulk of IDA's resources come from donor government contributions. These contributions come mainly from richer IDA members, but donor countries also include some that are current recipients of IBRD loans. Donors are asked every three years to replenish IDA funds. There have been 14 replenishments since IDA was established. In February 2005, donor representatives ("IDA Deputies"), concluding negotiations on the 14th replenishment, agreed on a framework for the projected programme and its financing needs. That replenishment made possible the commitment of SDRs worth some $32.5 billion to the world's poorest countries over the following three years — the largest expansion of IDA resources in two decades.

Negotiations for the 15th replenishment of IDA were launched in Paris in March 2007. One of the main issues under discussion is to ensure that IDA's future financial support for poor countries is not reduced as a result of debt cancellation under the Multilateral Debt Relief Initiative.

In fiscal 2007, IDA lending totalled $11.9 billion for 189 new operations in 64 countries. It has 166 members.

The Centre is an autonomous organization with close links to the Bank, and all of its members are also members of the Bank. Its Administrative Council, chaired by the World Bank's President, consists of one representative of each country that has ratified the Convention.

International Civil Aviation Organization (ICAO)
(www.icao.int)

The International Civil Aviation Organization was created in 1944 to promote the safe and orderly development of international civil aviation throughout the world. It sets standards and regulations necessary for aviation safety, security, efficiency and regularity, as well as for aviation environmental protection. It serves as the forum for cooperation in all fields of civil aviation among its 190 Contracting States.

ICAO has an Assembly, its sovereign body, comprising delegates from all Contracting States, and a Council of representatives of 36 nations elected by the Assembly. The Assembly meets at least once every three years: it decides ICAO policy and examines any matters not specifically referred to the Council. The Council is the executive body, and carries out Assembly directives.

Its budget for 2007 was $66.5 million. ICAO has over 700 staff members.

President of the Council: Mr. Roberto Kobeh González (Mexico)
Secretary General: Dr. Taïeb Chérif (Algeria)
Headquarters: 999 University Street, Montreal, Quebec H3C 5H7, Canada
Tel: (1-514) 954-8219; Fax: (1-514) 954-6077; Email: *icaohq@icao.int*

International Maritime Organization (IMO)
(www.imo.org)

The International Maritime Organization, which began functioning in 1959, is responsible for the safety and security of shipping engaged in international trade and for preventing marine pollution from ships.

IMO provides the machinery for governments to cooperate in formulating regulations and practices relating to technical matters affecting international shipping; to facilitate the adoption of the highest practicable standards of maritime safety and efficiency in navigation; and to protect the marine environment through prevention and control of pollution from ships.

More than 40 conventions and agreements and some 1,000 codes and recommendations have been produced by IMO and implemented globally.

In 1983, IMO established the World Maritime University in Malmö, Sweden, which provides advanced training for administrators, educators and others involved in shipping at the senior level. The IMO's International Maritime Law Institute (Valletta, Malta) was

Universal Postal Union (UPU)
(www.upu.int)

The Universal Postal Union is the specialized institution that regulates international postal services. Established by the Berne Treaty of 1874, it became a United Nations specialized agency in 1948.

The UPU plays a leadership role in promoting the continued revitalization of postal services. With 191 member countries, it is the primary vehicle for cooperation between postal services. It advises, mediates and renders technical assistance. Among its principal objectives are the promotion of universal postal service, growth in mail volumes through the provision of up-to-date postal products and services, and improvement in the quality of postal service for customers. In so doing, the UPU fulfils its basic mission of promoting and developing communication between all the people of the world.

The Universal Postal Congress is the supreme authority of the UPU. Meeting every five years, it examines strategic issues of concern to the postal sector and lays down the general programme of activities. The twenty-fourth Congress is to take place in Nairobi, Kenya, from 13 August to 3 September 2008.

UPU's annual budget is approximately CHF 37 million gross (around $30.4 million). Some 230 people, drawn from more than 45 countries, work at the UPU International Bureau.

Director-General: Mr. Eduaordo Dayan (France)
Headquarters: Weltpoststrasse 4, Case Postale 3000, Berne 15, Switzerland
Tel: (41-31) 350-3111; Fax: (41-31) 350-3110; Email: *info@upu.int*

World Meteorological Organization (WMO)
(www.wmo.ch)

The World Meteorological Organization, a United Nations specialized agency since 1951, provides authoritative scientific information on the state of the atmosphere, weather, freshwater resources, climate and related environmental issues.

Through international collaboration, WMO has developed and operates a global observing system and a network of global, regional and national centres, which provide weather, climate and hydrological forecasting services. This information system makes possible the rapid exchange of weather information and also promotes activities in operational hydrology.

WMO operates major programmes relating to weather, climate, atmospheric science, applied meteorology, the environment and water resources. These programmes provide the basis for better preparation and forewarning of most natural hazards, including heavy rain, strong winds, tropical cyclones, floods, sea surge, heat waves, droughts, El Niño and La Niña. They help save life and property, and improve our understanding of the environment and the climate. WMO has also drawn attention to issues of major concern, such as ozone layer depletion, global warming and diminishing water resources.

International Fund for Agricultural Development (IFAD)
(www.ifad.org)

Chronic hunger and malnutrition almost always accompany extreme poverty, and 75 per cent of the world's poorest people — almost 1 billion women, children and men — live in rural areas, depending on agriculture and related activities for their livelihoods. IFAD is an international financial institution and a specialized agency of the United Nations, dedicated to eradicating poverty in the rural areas of developing countries.

IFAD mobilizes resources from its 165 member countries to provide low-interest loans and grants to middle- and lower-income members to finance poverty reduction programmes and projects in the world's poorest communities. In 2007, IFAD adopted a debt sustainability framework based on a model developed by the International Development Association, to give grants instead of loans to countries with low debt sustainability. The framework is part of a unified effort by the world's largest multilateral financial institutions to ensure that essential financial assistance does not cause undue financial hardship for those countries most in need.

Partnerships are fundamental to IFAD's work. From its inception, IFAD has worked in partnership with national governments and international organizations. It also has strong relationships with national partners, including farmers' organizations and non-governmental organizations. Its partners in the international development community include other UN agencies, international financial institutions, research institutions and the private sector.

IFAD is financed by voluntary contributions from governments, special contributions, loan repayments and investment income. Since 1978, it has invested more than $9.5 billion in 731 projects and programmes that have reached more than 300 million poor rural people, and partners have contributed $16.1 billion in cofinancing. At the end of 2006, it was financing 186 ongoing programmes and projects worth $6.2 billion, of which IFAD had provided $2.9 billion and its partners about $3.3 billion.

IFAD's Governing Council is made up of all 165 member states and meets annually. The Executive Board, which consists of 18 members and 18 alternates, oversees IFAD's operations and approves loans and grants. At the end of 2006, IFAD had 436 staff members.

President: Mr. Lennart Båge (Sweden)
Headquarters: Via del Serafico 107, 00142 Rome, Italy
Tel: (39-06) 54-591; Fax: (39-06) 504-3463; Email: *ifad@ifad.org*

United Nations Industrial Development Organization (UNIDO)
(www.unido.org)

The mandate of the United Nations Industrial Development Organization is to promote industrial development and cooperation. Established by the General Assembly in 1966, it became a United Nations specialized agency in 1985.

UNIDO helps to improve the living conditions of people and promote global prosperity by offering tailor-made solutions for the sustainable industrial development of developing countries and countries in transition. It cooperates with governments, business associations and the private industrial sector to build industrial capabilities for meeting the challenges and spreading the benefits of the globalization of industry.

than 90 countries. Its total regular budget for 2007 was EUR 283.6 million; the target for additional, voluntary contributions to the Technical Co-operation Fund was $80 million.

Director General: Dr. Mohamed ElBaradei (Egypt)
Headquarters: PO Box 100, Wagramerstrasse 5, A-1400 Vienna, Austria
Tel: (43-1) 2600-0; Fax: (43-1) 2600-7; Email: *Official.Mail@iaea.org*

Preparatory Commission for the Comprehensive Nuclear-Test-Ban Treaty Organization (CTBTO)
(www.ctbto.org)

The Preparatory Commission for the Comprehensive Nuclear-Test-Ban Treaty Organization was established on 19 November 1996 at a Meeting of States Signatories to the Treaty held in New York. As an international organization financed by the States Signatories, it consists of two organs: a plenary body composed of all the States Signatories — also known as the Preparatory Commission — and the Provisional Technical Secretariat. The main task of the Preparatory Commission is to establish the global verification regime foreseen in the Treaty, so that it will be operational by the time the Treaty enters into force.

The Commission has three subsidiary bodies: Working Group A, on administrative and budgetary matters; Working Group B, on verification issues; and the Advisory Group on financial, budgetary and associated administrative issues. Its budget for 2007 was $48.3 million and EUR 48.6 million.

Executive Secretary: Mr. Tibor Tóth (Hungary)
Headquarters: Vienna International Centre, PO Box 1200, A-1400 Vienna, Austria
Tel: (43-1) 26030-6200; Fax: (43-1) 26030-5823; Email: *info@ctbto.org*

Organisation for the Prohibition of Chemical Weapons (OPCW)
(www.opcw.org)

The Organisation for the Prohibition of Chemical Weapons monitors the implementation of the Convention on the Prohibition of the Development, Production, Stockpiling and Use of Chemical Weapons and on their Destruction. The Convention, which entered into force on 29 April 1997, is the first multilateral disarmament and non-proliferation agreement that provides for the global elimination of an entire category of weapons of mass destruction, under stringent international verification and within prescribed timelines.

The OPCW is composed of 182 member states. Since 1997, member states have verifiably destroyed more than 25,020 metric tonnes of chemical agents — over 35 per cent of the total declared quantity of more than 71,000 metric tons (as of September 2007). That includes the destruction of more than one third of the 8 million declared munitions. Of the 65 former chemical weapons production facilities declared by 12 states parties under the Convention, over 93 per have been either destroyed or converted to use for permitted purposes.

OPCW inspectors have conducted more than 3,000 inspections at military and industrial plants in 80 countries. These missions ensure that chemical weapons production facilities are

World Trade Organization (WTO)
(www.wto.org)

The World Trade Organization was established in 1995, replacing the General Agreement on Tariffs and Trade (GATT) as the only international organization dealing with multilateral rules governing trade between nations. It is not a specialized agency, but has close cooperative arrangements and practices with the United Nations and UN agencies.

The purpose of the WTO is to help trade flow smoothly, in a system based on multilateral rules agreed to by all its members; to impartially settle trade disputes between governments; and to provide a forum for trade negotiations. At its heart are some 60 WTO agreements, the legal ground rules for international commerce and trade policy. The principles on which these agreements are based include: non-discrimination (the "most-favoured nation" clause and the national treatment provision), freer trade, encouraging competition, and special provisions for less developed countries. One of WTO's objectives is to gradually open trade for the benefit of all.

Since its establishment, the WTO has been the forum for successful negotiations to open markets in telecommunications, information technology equipment and financial services. It has been involved in settling close to 370 trade disputes, and continues to oversee implementation of the agreements reached in the 1986-1994 Uruguay Round of world trade talks. In 2001, at Doha, Qatar, the WTO launched a new round of multilateral trade negotiations known as the Doha Development Agenda. That round is still ongoing.

The WTO has 151 members. Its governing body, the Ministerial Conference, meets every two years; the General Council carries out the day-to-day work. WTO's budget for 2007 was CHF 182 million. It has a staff of some 664.

Director-General: Mr. Pascal Lamy (France)
Headquarters: Centre William Rappard, Rue de Lausanne 154,
CH-1211 Geneva 21, Switzerland
Tel: (41-22) 739-5111; Fax: (41-22) 731-4206;
Email: *enquiries@wto.org* (First go to *www.wto.org/english/info_e/cont_e.htm*)

INTERNATIONAL PEACE AND SECURITY

One of the primary purposes of the United Nations is the maintenance of international peace and security. Since its creation, the UN has often been called upon to prevent disputes from escalating into war, to persuade opposing parties to use the conference table rather than force of arms, or to help restore peace when armed conflict does break out. Over the decades, the UN has helped to end numerous conflicts, often through actions of the Security Council — the primary organ for dealing with issues of international peace and security.

During the 1990s, the end of the cold war led to an entirely new global security environment, one marked by a focus on internal rather than inter-state wars. In the early 21st century, new global threats emerged. The attacks of 11 September 2001 on the United States clearly demonstrated the challenge of international terrorism, while subsequent events heightened concern about the proliferation of nuclear weapons and the dangers from other non-conventional weapons, casting a shadow over people throughout the world.

The organizations of the UN system mobilized immediately in their respective spheres to step up action against terrorism. On 28 September, the Security Council adopted a wide-ranging resolution under the enforcement provisions of the UN Charter to prevent the financing of terrorism, criminalize the collection of funds for such purposes, and immediately freeze terrorist financial assets — establishing a Counter-Terrorism Committee to oversee its implementation.

The UN has also reshaped and enhanced the traditional range of instruments at its command, strengthening its peacekeeping capacity to meet new challenges, increasingly involving regional organizations, and enhancing its post-conflict peacebuilding capability. Civil conflicts have also raised complex issues regarding the adequate response of the international community, including the question of how best to assist civilian victims of war — a concept known as the "responsibility to protect". (See *box*)

To deal with civil conflicts, the Security Council has authorized complex and innovative peacekeeping operations. Since its establishment, the UN has played a major role in ending conflict and fostering reconciliation, including successful missions in El Salvador and Guatemala, in Cambodia and Mozambique, in Sierra Leone and Liberia and Tajikistan, to name but a few.

Other conflicts, however — such as in Somalia, Rwanda and the former Yugoslavia in the early 1990s — often characterized by ethnic violence and the lack of any internal power structure to deal with security issues, brought new challenges to United Nations peacemaking and peacekeeping.

Confronted with the problems encountered in these conflicts, the Security Council did not establish any new operation from 1995 to 1997. But soon the essential role of the UN was dramatically reaffirmed, as continuing crises in the Democratic Republic of the Congo, the Central African Republic, East Timor, Kosovo and Sierra Leone led the Council to establish five new missions as the decade drew to a close.

financial investment over the medium- to longer-term; extending the period of attention by the international community to post-conflict recovery; and developing best practices on issues that require extensive collaboration among political, military, humanitarian and development actors.

The concurrent General Assembly and Security Council resolutions establishing the Peacebuilding Commission also provided for establishment of a Peacebuilding Fund and a Peacebuilding Support Office. (See *box*, *The New Peacebuilding Architecture*, and *www.un.org/peace/peacebuilding*)

The Security Council, the General Assembly and the Secretary-General all play major, complementary roles in fostering peace and security. United Nations activities cover the principal areas of conflict prevention, peacemaking, peacekeeping, enforcement and peacebuilding. These types of engagement must overlap or take place simultaneously if they are to be effective. (For the UN role in maintaining peace and security, see *www.un.org/peace*)

The Security Council

The United Nations Charter — an international treaty — obligates member states to settle their disputes by peaceful means, in such a manner that international peace and security and justice are not endangered. They are to refrain from the threat or use of force against any state, and may bring any dispute before the Security Council.

The Security Council is the United Nations organ with primary responsibility for maintaining peace and security. Under the Charter, member states are obliged to accept and carry out its decisions. Recommendations of other United Nations bodies do not have the mandatory force of Security Council decisions, but can influence situations by expressing the opinion of the international community.

When a dispute is brought to its attention, the Council usually urges the parties to settle it by peaceful means. The Council may make recommendations to the parties for a peaceful settlement, appoint special representatives, ask the Secretary-General to use his good offices, and undertake investigation and mediation.

When a dispute leads to fighting, the Council seeks to bring it to an end as quickly as possible. Often the Council has issued ceasefire directives that have been instrumental in preventing wider hostilities. In support of a peace process, the Council may deploy military observers or a peacekeeping force to an area of conflict.

Under Chapter VII of the Charter, the Council is empowered to take measures to enforce its decisions. It can impose embargoes and sanctions, or authorize the use of force to ensure that mandates are fulfilled.

In some cases, the Council has authorized, under Chapter VII, the use of military force by a coalition of member states or by a regional organization or arrangement. But the Council takes such action only as a last resort, when peaceful means of settling a dispute have been and "make recommendations ... to the Members or to the Security Council or to both". The Assembly offers a means for finding consensus on difficult issues, providing a forum for the airing of grievances and diplomatic exchanges. To foster the maintenance of peace, it has held special sessions or emergency special sessions on such issues as disarmament, the question of Palestine and the situation in Afghanistan.

The General Assembly considers peace and security issues in its First (Disarmament and International Security) Committee and in its Fourth (Special Political and Decolonization) Committee. Over the years, the Assembly has helped promote peaceful relations among nations by adopting declarations on peace, the peaceful settlement of disputes and international cooperation.

The Assembly in 1980 approved the establishment in San José, Costa Rica, of the **University for Peace**, an international institute for studies, research and dissemination of knowledge on peace-related issues.

The Assembly has designated 21 September each year as the **International Day of Peace**.

Conflict prevention

The main strategies for preventing disputes from escalating into conflict, and for preventing the recurrence of conflict, are preventive diplomacy and preventive disarmament.

Preventive diplomacy refers to action to prevent disputes from arising, to resolve them before they escalate into conflicts, or to limit the spread of conflicts when they occur. It may take the form of mediation, conciliation or negotiation. Early warning is an essential component of prevention, and the United Nations carefully monitors political and other developments around the world to detect threats to international peace and security, thereby enabling the Security Council and the Secretary-General to carry out preventive action.

Envoys and special representatives of the Secretary-General are engaged in mediation and preventive diplomacy throughout the world. In some trouble spots, the mere presence of a skilled special representative can prevent the escalation of tension. This work is often undertaken in close cooperation with regional organizations.

Complementing preventive diplomacy, *preventive disarmament* seeks to reduce the number of small arms in conflict-prone regions. In El Salvador, Sierra Leone, Liberia and elsewhere, this has entailed demobilizing combat forces as well as collecting and destroying their weapons as part of an overall peace agreement. Destroying yesterday's weapons prevents their being used in tomorrow's wars.

Peacemaking

Peacemaking refers to the use of diplomatic means to persuade parties in conflict to cease hostilities and to negotiate the peaceful settlement of a dispute. The United Nations provides various means through which conflicts may be contained and resolved, and their root causes addressed. The Security Council may recommend ways to resolve a dispute or request the Secretary-General's mediation. The **Secretary-General** may take diplomatic initiatives to encourage and maintain the momentum of negotiations.

The Secretary-General plays a central role in peacemaking, both personally and by dispatching special envoys or missions for specific tasks, such as negotiation or fact-finding. Under the Charter, the Secretary-General may bring to the attention of the Security Council any matter that might threaten the maintenance of international peace and security.

To help resolve disputes, the Secretary-General may use his "good offices" for mediation or to exercise preventive diplomacy. The impartiality of the Secretary-General is one of the United Nations great assets. In many instances, the Secretary-General has been instrumental in averting a threat to peace or in securing a peace agreement.

For example, action by the Secretary-General and his envoy helped end, in 1996, the 36 year civil conflict in Guatemala. In the Democratic Republic of the Congo, the Secretary-General and his envoy helped negotiate the 2003 agreements that ended the country's civil war. Cases such as Tajikistan, El Salvador, Mozambique and Namibia reflect the many different ways the Secretary-General becomes involved as a peacemaker. Most recently, the Secretary-General has played a key role in the efforts to resolve the conflict in Darfur, in the Sudan, and the establishment of a new peacekeeping mission there — UNAMID.

Peacekeeping

United Nations peacekeeping operations are a crucial instrument at the disposal of the international community to advance peace and security. The role of UN peacekeeping was recognized in 1988, when United Nations peacekeeping forces received the Nobel Peace Prize.

While not specifically envisaged in the Charter, the UN pioneered peacekeeping in 1948 with the establishment of the United Nations Truce Supervision Organization in the Middle East. Since then, it has established a total of 63 — operations — 50 of these since 1988.[1] On 1 October 2007, there were 17 active peacekeeping operations. (See *box*)

Peacekeeping operations are deployed with the authorization of the Security Council and the consent of the host government and/or the main parties to the conflict. Peacekeeping has

---

[1] The intervention in Korea in 1950 was not a United Nations peacekeeping operation. In June 1950, the United States and the United Nations Commission on Korea informed the United Nations that the Republic of Korea had been attacked by forces from North Korea. The Security Council recommended that member states furnish the necessary assistance to the Republic of Korea to repel the attack and restore peace and security. In July, the Council recommended that member states providing military forces make them available to a unified command under the United States; 16 nations made troops available. This force, known as the United Nations Command and authorized by the Council to fly the United Nations flag, was not a United Nations peacekeeping operation, but an international force acting under a unified command. The Soviet Union, which had been absent from the Security Council in protest against the Chinese Nationalist government representing China at the United Nations, deemed the Council's decisions illegal on the grounds that two permanent members (the Soviet Union and China) were absent. Fighting continued until July 1953, when an armistice agreement was signed.

United Nations peacekeeping operations*

- United Nations Truce Supervision Organization (UNTSO, established 1948), in the Middle East (strength: military 152; civilian 225)

- United Nations Military Observer Group in India and Pakistan (UNMOGIP, 1949) (military 44; civilian 73)

- United Nations Peacekeeping Force in Cyprus (UNFICYP, 1964) (military 872; civilian police 66; civilian 145)

- United Nations Disengagement Observer Force (UNDOF, 1974), in the Syrian Golan Heights (military 1,047; civilian 140)

- United Nations Interim Force in Lebanon (UNIFIL, 1978) (military 12,341; civilian 908)

- United Nations Mission for the Referendum in Western Sahara (MINURSO, 1991) (military 214; police 6; civilian 247; UN Volunteers 24)

- United Nations Observer Mission in Georgia (UNOMIG, 1993) (military 134; police 18; civilian 282; UN Volunteers 1)

- United Nations Interim Administration Mission in Kosovo (UNMIK, 1999) (military 40; police 1,953; civilian 2,412; UN Volunteers 132)

- United Nations Observer Mission in the Democratic Republic of the Congo (MONUC, 1999) (military 17,359; police 1.049; civilian 3,021; UN Volunteers 571)

- United Nations Mission in Ethiopia and Eritrea (UNMEE, 2000) (military 503; civilian 343; UN Volunteers 63)

- United Nations Mission in Liberia (UNMIL, 2003) (military 12,438; police 1,148; civilian 1,453; UN Volunteers 238)

- United Nations Operation in Côte d'Ivoire (UNOCI, 2004) (military 8,034; police 1,182; civilians 989; UN Volunteers 284)

- United Nations Stabilization Mission in Haiti (MINUSTAH, 2004) (military 7,064; civilian police 1,923; civilian 1,663; UN Volunteers 199)

- United Nations Mission in the Sudan (UNMIS, 2005) (military 9,288; police 664; civilian 3,196; UN Volunteers 250)

- United Nations Integrated Mission in Timor-Leste (UNMIT, 2006) (military 33; civilian police 1,546; civilian 1,134; UN Volunteers 124)

- African Union-United Nations Hybrid Operation in Darfur (UNAMID, 2007) (military 7,509; police 1,704; civilian 960; UN Volunteers 129) (when fully deployed: military 19,555; police 6, 432; civilians 5,034; UN Volunteers 548)

- United Nations Mission in the Central African Republic and Chad (MINURCAT, 2007) (military 14; police 71; civilian 32; UN Volunteers 16) (when fully deployed: "a maximum of 300 police and 50 military liaison officers and an appropriate number of civilian personnel")

---

* As of 1 April 2008. For all operations, past and present, see Part Three (Appendices).

strategic oversight and operational political guidance. These changes were to be phased in over a period of 12 months.

The Under-Secretary-General in charge of DFS reports to and receives direction from the Under-Secretary-General for Peacekeeping Operations, in order to help ensure unity of command in UN peacekeeping.[2]

Peacekeeping operations can take many forms. They are constantly evolving in the light of changing circumstances. Among the tasks discharged by peacekeeping operations over the years are:

- *Maintenance of ceasefires and separation of forces.* By providing "breathing space", an operation based on a limited agreement between parties can foster an atmosphere conducive to negotiations.

- *Protection of humanitarian operations.* In many conflicts, civilian populations have been deliberately targeted as a means to gain political ends. In such situations, peacekeepers have been asked to provide protection and support for humanitarian operations. However, such tasks can place peacekeepers in difficult political positions, and can lead to threats to their security.

- *Implementation of a comprehensive peace settlement.* Complex, multidimensional operations, deployed on the basis of comprehensive peace agreements, can assist in such diverse tasks as providing humanitarian assistance, monitoring human rights, observing elections and coordinating support for economic reconstruction.

No catalogue of such roles can be exhaustive. Future conflicts are likely to continue to present complex challenges to the international community. An effective response will require courageous and imaginative use of the tools for peace.

Cooperating with regional and collective security organizations. In the search for peace, the United Nations has been increasingly cooperating with regional organizations and other actors and mechanisms provided for in Chapter VIII of the Charter.

It has worked closely with the Organization of American States (OAS) in Haiti; the European Union (EU) in the former Yugoslavia and the Democratic Republic of the Congo; the Economic Community of West African States (ECOWAS) in Liberia and Sierra Leone; and the African Union (AU) in Western Sahara, the Great Lakes region and Darfur — to name just a few.[3]

United Nations military observers have cooperated with peacekeeping forces of regional organizations in Liberia, Sierra Leone, Georgia and Tajikistan; and forces of the

---

[2] The Secretary-General's original detailed proposals are contained in his "Comprehensive report on strengthening the capacity of the United Nations to manage and sustain peace operations", of 13 April 2007 (document A/61/858).

[3] The Organization of African Union (OAU), originally established in 1963 to promote unity, solidarity and international cooperation among the newly independent African states, was reconstituted on 10 July 2002 as the African Union (AU) (*www.african-union.org*). Headquartered in Ethiopia, it has 53 members and is modelled after the European Union (EU) (*http://europa.eu*).

United Nations Political and Peacebuilding Missions*

- United Nations Political Office for Somalia (UNPOS, 1995) (civilian 28)
- United Nations Peacebuilding Support Office in Guinea-Bissau (UNOGBIS, 1999) (military advisers 2; police adviser 1; civilian 26; UN Volunteers 1)
- United Nations Special Coordinator for the Middle East (UNSCO, 1999) (civilian 50)
- United Nations Peacebuilding Office in the Central African Republic (BONUCA, 2000) (military advisers 5; police 6; civilian 79; UN Volunteers 3)
- Office of the Special Representative of the Secretary-General for West Africa (2001) (civilian 17)
- United Nations Assistance Mission in Afghanistan (UNAMA, 2002) (military observers 14; police 3; civilian 1,291; UN Volunteers 35)
- United Nations Assistance Mission for Iraq (UNAMI, 2003) (based in Iraq, Jordan and Kuwait) (military 224; civilian 632) (Authorized strength: 1,014)
- United Nations Integrated Office in Sierra Leone (UNIOSIL, 2006) (military observers 14; police 21; civilian 277; UN Volunteers 23)
- United Nations Integrated Office in Burundi (BINUB, 2007) (military observers 8; police 10; civilian 358; UN Volunteers 49)
- United Nations Political Mission in Nepal (UNMIN, 2007) (military observers 146; police 4; civilian 459; UN Volunteers 247)
- United Nations Special Coordinator of the Secretary-General for Lebanon (2007) (civilian 31)
- United Nations Regional Centre for Preventive Diplomacy for Central Asia (UNRCCA, 2007) (Proposed staffing complement 19)

---

* As of 1 April 2008.

Authorizing military action

When peacemaking efforts fail, stronger action by member states may be authorized under Chapter VII of the Charter. The Security Council has authorized coalitions of member states to use "all necessary means", including military action, to deal with a conflict — as it did to restore the sovereignty of Kuwait after its invasion by Iraq (1991); to establish a secure environment for humanitarian relief operations in Somalia (1992); to contribute to the protection of civilians at risk in Rwanda (1994); to restore the democratically elected government in Haiti (1994); to protect humanitarian operations in Albania (1997); and to restore peace and security in East Timor (1999 and 2006).

These actions, though sanctioned by the Security Council, were entirely under the control of the participating states. They were not United Nations peacekeeping operations — which are established by the Security Council and directed by the Secretary-General.

An interim administrator

The United Nations has sometimes played a role in helping to administer countries in transition. Requested to step in after a conflict, the Organization has carried out wide-ranging tasks in this new form of peacebuilding — on occasion taking up the full range of government powers while working with local political and civil leaders to build a self-sustaining government.

An example of such an administrative role took place in Cambodia in 1992- 1993, following years of civil war. As specified in the 1991 peace agreement, the Security Council established the United Nations Transitional Authority in Cambodia, which ran key sectors of the country's administration. After the 1993 elections, the mission relinquished its powers to the new government.

Another peacekeeping operation with administrative responsibilities was the United Nations Transitional Authority in Eastern Slavonia, Baranja and Western Sirmium, which was deployed from 1996 to 1998 to assist in the peaceful integration of that area into Croatia.

In 1999, the Security Council established the United Nations Interim Administration Mission in Kosovo, with legislative, executive and judiciary powers. The mission has been running the administration of the province, but progressively turning over these functions to authorities in Kosovo, pending its final status.

Also in 1999, the Security Council established the United Nations Transitional Administration in East Timor, with legislative and executive authority. The mission helped develop social services, assist in reconstruction and build capacity towards nationhood. The Territory attained independence in May 2002 as Timor-Leste.

governments, has assisted with elections in countries such as Nicaragua (1990), Angola (1992), Cambodia (1993), El Salvador, South Africa and Mozambique (1994), Eastern Slavonia (Croatia) (1997), the Central African Republic (1998 and 1999), Afghanistan (2004 and 2005), Iraq and Liberia (2005), and Haiti and the Democratic Republic of the Congo (2006). It also observed the 1993 referendum in Eritrea, and organized and conducted the 1999 popular consultation in East Timor and its 2001 and 2002 elections, which led to the independence of East Timor as Timor-Leste, as well as its elections in 2007.

The degree and type of United Nations involvement depends upon such factors as the requests received from governments, provisions of peace agreements, or mandates from the General Assembly or the Security Council. The UN has played a variety of roles, ranging from technical assistance to the actual conduct of the electoral process. In some cases, the UN will coordinate the activities of international observers. Typically, such observers follow the registration of voters, the electoral campaign and the organization of the polls.

Since 1992, the United Nations has provided various forms of electoral assistance to more than 107 countries — including advisory services, logistics, training, civic education, computer applications and short-term observation. The **Electoral Assistance Division** in the Department of Political Affairs (*www.un.org/Depts/dpa/ead*) serves as the focal point for electoral assistance within the UN system.

Africa: a United Nations priority

Africa remains an area of continuing major focus and action by the United Nations. The Organization has addressed the challenge posed by protracted conflicts and longstanding disputes on the continent in innovative ways and at the highest level. In their *Millennium Declaration* in September 2000, world leaders resolved to give full support, including special measures to help Africa tackle its peace and development issues. UN action for Africa over the years has included its campaign against apartheid in South Africa, active support for Namibia's independence, and some 25 peacekeeping operations in various countries on the continent.

Among these, a UN mission in Ethiopia and Eritrea helps maintain peace between those two countries. UN forces in Côte d'Ivoire since 2003 support peace agreements between divided parts of the country. A mission deployed in 2005 works to support the comprehensive peace agreement between north and south Sudan. In the Democratic Republic of the Congo, a major peacekeeping mission helped unify that giant country, which in 2006 enjoyed its first democratic elections since independence. In Liberia, a UN operation is helping that country restore stability and reconciliation after a 14-year civil war. And new peacekeeping operations have been authorized for Darfur, and for the Central African Republic and Chad.

In a 1998 report on the causes of conflict in Africa, the Secretary-General urged African nations to rely on political rather than military responses; embrace good governance, respect for human rights, democratization and accountable public administration; and enact reforms to promote economic growth. Subsequently, the Security Council adopted resolutions on the destabilizing effects of illicit arms flows, on arms embargoes, and on conflict prevention in Africa. And in January 2000, it held a month-long series of meetings on Africa, addressing such issues as conflict resolution, HIV/AIDS, refugees and internally displaced persons, and UN peace efforts.

The Secretary-General and his special representatives, advisers and envoys remain actively engaged in UN action for Africa, and the UN continues to act in close collaboration with the African Union and subregional organizations such as the Economic Community of West African States (ECOWAS) and the Southern African Development Community (SADC).

And since 2003, the Office of the Special Adviser on Africa (OSAA) has been working to enhance international support for African development and security, improve coordination of UN system support, and facilitate global deliberations on Africa, particularly with respect to a strategic framework adopted by African leaders in 2001 — the New Partnership for Africa's Development (NEPAD).

(For additional information, see *www.un.org/africa/osaa*).

Great Lakes region of Africa

Rwanda. United Nations involvement in Rwanda began in 1993, when Rwanda and Uganda requested the deployment of military observers along their common border to prevent military use of the area by the Rwandese Patriotic Front (RPF). In response, the Security Council established the **United Nations Observer Mission Uganda-Rwanda (UNOMUR)**.

Fighting had broken out in Rwanda in 1990 between the mainly Hutu government and the Tutsi-led RPF, operating from Uganda. A 1993 peace agreement provided for a transitional government and for elections. At the parties' request, the Security Council set up the **United Nations Assistance Mission for Rwanda (UNAMIR)** to help them implement it. But in early April 1994, the death of the Presidents of Rwanda and Burundi in a plane crash caused by rocket fire ignited weeks of intense and systemic waves of massacres by the Hutu-dominated army and militias, aimed at exterminating Tutsis and moderate Hutus.

UNAMIR sought to arrange a ceasefire, without success, and when some countries unilaterally withdrew their contingents, the Security Council reduced UNAMIR's strength from 2,548 to 270. Nevertheless, UNAMIR managed to shelter thousands of Rwandans. In May, the Council imposed an arms embargo against Rwanda and increased UNAMIR's strength to up to 5,500 troops, but it took nearly six months for member states to provide them. In July, RPF forces took control of Rwanda, ending the civil war and establishing a broad-based government.

From a population of 7.9 million, approximately 800,000 people had been murdered, some 2 million fled to other countries, and up to 2 million were internally displaced. A UN appeal raised $762 million to address the enormous humanitarian challenge.

In November 1994, the Council established the **International Criminal Tribunal for Rwanda (ICTR)** to prosecute those responsible for genocide and war crimes. By January 2007, it had indicted 90 individuals, handing down 25 judgements involving 31 accused; there were 28 detainees on trial, nine awaiting trial, and seven whose cases were pending appeal; 18 accused remained at large. Former President Jean Kambanda was convicted and sentenced to life in prison. The ICTR is set to end its term in 2008.

In 1996, at Rwanda's request, the Council terminated UNAMIR's mandate. In 1999, an independent inquiry commissioned by the Secretary-General found that responsibility for the failure to stop the genocide was shared by the UN Secretariat, the Security Council and the member states. He expressed deep remorse over the United Nations failure to stop the genocide, and restated his commitment to make sure the Organization never again fails to stop mass slaughter.

In 2003, a new constitution was adopted by referendum, Paul Kagame gained a landslide victory in presidential elections, and his RPF party won a large majority in the first multiparty, parliamentary elections since independence in 1962. To mark the tenth anniversary of the genocide in Rwanda, the General Assembly declared 7 April 2004 as an International Day of Reflection on the 1994 Genocide in Rwanda.

faction. Sixteen of Burundi's 17 provinces were now subject to sporadic fighting, looting and armed banditry. The UN withdrew its non-essential staff from Bujumbura.

Nevertheless, sustained efforts by South African President Thabo Mbeki and other regional leaders resulted in the signing between the transitional government and the CNDD/FDD of a Global Ceasefire Agreement in November 2003, as CNDD/FDD joined the transitional institutions. The Security Council urged Palipehutu-FNL (Rwasa), the only armed rebel group which had not yet joined the Arusha Agreement, to do so.

At long last there was real hope that a democratic Burundi would emerge from a decade of civil strife that had left between 250,000 and 300,000 people dead, and the presence of AMIB had played a key role in making it possible. But the Mission suffered from a serious lack of funds and logistics support. With legislative elections scheduled to take place before 31 October 2004, the AU requested that AMIB be taken over by the United Nations.

In May 2004, acting under the enforcement provisions of the UN Charter, the Security Council authorized the deployment, on 1 June, of the **United Nations Operation in Burundi (ONUB)** — to be composed, initially, of existing AMIB forces. On 1 June, more than 2,000 AMIB troops were "rehatted" as United Nations forces.

In February 2005, a successful referendum on Burundi's post-transitional constitution was held, followed by communal elections in June, and the election of Pierre Nkurunziza as the country's first post-transitional President in August. In June 2006, the government and the FNL signed an Agreement of Principles; it led to a ceasefire agreement in September, which the UN offered to help implement.

On 1 January 2007, ONUB was replaced with a small UN Integrated Office in Burundi (BINUB), to support the peace consolidation process and assist the government in such areas as strengthening national institutions, training the police, professionalizing the national defence force, completing demobilization and reintegration of former combatants, protecting human rights, reforming the justice and legal sector, and promoting economic growth and poverty reduction.

Democratic Republic of the Congo. Following the 1994 genocide in Rwanda and the establishment of a new government there, some 1.2 million Rwandese Hutus — including elements who had taken part in the genocide —fled to the Kivu provinces of eastern Zaire, an area inhabited by ethnic Tutsis and others. There, a rebellion began in 1996, pitting rebel forces led by Laurent Désiré Kabila against the army of President Mobutu Sese Seko. Kabila's forces, aided by Rwanda and Uganda, took the capital city of Kinshasa in 1997 and renamed the country the Democratic Republic of the Congo (DRC).

In 1998, a rebellion against the Kabila government started in the Kivus. Within weeks, the rebels had seized large areas of the country. Angola, Chad, Namibia and Zimbabwe promised President Kabila military support, but the rebels maintained their grip on the eastern regions. Rwanda and Uganda supported the rebel movement, the Congolese Rally for Democracy (RCD). The Security Council called for a ceasefire and the withdrawal of foreign forces, and urged states not to interfere in the country's internal affairs.

29 October, and resolution of a subsequent legal challenge, President Joseph Kabila was declared the winner. The entire electoral process represented one of the most complex votes the UN had ever helped organize.

Through MONUC, the UN remains actively involved in trying to resolve the conflict in the province of North Kivu between the national army and forces loyal to a dissident former general. In November 2007, the UN facilitated an agreement between the governments of the DRC and Rwanda to address the threat posed to the region by illegal local and foreign armed groups that still remained in the eastern DRC, including the former Hutu militias ("Interahamwe") and Rwandan Armed Forces ("ex-FAR").

Central African Republic. The conflict in the Central African Republic occurred when soldiers staged a series of mutinies in the mid-1990s. In 1998, following an intervention by troops from France, the former colonial power, and later by an African multinational force (MISAB), the UN established the **United Nations Mission in the Central African Republic (MINURCA)** — a peacekeeping operation with a mandate to help improve security in the capital, Bangui. Later, the United Nations also provided support for elections, which were concluded the following year. **The United Nations Peacebuilding Office in the Central African Republic (BONUCA)** was created in February 2000, following the withdrawal of MINURCA.

But unrest continued, and an attempted coup by army officers was put down in May 2001. Two years later, in March 2003, a group led by General François Bozizé forcefully took power through a coup d'état, ousting elected President Ange-Félix Patassé. The Security Council condemned the coup, stressing that the Bangui authorities must elaborate a plan for national dialogue, including a time frame for the holding of elections as soon as possible.

By the end of June, the UN Secretary-General reported that the new authorities envisaged a process of national dialogue, which led to two rounds of legislative and presidential elections in March and May 2005. In the final runoff ballot, General Bozizé was elected with 64.6 per cent of the vote. The newly elected National Assembly held its first regular session from 1 March to 30 May 2006.

International Conference on the Great Lakes Region. In view of the important regional dimension of the conflicts involving the Great Lakes countries, the Security Council, following the 1994 Rwanda genocide, called for the convening of an international conference on the region. At the end of the 1990s, the Office of the Special Representative of the Secretary-General for the Great Lakes was established. Located in Nairobi, Kenya, it played a key role in promoting dialogue. It was also to serve, with the African Union, as joint secretariat for the conference. The first International Conference on the Great Lakes Region was held in Dar es Salaam, Tanzania, in November 2004.

Meeting again in December 2006, the 11 regional heads of state and governments which had participated in the conference signed a Pact on Security, Stability and Development in the Great Lakes Region, concluding a four-year diplomatic process. The Pact provides a framework for the 11 signatories — Angola, Burundi, Central African Republic, Congo, Democratic Republic of

Yaoundé, Cameroon, and Abuja, Nigeria. The ensuing years saw slow progress and repeated delays until 12 June 2006, when the Presidents of both countries signed an agreement to end the border dispute over the Bakassi peninsula, following intense mediation by the Secretary-General. By 14 August, Nigeria had completely withdrawn its troops and formally transferred authority over the region to Cameroon. In October, the Secretary-General reported that steady progress was being made in marking their common boundary, under the supervision of the Mixed Commission.

Côte d'Ivoire. In December 1999, a group of officers and soldiers led by General Robert Guei overthrew Côte d'Ivoire's government. New presidential elections were scheduled for October 2000. Realizing that he was losing in the polls to Laurent Gbagbo, leader of the Front Populaire Ivorienne, Guei claimed victory on 23 October. Alassane Ouattara, leader of the Rassemblement Démocratique des Républicains, had been barred from contesting the elections under a new, controversial Constitution.

As thousands of people demonstrated against Guei's action in Abidjan, Gbagbo declared himself president, and Guei fled the city. Violent clashes ensued in the streets of the capital between Gbagbo's supporters, those backing Ouattara and security forces. Hundreds died. An independent commission established by the Secretary-General later concluded that the security forces had been repressing the protests and were implicated in the killings.

A national reconciliation process was launched under the chairmanship of former Prime Minister Seydou Diarra, and in August 2002, President Gbagbo formed a new, broad-based government. But tensions persisted. And on 19 September, groups of disgruntled military personnel attempted a coup and occupied the northern part of the country. The attempted coup resulted in a de facto partition of the country, with the government controlling the south, one rebel group controlling the north and north-east, and two other groups controlling the west. The fighting caused massive displacements.

The Economic Community of West African States (ECOWAS) established a peacekeeping force, which was deployed to monitor a ceasefire agreement between the government and one of the rebel groups. On 11 January 2003, the government and the remaining rebel groups agreed to a ceasefire.

From 15 to 23 January 2003, the government and rebel forces met in Linas-Marcoussis, France, and a peace agreement was reached, providing for the establishment of a government of national reconciliation. In keeping with the accord, President Gbagbo established the national reconciliation government on 13 March, with Seydou Diarra as Prime Minister with enlarged powers. On 3 May, the Forces armées nationales de Côte d'Ivoire and the Forces Nouvelles — comprising the three rebel groups — signed a ceasefire agreement that covered the whole country.

On 13 May 2003, the Security Council established the **United Nations Mission in Côte d'Ivoire (MINUCI)**, consisting of up to 76 military liaison officers and a civilian component, to facilitate implementation of the Linas-Marcoussis Agreement. In September, however, the Forces Nouvelles rejected President Gbagbo's appointment of defence and

But the fighting continued, and on 23 July, with rebel mortars pounding the capital, hundreds of hungry, terrified refugees scrambled for safety inside the walls of the UN compound. ECOWAS decided to send in a vanguard force of 1,000 to 1,500 troops. Upon their arrival, reinforcements from the United States and other countries would move in to prepare for a UN mission.

On 1 August, the Security Council authorized the ECOWAS multinational force. Three days later, the UN airlifted the first of two battalions to Liberia's main airport. Taking advantage of a lull in the violence, UN and other relief agencies began rushing food and medical supplies to hundreds of thousands of desperate people crowding the streets of Monrovia.

President Taylor resigned his office on 11 August, and departed for exile in Nigeria. His Vice-President, Moses Blah, succeeded him, to head an interim government. Days later, the Secretary-General's special representative secured a signed agreement by the parties to ensure free and unimpeded access of humanitarian aid to all territories under their control, and to guarantee the security of aid workers. They also signed a comprehensive peace agreement.

On 19 September 2003, the Security Council established the **United Nations Mission in Liberia (UNMIL)** — with up to 15,000 military personnel and over 1,000 civilian police officers — to take over from the ECOWAS force on 1 October, and to replace UNOL. Its mandate included: monitoring the ceasefire; assisting in the disarmament, demobilization, reintegration and repatriation (DDDR) of all armed parties; providing security at key government installations and vital infrastructure; protecting UN staff, facilities and civilians; and assisting in humanitarian aid and human rights. UNMIL was also mandated to help the transitional government develop a strategy to consolidate its institutions, with a view to holding free and fair elections by October 2005.

As scheduled, 3,500 ECOWAS soldiers were "rehatted" with the UN blue helmet. Within two weeks, the parties declared Monrovia a "weapons-free zone". On 14 October, the national transitional government was installed, led by Chairman Gyude Bryant. On 17 October, former President Blah turned over a large quantity of arms to UN peacekeepers, declaring: "We do not want to fight anymore".

The DDDR process was launched on 1 December. Over the next 12 months, nearly 100,000 Liberians turned in guns, ammunition, rocket-propelled grenades and other weapons. On 3 November 2004, Liberia's warring militias formally disbanded in a ceremony at UNMIL headquarters in Monrovia. By the end of February 2006, more than 300,000 internally displaced Liberians had been returned to their home villages.

After 15 years of conflict, the people of Liberia, with UN assistance, held their first post-war elections. Turning out in massive numbers on 12 October 2005 — and later in a run-off between the top two contenders — they elected Ellen Johnson-Sirleaf as President, with 59.4 per cent of the vote. She took office on 16 January 2006 and set up a Truth and Reconciliation Commission to heal the country's wounds.

Although major challenges remain, Liberia has been making steady progress towards peaceful nationhood. As a result, the Council, on 20 September 2007, endorsed Secretary-General

overthrew the government. In 1995, the Secretary-General appointed a special envoy who, working with the OAU and the Economic Community of West African States (ECOWAS), negotiated a return to civilian rule. Following elections in 1996, in which the RUF did not participate, the army relinquished power to the winner, Ahmad Tejan Kabbah. The special envoy then helped negotiate the 1996 Abidjan Peace Accord between the government and the RUF. But in 1997, in another military coup, the army joined with the RUF to form a ruling junta. President Kabbah went into exile, and the Security Council imposed an oil and arms embargo — authorizing ECOWAS to ensure its implementation using troops of its monitoring group, ECOMOG.

When supporters of the junta attacked ECOMOG in 1998, its military response led to the junta's collapse. President Kabbah was returned to office, and the Council ended the embargo. In June, the Council established the **United Nations Observer Mission in Sierra Leone (UNOMSIL)** to monitor the security situation, the disarmament of combatants, and restructuring of the security forces. Unarmed UNOMSIL teams, under ECOMOG protection, documented atrocities and human rights abuses.

The rebel alliance soon gained control of more than half of the country, and in a January 1999 overran most of the capital, Freetown. Later that month, ECOMOG troops retook Freetown and reinstalled the government. The fighting had resulted in 700,000 internally displaced persons (IDPs) and 450,000 refugees. The special representative, in consultation with West African states, began diplomatic efforts to open up a dialogue with the rebels. These negotiations led in July to the Lomé Peace Agreement – to end the war and form a government of national unity.

The Security Council replaced UNOMSIL in October with the larger **United Nations Mission in Sierra Leone (UNAMSIL)**, to help the parties put the agreement into effect and assist in disarming, demobilizing and reintegrating some 45,000 combatants. In February 2000, following the announced withdrawal of ECOMOG, UNAMSIL's strength was increased to 11,000 troops. But in April, when the RUF attacked UN forces after ex-combatants came forward to disarm, four peacekeepers were killed and nearly 500 UN personnel taken hostage.

In May, British troops serving under a bilateral arrangement secured the capital and its airport, and assisted in capturing the RUF leader, Foday Sankoh, who was arrested by the police. By the end of the month, around half of the UN hostages had been released. The Council increased UNAMSIL's strength to 13,000 troops to help restore peace, and in July UNAMSIL rescued the remaining hostages. In August, the Council began the process of setting up a special court to try those responsible for war crimes.

UNAMSIL completed its deployment to all areas of the country in November 2001, and the disarmament process was completed in January. Following presidential and parliamentary elections in May 2002, the Mission focused on extension of state authority throughout the country, the reintegration of ex-combatants, and the resettlement of IDPs and returnees. The IDP resettlement was completed in December, the repatriation of some 280,000 Sierra

African Union Mission in the Sudan (AMIS) was deployed as a monitoring mission, and a **United Nations Advance Mission in the Sudan (UNAMIS)** was established to prepare for introduction of a peace operation.

Over 2 million people died, 4 million were uprooted and some 600,000 others fled the country, until the signing of the **Comprehensive Peace Agreement (CPA)** on 9 January 2005. The CPA covered security arrangements, power-sharing in the capital, some autonomy for the south, and more equitable distribution of economic resources, including oil. Under its terms, interim institutions would govern for six-and-a-half years, observed by international monitors. Then, in an internationally monitored referendum, the people of southern Sudan would vote for Sudanese unity or secession.

On 24 March 2005, the Security Council established the **United Nations Mission in the Sudan (UNMIS)**, with a mandate to support implementation of the CPA; facilitate and coordinate humanitarian assistance and the voluntary return of refugees and internally displaced persons; and assist the parties in mine action. It was also to contribute to protecting and promoting human rights, and coordinate international efforts to protect civilians — with particular attention to vulnerable groups.

During the same period, the African Union (AU) increased AMIS to a total authorized strength of 6,171 military personnel and 1,560 civilian police — "to promote a more secure environment and confidence-building measures, as well as protect civilians and humanitarian operations".

In September 2005, a Government of National Unity was established. Although the parties were respecting the letter of the CPA on the whole, the spirit of cooperation, inclusiveness and transparency was less than had been hoped. The continuing crisis in Darfur was also having a direct and negative effect on its implementation.

The UN role in Darfur. Ethnic, economic and political tensions had long combined with competition over scarce resources to fuel violence in Darfur. In 2003, the government's decision to deploy its national armed forces and to mobilize local militia in response to attacks by the Sudan Liberation Movement/Army (SLM/A) and the Justice and Equality Movement (JEM) took that violence to unprecedented levels. Indiscriminate air bombardment by Sudan's armed forces, along with attacks by the Janjaweed and other militias, left villages across the region razed to the ground. Civilians were murdered, women and girls raped, children abducted, and food and water sources destroyed.

In July 2004, the African Union (AU) had launched negotiations at inter-Sudanese peace talks in Abuja, while deploying 60 military observers and 310 protection troops to Darfur to monitor compliance with a humanitarian ceasefire agreement that had been signed in April by the government, SLM/A and JEM. Meanwhile, the UN and non-governmental organizations launched a massive humanitarian operation.

In January 2005, a Commission of Inquiry established at the request of the Security Council reported that while the Sudanese government had not pursued a policy of genocide

The African Union-United Nations Hybrid Operation in Darfur: the UN's First Hybrid Peacekeeping Mission

By early 2007, the conflict in the Darfur region of the Sudan had killed over 200,000 people and uprooted 2.5 million more, in a situation rife with alleged war crimes and crimes against humanity.

As the International Criminal Court began to address the matter, the Security Council, on 31 July 2007, established the first-ever hybrid force involving the United Nations — the **African Union-United Nations Hybrid Operation in Darfur (UNAMID)**. It combines UN forces with those of the former African Union Mission in Sudan (AMIS) in a new, comprehensive operation aimed at bringing peace to that troubled part of the world.

When fully deployed, UNAMID will be the largest peacekeeping operation ever, with 19,555 military personnel and 3,772 police, as well as 19 formed police units with up to 140 personnel each (a total of 2,660 personnel). Its rapid deployment aims at enabling it to assume authority from AMIS as soon as possible and no later than then end of 2007, with a view to achieving full operational capacity and force strength as soon as possible thereafter. Its mandate includes:

- facilitating full humanitarian access throughout Darfur;

- helping protect civilian populations under imminent threat of violence;

- verifying compliance with ceasefire agreements;

- assisting in implementation of the Darfur Peace Agreement;

- helping to ensure that the political process is inclusive;

- supporting AU-UN joint mediation to broaden and deepen the peace process;

- contributing to a secure environment for economic reconstruction and development, and for the sustainable return of internally displaced persons and refugees to their homes;

- helping promote respect for and protection of human rights and fundamental freedoms in Darfur;

- helping promote the rule of law in Darfur, including support for strengthening an independent judiciary and the prison system

- assisting in development of the legal framework, with Sudanese authorities;

- monitoring and reporting on the security situation at Sudan's borders with Chad and the Central African Republic.

In June 2006, the TFG and the Union of Islamic Courts pledged mutual recognition, continued dialogue, and to refrain from actions that might increase tensions. But on 11 July, the Secretary-General's special representative said that hardliners within the Islamic Courts posed a threat to the peace process and in particular to the Transitional Federal Institutions, which had its interim seat in Baidoa. On 20 July, forces loyal to the Islamic Courts advanced on a town some 60 kilometres from Baidoa.

On 6 December, the Security Council authorized IGAD and all AU member states to establish a protection and training mission in Somalia. Its mandate included: monitoring progress by the parties in implementing agreements; maintaining security in Baidoa; protecting members and infrastructure of the Transitional Federal Institutions and Government; training their security forces to provide their own security; and helping re-establish Somalia's national security forces.

With hundreds of thousands fleeing heavy fighting in Mogadishu, the Security Council, on 20 February 2007, authorized the AU to establish a wider operation, known as **AMISOM**, for an initial period of six months. Replacing the IGAD mission, it was authorized to take all necessary measures to fulfil its mandate, which included: supporting the safe passage and protection of those involved with the process of dialogue and national reconciliation; protecting the Transitional Federal Institutions; assisting with the re-establishment and training of all-inclusive Somali security forces; and helping to create security for the provision of humanitarian assistance.

On 20 August, the Council extended AMISOM for an additional six months, and approved continued contingency planning for a possible UN operation. But in November, Secretary-General Ban Ki-moon reported that deploying such a mission was neither realistic nor viable, given the marked deterioration in the political and security situation. Meanwhile, the UN would continue to focus on encouraging dialogue between the TFG and opposition groups and on strengthening AMISOM.

As for the humanitarian situation, UNHCR reported that 1 million people had been displaced by the recent violence — 600,000 of them fleeing Mogadishu. (See also the UNPOS website: *www.un-somalia.org*)

Ethiopia-Eritrea. With the collapse of the military government in Ethiopia in 1991, the Eritrean People's Liberation Front (EPLF) announced the formation of a provisional government and the holding of a referendum to determine the wishes of the Eritrean people regarding their status in relation to Ethiopia. In response to a request from its referendum commission, the General Assembly established the **United Nations Observer Mission to Verify the Referendum in Eritrea (UNOVER)**, to observe the organization and holding of the 1993 referendum. With 99 per cent of the voters favouring independence, Eritrea declared independence shortly thereafter and joined the UN.

In May 1998, fighting broke out between Ethiopia and Eritrea over disputed border areas. The Security Council demanded an end to the hostilities and offered technical support for the

The United Nations became involved in Central America in 1989, when Costa Rica, El Salvador, Guatemala, Honduras and Nicaragua requested its assistance in their agreement to end the conflicts that plagued the region, promote democratic elections and pursue democratization and dialogue. The Security Council established the **United Nations Observer Group in Central America (ONUCA)** to verify compliance with commitments to cease assistance to irregular and insurrectionist forces, and not allow the territory of any country to be used for attacks into other countries.

Nicaragua. The five countries also agreed to draw up a plan for demobilizing the Nicaraguan resistance, and the Nicaraguan government announced it would hold elections under international and United Nations monitoring. The **United Nations Observation Mission for the Verification of Elections in Nicaragua (ONUVEN)** observed the preparation and holding of the 1990 elections — the first to be observed by the UN in an independent country. Its success helped create conditions for the voluntary demobilization of the "contras", which was overseen by ONUCA in 1990.

El Salvador. In El Salvador, negotiations brokered by the Secretary-General and his personal representative culminated in the 1992 peace accords, which put an end to a 12-year conflict that had claimed some 75,000 lives. The **United Nations Observer Mission in El Salvador (ONUSAL)** monitored the accords, including the demobilization of combatants and both parties' compliance with their human rights commitments. ONUSAL also assisted in bringing about reforms needed to tackle the root causes of the civil war — such as judicial reforms and the establishment of a new civilian police force. At the request of the government, ONUSAL observed the 1994 elections. Its mandate ended in 1995.

Guatemala. At the request of the government and the Guatemalan National Revolutionary Unity (URNG), the United Nations in 1991 began to assist in talks aimed at ending that country's civil war, which had lasted over three decades and resulted in some 200,000 people killed or missing. In 1994, the parties concluded accords providing for the UN to verify all agreements reached and to establish a human rights mission. The General Assembly thus established the **United Nations Human Rights Verification Mission in Guatemala (MINUGUA)**.

In December 1996, a ceasefire was reached and the parties signed a peace agreement, ending the last and longest of Central America's conflicts. For the first time in 36 years, the region was at peace. MINUGUA remained until November 2004 to verify compliance with the accords, while UN agencies continued to address the social and economic roots of conflict throughout the region.

Haiti. In 1990, following the departure of "life president" Jean-Claude Duvalier and a series of short-lived governments, Haiti's provisional government asked the UN to observe that year's elections. The **United Nations Observer Group for the Verification of the Elections in Haiti (ONUVEH)** observed the preparation and holding of the elections, in which Jean-Bertrand Aristide was elected President. But a military coup in 1991 ended democratic rule, police element to adjust to the changing circumstances. For while gang violence had been significantly curtailed, the threat of civil unrest remained — owing to the persistence of a deep socio-economic divide. As the poorest country in the Western Hemisphere, Haiti's difficulties are exacerbated by its economic and social plight.

Asia and the Pacific

The Middle East

The United Nations has been concerned with the question of the Middle East from its earliest days. It has formulated principles for a peaceful settlement and dispatched various peacekeeping operations, and continues to support efforts towards a just, lasting and comprehensive solution to the underlying political problems.

The question has its origin in the issue of the status of Palestine. In 1947, Palestine was a Territory administered by the United Kingdom under a mandate from the League of Nations. It had a population of some 2 million — two thirds Arabs and one third Jews. The General Assembly in 1947 endorsed a plan, prepared by the United Nations Special Committee on Palestine, for the partition of the Territory. It provided for creating an Arab and a Jewish state, with Jerusalem under international status. The plan was rejected by the Palestinian Arabs, the Arab states and other states.

On 14 May 1948, the United Kingdom relinquished its mandate and the Jewish Agency proclaimed the state of Israel. The following day, the Palestinian Arabs, assisted by Arab states, opened hostilities against the new state. The hostilities were halted through a truce called for by the Security Council and supervised by a mediator appointed by the General Assembly, assisted by a group of military observers which came to be known as the **United Nations Truce Supervision Organization (UNTSO)** — the first United Nations observer mission.

As a result of the conflict, some 750,000 Palestine Arabs lost their homes and livelihoods and became refugees. To assist them, the General Assembly in 1949 established the **United Nations Relief and Works Agency for Palestine Refugees in the Near East (UNRWA)**, which has since been a major provider of assistance and a force for stability in the region.

The conflict remaining unresolved, Arab-Israeli warfare erupted again in 1956, 1967 and 1973, each time leading member states to call for United Nations mediation and peacekeeping missions. The 1956 conflict saw the deployment of the first full-fledged peacekeeping force — the **United Nations Emergency Force (UNEF I)** — which oversaw troop withdrawals and contributed to peace and stability.

The 1967 war involved fighting between Israel and Egypt, Jordan and Syria, during which Israel occupied the Sinai Peninsula, the Gaza Strip, the West Bank of the Jordan River, including East Jerusalem, and part of Syria's Golan Heights. The Security Council called for pulled out, the Council endorsed the Secretary-General's plan to assist Lebanon in re-establishing its authority. It subsequently commended Lebanon for taking steps to "ensure the return of its effective authority" throughout the south of the country. Nevertheless, the situation along the "blue line" marking Israel's withdrawal from southern Lebanon remained precarious.

On 14 February 2005, tensions escalated when former Lebanese Prime Minister Rafik Hariri was assassinated. In November, the Security Council supported establishment of a special tribunal to try those allegedly responsible for the assassination. In April, the UN verified withdrawal of Syrian troops, military assets and intelligence operations from Lebanon. In May and June, parliamentary elections were held with UN assistance.

Serious violations of the "blue line" continued through 2005 and 2006. Israeli forces violated Lebanese air space, including overflights of Beirut, while Hizbollah launched mortar rounds, missiles and rockets on Israeli Defence Force positions in the Shaba'a Farms area of the Syrian Golan — occupied by Israel since 1967 and claimed by Hizbollah as Lebanese territory.

When two Israeli soldiers were seized by Hizbollah militants on 12 July 2006, Israel responded with massive air attacks; Hizbollah responded with rocket attacks in northern Israel. By the time the fightnig was over, some 1,200 Lebanese — nearly all civilians — had been killed and 4,100 wounded, as well as more than 40 Israeli civilians and 120 soldiers killed. More than a quarter of Lebanon's population had been forced to flee their homes. Physical damage in Lebanon was estimated at $3.6 billion, including 30,000 homes damaged or destroyed.

The fighting ended on 14 August 2006, by the terms of Security Council resolution 1701. It called for an immediate cessation of hostilities — to be followed by deployment of Lebanese troops; a significantly expanded UNIFIL peacekeeping presence across southern Lebanon; and the withdrawal of Israeli forces from the same area. As the resolution was progressively implemented, massive amounts of UN aid came pouring into the country. Meanwhile, European countries rejoined UN peacekeeping for the first time in years, as blue helmets from Italy, France, Germany and Spain joined contingents from Ghana, India and Indonesia already on the ground.

A significant problem facing UNIFIL was the deadly risk posed to civilians by active remnants of cluster bombs. Up to 1 million pieces of unexploded ordnance were left in southern Lebanon from the 34-day war, with a density higher than in Kosovo and Iraq. UNIFIL mine-clearance activities have cost a number of peacekeepers their lives.

By March 2007, UNIFIL was close to its maximum strength of 15,000, with nearly 13,000 troops and sailors from 30 countries patrolling on land and sea. Its deminers had already destroyed more than 25,000 explosive devices. UNIFIL peacekeepers were also engaged in daily humanitarian work, including medical and dental aid.

In April, concerned at reported breaches of its arms embargo across the Lebanese-Syrian border, the Security Council invited the Secretary-General to send an independent mission to

In September, a new wave of protests and violence began in the occupied Palestinian territory. The Security Council repeatedly called for an end to the violence and affirmed the vision of two states, Israel and Palestine, living side by side within secure and recognized borders. But between October 2000 and January 2003, nearly 10,000 people lost their lives in the conflict.

International efforts to bring the two parties back to the negotiating table were increasingly carried out through the mechanism of "the Quartet" — composed of the United States, the United Nations, the European Union and the Russian Federation. In April 2003, the Quartet presented its "Road Map" to a permanent two-state solution — a plan with distinct phases and benchmarks, calling for parallel and reciprocal steps by the two parties, to resolve the conflict by 2005. It also envisaged a comprehensive settlement of the Middle East conflict, including the Syrian-Israeli and Lebanese-Israeli tracks. The Council endorsed the Road Map in its resolution 1515 (2003), and both parties accepted it.

Nevertheless, the last half of 2003 saw a sharp escalation of violence. The UN special coordinator for the Middle East peace process said neither side had actively addressed the other's concerns: for Israel, security and freedom from terrorist attack; for Palestinians, a viable and independent state based on pre-1967-war borders. Palestinian suicide bombings continued, and Israel pressed on with construction of a "separation barrier" in the West Bank — later held to be contrary to international law under an advisory opinion of the International Court of Justice requested by the General Assembly.

In February 2004, Israeli Prime Minister Ariel Sharon announced that Israel would withdraw its military and settlements from the Gaza Strip. In November 2004, Palestinian Authority President Yasser Arafat died, and was replaced in January 2005 by Mahmoud Abbas, in elections conducted with UN technical and logistic support. In February, Prime Minister Sharon and President Abbas met directly in Egypt, and announced steps to halt the violence. They met again in June, in Jerusalem, and by September Israel's withdrawal was completed. At last, genuine progress towards a negotiated solution seemed possible — until two significant events changed the political landscape.

On 4 January 2006, Prime Minister Sharon suffered a massive stroke and fell into a coma. And in legislative elections on 25 January, the Palestinian people voted the militant Hamas faction into power. Despite appeals from the Quartet and others, Hamas did not formally recognize Israel's right to exist.

The Israeli government, now led by Ehud Olmert — who was formally elected as Prime Minister on 15 April — took the position that the entire Palestinian Authority, including the Presidency, had now become a terrorist entity, and imposed a freeze on Palestinian tax revenues. As the year progressed, violence escalated, including the launching of rockets from Gaza into Israel, and major Israeli reprisal operations.

International aid donors balked at funding the Hamas-led government as long as it did not commit to renouncing violence, recognizing Israel's right to exist, and abiding by previously signed agreements. The humanitarian situation in the West Bank and Gaza became the forced displacements of civilian populations, summary executions, abuse and arbitrary detention of civilians, violence against women and girls, and indiscriminate bombing.

The Taliban's religious intolerance also aroused widespread condemnation. In March 2001, they blew up two statues of the Buddha carved out of the sandstone cliff-face in the Bamiyan Valley some 1,300 years ago, including the largest statue of the Buddha in the world. In May, an edict required Hindu women to veil themselves like their Muslim counterparts, and all non-Muslims were required to wear identity labels. In August, eight international aid workers were arrested and subsequently put on trial for "promoting Christianity".

Their trial was under way on 11 September, when members of bin Laden's AlQaeda organization hijacked four commercial jets in the United States, crashing two into the World Trade Center in New York City, one into the Pentagon in the US capital, and the fourth into a field in Pennsylvania when passengers tried to stop them. Some 3,000 people were killed. In the days that followed, the US administration issued an ultimatum to the Taliban: turn over bin Laden and close the terrorist operations in Afghanistan or risk a massive military assault. The Taliban refused.

On 7 October, forces of the United States and United Kingdom unleashed missile attacks against Taliban military targets and bin Laden's training camps in Afghanistan. Two weeks of bombings were followed by the deployment of US ground forces. In December, Afghan militiamen, supported by American bombers, began an offensive strike on a suspected mountaintop stronghold of bin Laden and al-Qaeda forces in Tora Bora, in eastern Afghanistan near the Pakistan border.

In the weeks following 11 September, the Security Council supported efforts of the Afghan people to replace the Taliban regime, as the UN continued to promote dialogue among Afghan parties aimed at establishing a broad-based, inclusive government. A UN-organized meeting of Afghan political leaders in Bonn concluded on 5 December with agreement on a provisional arrangement, pending re-establishment of permanent government institutions. As a first step, the Afghan Interim Authority was established.

On 20 December 2001, the Security Council, by resolution 1386, authorized the establishment of an **International Security Assistance Force (ISAF)** to help the Authority maintain security in Kabul and its surrounding areas. On 22 December, the internationally recognized administration of President Rabbani handed power to the new Afghan Interim Authority headed by Chairman Hamid Karzai, and the first ISAF troops were deployed.

In January 2002, an International Conference on Reconstruction Assistance to Afghanistan, held in Tokyo, garnered pledges of over $4.5 billion. It was announced that an Emergency Loya Jirga (Pashto for "Grand Council") — a traditional forum in which tribal elders come together and settle affairs — would be constituted to elect a head of state for the transitional administration and determine its structure and key personnel. The Security Council, welcoming the positive changes in Afghanistan as a result of the collapse of the Taliban, adjusted its sanctions to reflect the new realities, targeting al-Qaeda and its supporters.

On 27 September 2007, the Security Council voiced concern about the increased violence and terrorism, as it approved the extension of ISAF for another year. Addressing this situation, Secretary-General Ban Ki-moon said the key to sustaining security gains in the long term lay in increasing the capability, autonomy and integrity of the Afghan National Security Forces, and especially the Afghhan National Police.

Iraq

The United Nations response to Iraq's invasion of Kuwait in 1990, and the situation following the collapse of Saddam Hussein's regime in 2003, illustrate the scope of the challenges the UN faces in seeking to restore international peace and security.

The Security Council, by its resolutions 660 of 2 August 1990 and 661 of 6 August, immediately condemned the invasion of Kuwait, demanded Iraq's withdrawal and imposed sanctions against Iraq, including a trade and oil embargo.

On 29 November, the Security Council set 15 January 1991 as the deadline for Iraq's compliance with resolution 660, and authorized member states to use "all necessary means" to restore international peace and security. On 16 January 1991, multinational forces authorized by the Council but not under UN direction or control launched military operations against Iraq. Hostilities were suspended in February, after the Iraqi forces withdrew from Kuwait. By its resolution 687 of 8 April 1991, the Council set the terms of the ceasefire.

Deciding that Iraq's weapons of mass destruction should be eliminated, the Council established the **United Nations Special Commission (UNSCOM)** on the disarmament of Iraq, with powers of no-notice inspection, and entrusted the **International Atomic Energy Agency (IAEA)** with similar verification tasks in the nuclear sphere, with UNSCOM assistance. It also established a demilitarized zone along the Iraq-Kuwait border. Resolution 689 set up the **United Nations Iraq-Kuwait Observation Mission (UNIKOM)**, to monitor it.

The Council established an **Iraq-Kuwait Boundary Demarcation Commission**, whose boundary decisions were accepted by Iraq in 1994. It also established a **United Nations Compensation Commission** to process claims and compensate governments, nationals or corporations for any loss or damage resulting from Iraq's invasion of Kuwait, out of a percentage of the proceeds from sales of Iraqi oil. Thus far, the Commission has approved a total of $52.4 billion in claims, of which $22.5 billion has been paid out. It continues to process payments, as Iraq continues to pay 5 per cent of its oil revenue to the Compensation Fund.

Concerned about the severe humanitarian impact of economic sanctions on the Iraqi people, the Council, on 17 December 1995, created an "oil-for-food" programme to offer them a degree of relief. Established under its resolution 986, it monitored sales of oil by the government of Iraq to purchase food and humanitarian supplies, and managed the distribution of food in the country. It served as the sole source of sustenance for 60 per cent of Iraq's estimated 27 million people.

In the course of their inspections, UNSCOM and the IAEA uncovered and eliminated large quantities of Iraq's banned weapons programmes and capabilities in the nuclear, chemical

Oil for Food: Fact and Fiction

From December 1995 to November 2003, the United Nations "oil-for-food" programme provided humanitarian relief to 27 million Iraqis. It was unique — a stand-alone programme of immense scale and complexity that was the sole source of sustenance for 60 per cent of the people. Their daily caloric intake increased dramatically under the programme, and between 1996 and 2002, malnutrition rates among children under the age of five in central and southern Iraq were cut in half. The Security Council, which established the programme, also set up a Committee to monitor all contracts awarded under it.

When the programme ended, income from the sale of oil under its purview, including income from interest and currency gains, totalled $69.5 billion. Of that amount, $47.6 billion funded humanitarian activities, and $18 billion went to the UN Compensation Commission — to be paid out to persons harmed during Iraq's 1990 invasion of Kuwait. Approximately half a billion dollars supported the work of UNSCOM and UNMOVIC, which monitored Iraqi weapons systems and materials, and oversaw the destruction of all items proscribed under the Iraq-Kuwait ceasefire agreement.

In 2004, allegations began to surface claiming corruption and mismanagement in the operation of the programme. In response, then Secretary-General Kofi Annan appointed Paul Volcker, former Chairman of the United States Federal Reserve Board, to lead an Independent Investigation Committee. The other members of the panel were South African Justice Richard Goldstone and Swiss Professor of Criminal Law Mark Pieth. It was tasked to carry out a thorough and independent probe of the programme, and was provided unprecedented access, as well as the UN's complete cooperation. Over a year and a half of work, the Committee released five interim reports that painted a broad picture of the programme, focusing on management and oversight failures. The final report was released in October 2005.

The panel found that 2,200 companies from some 60 countries had been involved in illicit payments **outside** the purview of the oil-for-food monitoring mechanism. In contrast to the $147,000 alleged to have been misappropriated by a UN official, the Iraqi government's **total** illicit revenue from August 1990 through March 2003 was estimated by the US Central Intelligence Agency (CIA) at **$10.9 billion**. Some $8 billion of that amount came from exports under trade protocols which were known, and in some cases condoned, by the states members of the Security Council. Smuggling — outside the purview of the oil-for-food mechanism or before it was put in place — was estimated at $1.74 billion.

With regard to the Secretariat's administration of the programme, the panel found there had been mismanagement by the head of the Office of the Iraq Programme. The Volcker panel alleged that the former head of OIP had taken $147,000 in bribes during his tenure — a charge he disputed. Nevertheless, the Secretary-General lifted his immunity from prosecution immediately. The panel also looked into allegations regarding the Secretary-General and concluded that he had not been involved in procurement decisions.

Since the release of the Volcker report, several management reform initiatives have been implemented to strengthen ethical conduct, internal oversight and accountability, as well as transparency, financial disclosure and "whistleblower" protection.

At the expanded ministerial meeting of Iraq and its neighbours held on 4 May 2007 in Sharm el-Sheikh, Egypt, the participants agreed to establish three working groups on issues of common concern, including energy, border security and refugees and internally displaced persons (IDPs). The UN was asked to provide technical assistance and expertise for these working groups. At the expanded ministerial meeting held in November 2007 in Istanbul, the participants endorsed the establishment of an ad hoc mechanism in Baghdad to coordinate and support the process of regional dialogue. The support mechanism would be led by the Iraqi government and be provided with strong UN assistance.

Although there have been improvements in the security situation since in mid-2007, Iraqi civilians, including women and children, have continued to be victims of terrorist acts, roadside bombs, drive-by shootings, cross-fire between rival gangs or between police and insurgents, kidnappings, military operations, crime and police abuse. Mass arrests by Iraqi security and multinational forces during military operations under the jurisdiction of the multinational forces had resulted in large numbers of detainees. Daily living conditions had become dismal, marked by intermittent water and electricity, chronic malnutrition among children, and more illiteracy among youth than ever before.

There were, however, a number of positive developments in 2007. On 3 March, the **International Compact with Iraq** was official launched, with world leaders gathered in Sharm el-Sheik, Egypt, pledging over $30 billion in specific financial commitments to Iraq's five-year plan for peace and development, including debt relief. On 10 August, the Security Council, by its resolution 1770, voted unanimously to renew and expand the mandate of UNAMI, paving the way for the UN to enhance its role in such key areas as national reconciliation, regional dialogue, humanitarian assistance and human rights. Nevertheless, the security situation continued to limit UN presence on the ground.

Earlier, on 29 June 2007, the Security Council, expressing its gratitude for the "comprehensive contributions" made by UNMOVIC and the IAEA, formally terminated their respective mandates in Iraq.

India and Pakistan

The United Nations is actively committed to promoting harmonious relations between India and Pakistan, which have been troubled by the decades-old dispute over Kashmir. The issue dates back to the 1940s, when the princely state of Jammu and Kashmir became free to accede to India or Pakistan under the partition plan and the India Independence Act of 1947. The Hindu Maharaja of mostly Muslim Jammu and Kashmir signed his state's instrument of accession to India.

The Security Council first discussed the issue in 1948, following India's complaint that tribesmen and others, with Pakistan's support and participation, were invading Jammu and Kashmir and fighting was taking place. Pakistan denied the charges and declared Jammu and Kashmir's accession to India illegal.

February 2000. UNMOT withdrew in May, and was replaced by the much smaller UN Tajikistan Office of Peacebuilding (UNTOP), with a mandate to help consolidate peace and promote democracy. UNTOP completed its work on 31 July 2007.

Even as the closure of UNTOP ended one chapter in UN political assistance to Central Asia, a new one began in December 2007 with the inauguration of the **United Nations Regional Centre for Preventive Diplomacy for Central Asia**. Based in Ashgabat, the capital of Turkmenistan, the Centre was established to help the governments of the region to peacefully and cooperatively manage an array of common challenges and threats — including terrorism, drug trafficking, organized crime and environmental degradation.

The Centre, which represents the culmination of several years of consultations between the UN and the five Central Asian countries, will offer governments its assistance in a number of areas, including: building capacity to prevent conflict peacefully; facilitating dialogue; and catalyzing international support for specific projects and initiatives. The Centre will cooperate closely with the existing UN programmes and agencies in Central Asia, as well as with regional organizations.

Cambodia

Prior to implementation of the UN-brokered 1991 Paris Peace Agreements, Cambodia was in a state of deep internal conflict and relative isolation. Since its emergence from French colonialism in the 1950s, the country had suffered the spillover of the Viet Nam war in the 1960s and 1970s, followed by devastating civil conflicts and the genocidal totalitarian rule of Pol Pot. Under his "Khmer Rouge" regime from 1975 through 1979, nearly 2 million people perished of murder, disease or starvation, many on Cambodia's infamous "killing fields".

In 1993, with help from the **United Nations Transitional Authority in Cambodia (UNTAC)**, Cambodia held its first democratic elections. Since then, UN agencies and programmes have assisted the government in strengthening reconciliation and development, and the Office of the UN High Commissioner for Human Rights and the Secretary-General's special representative have helped it promote and protect those rights — cornerstones of the rule of law and democratic development.

In May 2003, agreement was reached with the government for the UN to help it set up and run a special court to prosecute crimes committed under the Khmer Rouge. Established on 29 April 2005, its judges and prosecutors were sworn in during July 2006. By 13 June 2007, they had agreed on its internal rules. Beginning in July, the Extraordinary Chambers in the Courts of Cambodia issued its first charges for crimes against humanity, taking several persons charged into provisional detention. (See also the section on international tribunals in chapter 6.)

Myanmar

Since Myanmar's military leadership voided the results of democratic elections in 1990, the UN has sought to help bring about a return to democracy and improvements in its human rights situation though an all-inclusive process of national reconciliation. In 1993, the code of conduct of the ceasefire, as well as all the human rights provisions of the peace agreement. Through its reports and statements, the office plays an active role in persuading Nepali security forces and Maoists to exercise restraint and avoid deliberately targeting civilian populations.

The UN had been engaged for several years in political efforts to end the hostilities in Nepal and encourage a negotiated political solution. In July 2006, following a request by the government for UN assistance, the Secretary-General dispatched a pre-assessment mission to the country. In August, the government and the Maoists sent identical letters to the Secretary-General requesting UN assistance in monitoring of the ceasefire code of conduct; observing elections for the constituent assembly; deploying qualified civilian personnel to monitor and verify the confinement of Maoist combatants and their weapons in designated cantonment areas; and monitoring the Nepal Army to ensure that it remains within its barracks and that its weapons are not used.

In August 2006, the Secretary-General appointed Ian Martin as his personal representative in Nepal in support of the peace process. Mr. Martin and his team were instrumental in helping the parties find common ground on key elements, including organization of the elections for the constituent assembly, the management of arms and armies, and reaching consensus on the United Nations role in the peace process.

In November, the government reiterated the two sides' request for UN assistance. The Secretary-General requested that the Security Council dispatch a technical assessment mission to Nepal, with a view to developing a full concept of operations. Such an operation would include a UN political mission to deliver the assistance requested by the parties, as well as the advance deployment of 35 civilian monitors and 25 electoral advisors. Through a presidential statement on 1 December, the Council endorsed this request. On 23 January 2007, the Council adopted resolution 1740, establishing the United Nations Mission in Nepal (UNMIN). Mr. Martin was subsequently appointed as the special representative of the Secretary-General.

Since its establishment, UNMIN has been active on various fronts. Its arms monitors have supervised the registration of Maoist weapons and combatants, a process to be completed by the end of 2007. UNMIN electoral experts have assisted Nepal's Election Commission by providing technical support for the planning, preparation and conduct of the election of the constituent assembly. A small team of UN electoral monitors independent from UNMIN has been involved in reviewing all technical aspects of the electoral process and reporting on the conduct of the election. Meanwhile, UNMIN civil affairs officers have provided the Mission with the ability to engage communities outside Kathmandu, and to help create a climate conducive to a peaceful election.

By the end of 2007, Nepal was standing on a path to peace, with the United Nations providing its continued support for that process, despite difficulties in implementing certain aspects of the Comprehensive Peace Agreement and two postponements during the year of the planned electionn for the constituent assembly.

external security. Upon completing its work in May 2005, UNMISET was replaced by a **United Nations Office in Timor-Leste (UNOTIL),** which worked for the next year to support the development of critical state institutions, the police and the border patrol unit, and to provide training in democratic governance and the observance of human rights.

However, the dismissal of nearly 600 members of the Timorese armed forces in March 2006 triggered a violent crisis that peaked in May, resulting in casualties. The government requested, and the Security Council endorsed, the deployment of international police and military assistance to secure critical locations and facilities. The Secretary-General sent his special envoy to help diffuse the crisis and to find a political solution. Following extensive negotiations among the political actors, a new government was formed in July, and elections were scheduled for May 2007, in accordance with the constitution.

Subsequently, the Security Council, on 25 August 2007, established a new and expanded operation, the **United Nations Integrated Mission in Timor-Leste (UNMIT)**, to support the government in "consolidating stability, enhancing a culture of democratic governance, and facilitating dialogue among Timorese stakeholders". Since then, stability in the country has been largely maintained, and presidential and parliamentary elections were held in a generally calm security environment in May and August 2007, respectively.

Europe

Cyprus

The **United Nations Peacekeeping Force in Cyprus (UNFICYP)** was established in 1964 to prevent a recurrence of fighting between the Greek Cypriot and Turkish Cypriot communities and to contribute to the maintenance and restoration of law and order and a return to normal conditions.

In 1974, a coup d'état by Greek Cypriot and Greek elements favouring union of the country with Greece was followed by military intervention by Turkey and the de facto division of the island. Since 1974, UNFICYP has supervised a de facto ceasefire which came into effect on 16 August 1974, and maintained a buffer zone between the lines of the Cyprus National Guard and of the Turkish and Turkish Cypriot forces. In the absence of a political settlement, UNFICYP continues its presence on the island.

The Secretary-General has used his good offices in search of a comprehensive settlement, hosting proximity talks between the two leaders in 1999 and 2000, followed by intensive direct talks beginning in January 2002. In November, he submitted a comprehensive proposal aimed at bridging the gaps between them, but agreement could not be reached on submitting it to referendums on each side in time to allow a reunited Cyprus to sign the Treaty of Accession to the European Union (16 April).

The talks were suspended in March 2003. In April, the Turkish Cypriot authorities began to open crossing points for public travel by Greek Cypriots to the north and Turkish Cypriots to the south for the first time in nearly three decades. As UN engineers worked to improve the roads, the Security Council authorized an increase in UNFICYP's civilian police component to

The Balkans

Former Yugoslavia. The Federal Republic of Yugoslavia was a founding member of the United Nations. In 1991, two republics of the federation, Slovenia and Croatia, declared independence. Croatian Serbs, supported by the national army, opposed the move, and war broke out between Serbia and Croatia. Responding, the Security Council imposed an arms embargo on Yugoslavia, and the Secretary-General appointed a personal envoy to support peace efforts by the European Community.

To create conditions for a settlement, the Security Council in 1992 established the **United Nations Protection Force (UNPROFOR)**, initially in Croatia. But the war extended to Bosnia and Herzegovina, which had also declared independence — a move supported by Bosnian Croats and Muslims but opposed by Bosnian Serbs. The Serb and Croatian armies intervened, and the Council imposed economic sanctions on the Federal Republic of Yugoslavia, consisting by then of Serbia and Montenegro.

The war intensified, generating the largest refugee crisis in Europe since the Second World War. Faced with widespread reports of "ethnic cleansing", the Security Council in 1993 created, for the first time, an international court to prosecute war crimes. It also declared certain places as "safe areas", in an attempt to insulate them from the fighting.

UNPROFOR sought to protect the delivery of humanitarian aid in Bosnia and to protect Sarajevo, its capital, as well as other "safe areas". But while peacekeeping commanders requested 35,000 troops, the Security Council authorized only 7,600. To deter continuing attacks against Sarajevo, the North Atlantic Treaty Organization (NATO) in 1994 authorized air strikes at the Secretary-General's request. Bosnian Serb forces detained some 400 UNPROFOR observers, using some as "human shields".

Fighting intensified in 1995. Croatia launched major offensives against its Serb-populated areas. NATO responded to Bosnian Serb shelling of Sarajevo with massive air strikes. Bosnian Serb forces took over the "safe areas" of Srebrenica and Zepa. They killed some 7,000 unarmed men and boys in Srebrenica, in the worst massacre in Europe since the Second World War. In a 1999 report, the Secretary-General acknowledged the errors of the UN and member states in their response to the ethnic cleansing campaign that culminated in Srebrenica. The tragedy, he said, "will haunt our history forever".

At the talks in Dayton, Ohio, in 1995, agreement was reached between Bosnia and Herzegovina, Croatia and Yugoslavia, ending the 42-month war. To ensure compliance, the Security Council authorized a multinational, NATO-led, 60,000-strong Implementation Force.

The Council also established a UN International Police Task Force. It later became part of a larger **United Nations Mission in Bosnia and Herzegovina (UNMIBH)**, which facilitated the return of refugees and displaced persons, fostered peace and security, and helped build up state institutions. In 1996, the Council established the **United Nations Mission of Observers in Prevlaka (UNMOP)**, to monitor the demilitarization of the Prevlaka peninsula, a strategic area in Croatia contested by Yugoslavia. UNMIBH and UNMOP completed their work at the end of 2002.

during a "systematic attack directed against the Kosovo Albanian civilian population of Kosovo". When the defence had nearly completed its response, Milosovic died of natural causes while in detention, on 11 March 2006. He had been facing 66 counts for genocide, crimes against humanity and war crimes in Croatia, Bosnia and Herzegovina and Kosovo.

The Security Council lifted its arms embargo in September 2001. In November, a 120-member Kosovo Assembly was elected which, in March 2002, elected the province's first President and Prime Minister. In December, UNMIK completed the transfer of specific responsibilities to local provisional institutions, though it retained control over security, foreign relations, protection of minority rights, and energy — pending determination of the province's final status.

During 2006, the Secretary-General's special envoy, former Finnish President Martti Ahtisaari, conducted four rounds of direct negotiations between the parties and the first high-level meeting between top Serbian and Kosovar leaders, but Kosovo's ethnic Albanian government and Serbia remained completely at odds. In February 2007, he presented his final status plan as "a compromise proposal", but the parties were unmoved. He subsequently reported that the only viable option for Kosovo was independence — which had been consistently opposed by Serbia.

In August 2007, Secretary-General Ban Ki-moon welcomed an agreement to have a troika composed of the European Union, Russia and the United States lead further negotiations on Kosovo's future status. (See *www.unmikonline.org*)

Disarmament

(http://disarmament.un.org)

Since the birth of the United Nations, the goals of multilateral disarmament and arms limitation have been central to its efforts to maintain international peace and security. The Organization has given highest priority to reducing and eventually eliminating nuclear weapons, destroying chemical weapons and strengthening the prohibition against biological weapons — all of which pose the greatest threat to humankind. While these objectives have remained constant over the years, the scope of deliberations and negotiations is changing as political realities and the international situation evolve.

The international community is now considering more closely the excessive and destabilizing proliferation of small arms and light weapons and has mobilized to combat the massive deployment of landmines — phenomena that threaten the economic and social fabric of societies and kill and maim civilians, too many of whom are women and children. Consideration is also being given to the need for multilaterally negotiated norms against the spread of ballistic missile technology, the explosive remnants of war, and the impact of new information and telecommunications technologies on international security.

The tragic events of 11 September 2001 in the United States, and subsequent terrorist attacks in a number of countries, underlined the potential danger of weapons of mass

- 1993 *Chemical Weapons Convention (CWC)*: prohibits the development, production, stockpiling and use of chemical weapons and requires their destruction.
- 1995 *Southeast Asia Nuclear-Weapon-Free Zone Treaty (Treaty of Bangkok)*: bans the development or stationing of nuclear weapons on the territories of the states party to the treaty.
- 1996 *African Nuclear-Weapon-Free Zone Treaty (Treaty of Pelindaba)*: bans the development or stationing of nuclear weapons on the African continent.
- 1996 *Comprehensive Nuclear-Test-Ban Treaty (CTBT)*: places a worldwide ban on nuclear test explosions of any kind and in any environment.
- 1997 *Mine-Ban Convention*: prohibits the use, stockpiling, production and transfer of antipersonnel mines and provides for their destruction.
- 2005 *International Convention for the Suppression of Acts of Nuclear Terrorism (Nuclear Terrorism Convention)*: outlines specific acts of nuclear terrorism, aims to protect a broad range of possible targets, bring perpetrators to justice and promote cooperation among countries.
- 2006 *Central Asia Nuclear-Weapon-Free Zone Treaty*: comprising the five central Asian states — Kazakhstan, Kyrgyzstan, Tajikistan, Turkmenistan and Uzbekistan.

(For status of ratification of these agreements, see *http://disarmament.un.org/TreatyStatus.nsf*)

destruction falling into the hands of non-state actors. The attack could have had even more devastating consequences had the terrorists been able to acquire and use chemical, biological or nuclear weapons. Reflecting these concerns, the General Assembly adopted at its fifty-seventh session in 2002, for the first time, a resolution on measures to prevent terrorists from acquiring weapons of mass destruction and their means of delivery.

In 2004, the Security Council took its first formal decision on the danger of the proliferation of weapons of mass destruction, particularly to non-state actors. Acting under the enforcement provisions of the UN Charter, the Council unanimously adopted resolution 1540, obliging states to refrain from any support for non-state actors in the development, acquisition, manufacture, possession, transport, transfer or use of nuclear, chemical and biological weapons and their means of delivery. The resolution imposes far-reaching obligations on all states to establish domestic measures to prevent the proliferation of nuclear, chemical and biological weapons, and their means of delivery, including the establishment of appropriate controls over related materials.

Subsequently, the General Assembly adopted the *International Convention for the Suppression of Acts of Nuclear Terrorism*, which was opened for signature in September 2005.

In addition to its role in the actual disarmament of weapons and in verifying compliance, the United Nations plays an essential role in multilateral disarmament by assisting member states in establishing new norms and in strengthening and consolidating existing agreements. One of the most effective means of deterring the use or threatened use of weapons of mass

Bilateral agreements

The 1972 Treaty on the Limitation of Anti-Ballistic Missile Systems (ABM Treaty) limited the number of anti-ballistic missile systems of the United States and the Soviet Union to one each. A 1997 "demarcation" agreement between the United States and the Russian Federation distinguished between "strategic", or long-range ABMs, which were prohibited, and "non-strategic", or shorter-range ABMs, which were not. The Treaty ceased to be in effect as of 13 June 2002, when the United States withdrew from it.

The 1987 United States-Soviet Union Intermediate- and Shorter-Range Nuclear Forces Treaty (INF Treaty) eliminated an entire class of nuclear weapons, which includes all land-based ballistic and cruise missiles with a range of 500 to 5,500 km. By the end of 1996, all the weapons slated for destruction under the provisions of the Treaty had been eliminated.

The 1991 United States-Soviet Union Strategic Arms Limitation and Reduction Treaty (START I) placed a ceiling of 6,000 warheads on 1,600 deployed long-range nuclear missiles for each side by 2001, thereby reducing the 1991 stockpile levels by about 30 per cent.

The 1992 Lisbon Protocol to START I committed the Russian Federation, Belarus, Kazakhstan and Ukraine, as successor states to the Soviet Union, to abide by the START I Treaty; Belarus, Kazakhstan and Ukraine were to adhere to the NPT as nonnuclear-weapon states. By 1996, these three states had removed all nuclear weapons from their territories.

The 1993 Strategic Arms Limitation and Reduction Treaty II (START II) committed both parties to reduce the number of warheads on long-range nuclear missiles to 3,500 on each side by 2003, and eliminated ICBMs (intercontinental ballistic missiles) equipped with MIRVs (multiple independently targetable re-entry vehicles). A 1997 agreement extended the deadline for destruction of the launching systems — missile silos, bombers and submarines — to the end of 2007.

On 24 May 2002, the Presidents of the Russian Federation and the United States signed the Strategic Offensive Reductions Treaty (SORT), also known as the Moscow Treaty, agreeing to limit the level of their deployed strategic nuclear warheads to between 1,700 and 2,200. The Treaty will remain in force until December 2012, and may be extended or superseded by agreement of the parties.

Bilateral agreements on nuclear weapons. While international efforts to contain nuclear weapons continue in different forums, it has been generally understood that the nuclear-weapon powers hold special responsibility for maintaining a stable international security environment. During and after the cold war, the two major powers arrived at agreements that have significantly reduced the threat of nuclear war.

Multilateral agreements on nuclear weapons and non-proliferation. The *Treaty on the Non-Proliferation of Nuclear Weapons (NPT)*, the most universal of all multilateral disarmament treaties, was first opened for signature in 1968 and came into force in 1970. The NPT is

Subsequently, four additional zones were established — in the South Pacific *(Treaty of Rarotonga,* 1985), South-East Asia *(Treaty of Bangkok,* 1995), Africa *(Treaty of Pelindaba,* 1996), and Central Asia *(Central Asia Nuclear-Weapon-Free Zone Treaty,* 2006). Proposals have also been made for establishing nuclear-weapon-free zones in Central Europe and South Asia, as well as for a zone free of weapons of mass destruction in the Middle East. The concept of an individual country as a nuclear-weapon-free zone was acknowledged by the international community in 1998, when the General Assembly supported Mongolia's self-declaration of its nuclear-weapon-free status.

Preventing nuclear proliferation. The International Atomic Energy Agency (IAEA) plays a prominent role in international efforts to prevent the proliferation of nuclear weapons — serving as the world's inspectorate for the application of nuclear safeguards and verification measures covering civilian nuclear programmes.

Under agreements concluded with states, IAEA inspectors regularly visit nuclear facilities to verify records on the whereabouts of nuclear material, check IAEAinstalled instruments and surveillance equipment and confirm inventories of nuclear material. Taken together, these and other safeguards measures provide independent, international verification that governments are abiding by their commitment to peaceful uses of nuclear energy.

To verify the implementation of the 238 safeguards agreements in force in 155 states (and in Taiwan, China) during 2006, IAEA experts conducted a total of 1,733 safeguards inspections. Their aim was to ensure that the nuclear material held in some 900 nuclear installations in more than 70 countries was not diverted away from legitimate peaceful uses to military purposes. Through such annual inspections, IAEA contributes to international security and reinforces efforts to halt the spread of arms and move towards a world free of nuclear weapons.

Various types of safeguards agreements can be concluded with IAEA. Those in connection with the NPT, the *Model Protocol Additional to Existing Safeguards Agreements,* as well as those relating to the *Treaty of Tlatelolco,* the *Treaty of Pelindaba* and the *Treaty of Rarotonga* require non-nuclear-weapon states to submit their entire nuclear-fuel-cycle activities to IAEA safeguards. Other agreements cover safeguards at single facilities. IAEA safeguards under the NPT are an integral part of the international regime for non-proliferation and play an indispensable role in ensuring the implementation of the Treaty. (See *www.iaea.org*)

Removing the threat of chemical and biological weapons

The entry into force of the *Chemical Weapons Convention (CWC)* in 1997 completed a process that started in 1925, when the *Geneva Protocol* prohibited the use of poison gas weapons. The Convention created, for the first time in the history of international arms control, a stringent international verification regime (involving collection of information on chemical facilities and routine global inspections) to oversee compliance with treaty obligations by states parties to the Convention. Established for that purpose at The Hague in the Netherlands, the **Organisation**

In 2001, an international Conference on the Illicit Trade in Small Arms and Light Weapons in All Its Aspects was held at the United Nations. Under its resulting programme of action, members agreed to ensure that licensed manufacturers apply a reliable marking on each small arm and light weapon in the production process; to keep comprehensive and accurate records on the manufacture, holding and transfer of such weapons under their jurisdiction; to strengthen their ability to cooperate in identifying and tracing the illicit trade of such weapons; and to guarantee that all small arms and light weapons thus confiscated, seized or collected are destroyed.

The result was a huge increase in government anti-trafficking activities. In the five years following adoption of the programme, nearly 140 countries had reported on illegal gun trafficking, while a third of all states had made efforts to collect weapons from those not legally entitled to hold them. There was also increased cooperation among and within regions to stem the flow of illicit weapons across national borders. From 26 June to 7 July 2006, more than 2,000 representatives from governments, international and regional organizations and civil society took part in a two-week event at UN Headquarters to review implementation of the programme of action, and to draw increased world attention to the issue.

Since the uncontrolled spread of illicit small arms impacts many aspects of the United Nations work — from children to health to refugees to development — a mechanism called "Coordinating Action on Small Arms" was put in place in 1998 to guarantee that the UN system addressed the many sides of small arms control in a coordinated manner. A comprehensive global effort to address the small arms scourge was also launched and sustained by civil society — through research, the promotion of coordinated national action, and global lobbying for an international convention on the arms trade.

Anti-personnel mines. The growing proliferation and indiscriminate use of anti-personnel landmines around the world has been a particular focus of attention. In 1995, a review of the *Convention on Certain Conventional Weapons (CCW)* — also known as the *Inhumane Weapons Convention* — produced *Amended Protocol II*, which entered into force on 3 December 1998, strengthening restrictions on certain uses, transfers and types (self-destroying and detectable) of landmines. Currently 86 states are bound by this *Protocol*.

Not satisfied with what they considered an inadequate response to a serious humanitarian crisis, a group of like-minded states negotiated an agreement on a total ban on all anti-personnel landmines — the *Convention on the Prohibition of the Use, Stockpiling, Production and Transfer of Anti-personnel Mines and on Their Destruction (Mine-Ban Convention)*, which was opened for signature in 1997 and entered into force on 1 March 1999. As of August 2007, 155 states had become parties to it.

The successful implementation of both instruments led to the destruction of stockpiles, mine clearance in affected countries, and fewer new victims. *Landmine Monitor Report, 2006* states that as of July 2006, it appears that 138 of the states parties to the Convention do not have stockpiles of anti-personnel mines (see *www.icbl.org*), and that states parties collectively had destroyed more than 39.5 million anti-personnel mines.

The fight against landmines

Since the 1980s, the United Nations has been addressing the problems posed by millions of landmines scattered in some 78 countries. Every year, they kill 15,000 to 20,000 people — most of them children, women and the elderly — and those who are not killed are often severely maimed. Years, and even decades after conflicts have ended, landmines continue to wreak havoc on civilian populations. And yet landmines continue to be used as weapons of war.

In the legal sphere, the UN–sponsored *Inhumane Weapons Convention* (1980) was strengthened in 1996 to include mine use in internal conflicts and to require that all mines be detectable. The 1997 landmark *Convention on the Prohibition of the Use, Stockpiling, Production and Transfer of Anti-personnel Mines and on Their Destruction (Mine-Ban Convention)* banned the production, use and export of these weapons.

On the ground, 14 UN agencies, programmes, departments and funds are active in mine-related service. They find and destroy landmines and explosive remnants of war; assist victims; teach people how to remain safe in mine-affected areas; destroy stockpiles; and encourage universal participation in international agreements such as the *Mine-Ban Convention*.

The United Nations Mine Action Service (UNMAS) coordinates all mine-related activities of the UN system. It develops policies and standards, conducts ongoing assessment and monitoring of the threat posed by mines and unexploded ordnance, collects and disseminates information, mobilizes resources, and engages in advocacy in support of the global ban on antipersonnel landmines. It is also responsible for the provision of mine-action assistance in humanitarian emergencies and for peacekeeping operations. (See *www.mineaction.org*)

Reflecting the importance of preventing the militarization of outer space, the General Assembly's first special session on disarmament (1978) called for international negotiations on the issue. Since 1982, the Conference on Disarmament has had on its agenda an item entitled "Prevention of an arms race in outer space", but little progress has been made to date in negotiating a multilateral agreement, owing to continuing differences in perception among its members.

Relationship between disarmament and development. The question of promoting economic and social progress, especially for less developed nations, by using the resources released through general disarmament under a system of effective international control has long been debated among member states. Eventually, an international conference on the relationship between disarmament and development was held in 1987. In its resolution 61/53 of 6 December 2006, the General Assembly urged the international community to devote part of the resources made available through disarmament and arms limitation agreements to economic and social development, with a view to reducing the gap between developed and developing countries.

Regional approaches to disarmament. The United Nations supports initiatives towards disarmament undertaken at the regional and subregional levels, promoting

The main intergovernmental body in this field is the **United Nations Committee on the Peaceful Uses of Outer Space**. It reviews the scope of international cooperation in peaceful uses of outer space, devises programmes and directs United Nations technical cooperation, encourages research and dissemination of information, and contributes to the development of international space law. Set up by the General Assembly in 1959, it is made up of 69 member states. A number of international organizations, both intergovernmental and non-governmental, have observer status with the Committee.

The Committee has two subcommittees:

- The **Scientific and Technical Subcommittee** is the focal point of international cooperation in space technology and research.

- The **Legal Subcommittee** works to ensure the development of a legal framework concomitant with the rapid technological development of space activities.

The Committee and its subcommittees meet annually to consider questions put before them by the General Assembly, reports submitted to them and issues raised by member states. Working on the basis of consensus, the Committee makes recommendations to the General Assembly.

Legal instruments

The work of the Committee and its Legal Subcommittee has resulted in the adoption by the General Assembly of five legal instruments, all of which are in force:

- The 1966 *Treaty on Principles Governing the Activities of States in the Exploration and Use of Outer Space, including the Moon and Other Celestial Bodies (Outer Space Treaty)* provides that space exploration shall be carried out for the benefit of all countries, irrespective of their degree of development. It seeks to maintain outer space as the province of all humankind, free for exploration and use by all states, solely for peaceful purposes, and not subject to national appropriation.

- The 1967 *Agreement on the Rescue of Astronauts, the Return of Astronauts and the Return of Objects Launched into Outer Space (Rescue Agreement)* provides for aiding the crews of spacecraft in case of accident or emergency landing, and establishes procedures for returning to the launching authority a space object found beyond the territory of that authority.

- The 1971 *Convention on International Liability for Damage Caused by Space Objects (Liability Convention)* provides that the launching state is liable for damage caused by its space objects on the earth's surface, to aircraft in flight, and to space objects of another state or persons or property on board such objects.

- The 1974 *Convention on Registration of Objects Launched into Outer Space (Registration Convention)* provides that launching states maintain registries of space objects and provide information on objects launched to the United Nations. Under this Convention, the Office for Outer Space Affairs maintains a United Nations Registry on objects launched

- The *Principles governing the use by states of artificial earth satellites for international direct television broadcasting* (1982) recognize that such use has international political, economic, social and cultural implications. Such activities should promote the dissemination and exchange of information and knowledge, foster development, and respect the sovereign rights of states, including the principle of non-intervention.

- The *Principles relating to remote sensing of the earth from outer space* (1986) state that such activities are to be conducted for the benefit of all countries, respecting the sovereignty of all states and peoples over their natural resources, and for the rights and interests of other states. Remote sensing is to be used to preserve the environment and to reduce the impact of natural disasters.

- The *Principles on the use of nuclear power sources in outer space* (1992) recognize that such sources are essential for some space missions, but that their use should be based on a thorough safety assessment. The Principles provide guidelines for the safe use of nuclear power sources and for notification of a malfunction of a space object where there is a risk of re-entry of radioactive material to the earth.

- The *Declaration on international cooperation in the exploration and use of outer space for the benefit and in the interest of all states, particularly developing countries* (1996) provides that states are free to determine all aspects of their participation in international space cooperation on an equitable and mutually acceptable basis, and that such cooperation should be conducted in ways that are considered most effective and appropriate by the countries concerned.

Office for Outer Space Affairs

The Vienna-based **United Nations Office for Outer Space Affairs** serves as the secretariat for the Committee on the Peaceful Uses of Outer Space and its subcommittees, and assists developing countries in using space technology for development.

The Office disseminates space-related information to member states through its International Space Information System, and maintains the United Nations Register on Objects Launched into Outer Space. Through its *United Nations Programme on Space Applications,* the Office works to improve the use of space science and technology for the economic and social development of all nations, in particular developing countries. Under this programme, it also provides technical advisory services to member states in conducting pilot projects, and undertakes training and fellowship programmes in such areas as remote sensing, satellite communication, satellite meteorology, satellite navigation, basic space science and space law.

The Office is a cooperating body to the International Charter, "Space and Major Disasters" — a mechanism through which UN agencies can request satellite imagery to support their response to disasters. The Office also serves as secretariat to the International Committee on Global Navigation Satellite Systems — an informal body that promotes cooperation on civil satellite-based positioning, navigation, timing and value-added services, as well as on the

ECONOMIC AND SOCIAL DEVELOPMENT

Although most people associate the United Nations with the issues of peace and security, the vast majority of the Organization's resources are in fact devoted to advancing the Charter's pledge to "promote higher standards of living, full employment, and conditions of economic and social progress and development". United Nations development efforts have profoundly affected the lives and well-being of millions of people throughout the world. Guiding the United Nations endeavours is the conviction that lasting international peace and security are possible only if the economic and social well-being of people everywhere is assured.

Many of the economic and social transformations that have taken place globally since 1945 have been significantly affected in their direction and shape by the work of the United Nations. As the global centre for consensus-building, the UN has set priorities and goals for international cooperation to assist countries in their development efforts and to foster a supportive global economic environment.

Since the 1990s, the UN has provided a platform for formulating and promoting key new developmental objectives on the international agenda, through a series of global conferences. It has articulated the need for incorporating issues such as the advancement of women, human rights, sustainable development, environmental protection and good governance into the development paradigm.

This global consensus was also expressed through a series of *international development decades*, the first beginning in 1961. These broad statements of policy and goals, while emphasizing certain issues of particular concern in each decade, consistently stressed the need for progress on all aspects of development, social as well as economic, and the importance of narrowing the disparities between industrialized and developing countries. As the twentieth century came to an end, the focus shifted to implementing these commitments in an integrated and coordinated manner.

At their Millennium Summit in 2000, member states adopted a set of wide-ranging **Millennium Development Goals (MDGs)**, supported by a series of specific, attainable targets. Together, the goals and targets aim at: eradicating extreme poverty and hunger; achieving universal primary education; promoting gender equality and the empowerment of women; reducing child mortality; improving maternal health; combating HIV/AIDS, malaria and other diseases; ensuring environmental sustainability; and developing a global partnership for development. The international community recommitted itself to those goals during a World Summit in 2005, aimed at reviewing and moving ahead with the outcome of the Millennium Summit.

Coordinating development activities

Despite advances on many fronts, gross disparities in wealth and well-being continue to characterize the world. Reducing poverty and redressing inequalities, both within and between countries, remain fundamental goals of the United Nations.

The UN system works in a variety of ways to promote its economic and social goals — by formulating policies, advising governments on their development plans, setting international norms and standards, and mobilizing funds for development programmes. Through the work of its various funds and programmes and its family of specialized agencies in areas as diverse as education, air safety, environmental protection and labour conditions, the UN touches the lives of people everywhere.

In 2005, the UN system spent $13.7 billion on operational activities for development. An additional $13.6 billion went for global humanitarian funding — nearly half of which was in response to the Indian Ocean tsunami and an earthquake in South Asia.

The **Economic and Social Council (ECOSOC)** is the principal body coordinating the economic and social work of the United Nations and its operational arms. It is also the central forum for discussing international economic and social issues and for formulating policy recommendations (see *www.un.org/docs/ecosoc*).

Under ECOSOC, the **Committee for Development Policy**, made up of 24 experts working in their personal capacity, acts as an advisory body on emerging economic, social and environmental issues. It also sets the criteria for the designation of least developed countries. The UN category of "least developed countries" was established by the General Assembly in the 1970s, based on UNCTAD's early work on the differing characteristics and stages of development of developing countries.

The **United Nations Development Group**, comprised of Secretariat bodies as well as the development funds and programmes, assists in the management and coordination of development work within the Organization (see *www.undg.org*). This executive body works to enhance cooperation between policy-making entities and the distinct operational programmes. The **Executive Committee on Economic and Social Affairs**, comprised of Secretariat bodies and including the regional commissions, is also an instrument for policy development and management (see *www.un.org/esa/ecesa*).

Within the United Nations Secretariat, the **Department of Economic and Social Affairs (DESA)** gathers and analyses economic and social data; carries out policy analysis and coordination, and provides substantive and technical support to member states in the social and economic sphere (see *www.un.org/esa/desa*). Its substantive support to intergovernmental processes facilitates member states' role in setting norms and standards and in agreeing on common courses of action in response to global challenges. DESA provides a crucial interface between global policies and national action, and among research, policy and operational activities.

> ## The United Nations competitive advantage
>
> The United Nations system has unique strengths in promoting development:
>
> - Its *universality:* all countries have a voice when policy decisions are made.
>
> - Its *impartiality:* it does not represent any particular national or commercial interest, and can thus develop special relations of trust with countries and their people to provide aid with no strings attached.
>
> - Its *global presence:* it has the world's largest network of country offices for delivering assistance for development.
>
> - Its *comprehensive mandate,* encompassing development, security, humanitarian assistance, human rights and the environment.
>
> - Its *commitment* to "the peoples of the United Nations".

true for the least developed countries (LDCs), which include 50 nations whose extreme poverty and indebtedness have marginalized them from global growth and development. These nations, 34 of which are in Africa, are given priority attention in several United Nations assistance programmes.

Small island developing states, landlocked developing countries and countries with economies in transition also suffer from critical problems requiring special attention from the international community. These, too, are given priority in the assistance programmes of the UN system, as well as through official development assistance (ODA) from member states.

Of the world's 31 landlocked developing countries, 16 are LDCs. Of the 38 small island developing states, 10 are LDCs.

In 1970, the General Assembly set an ODA target of 0.7 per cent of gross national product (GNP) — now referred to as gross national income (GNI)[1]. For years, the collective effort of members of the Development Assistance Committee (DAC) of the Organisation for Economic Co-operation and Development (OECD), now comprising 22 industrialized countries, hovered at around half that level.

During the 1990s, ODA fell sharply, bringing it to an all-time low. Within the reduced total, however, more assistance went to basic social services — up from 4 per cent of ODA in 1995, to 14 per cent by the year 2000 (nearly $4 billion). And more than four-fifths of aid was no longer tied to the procurement of goods and services in the donor country.

ODA levels began to recover during the new century. Among DAC members, total ODA was up to 0.30 per cent of combined GNI in 2006, at $103.9 billion. To date, only five countries — Denmark, Luxembourg, the Netherlands, Norway and Sweden — have met and maintained the 0.7 per cent target for ODA.

---

[1] GDP is the sum of value added by all resident producers plus any product taxes (less subsidies) not included in the valuation of output. GNI is GDP plus net receipts of primary income (compensation of employees and property income) from abroad.

International Conference on Financing for Development
(www.un.org/esa/ffd)

The International Conference on Financing for Development was held from 18 to 22 March 2002 in Monterrey, Mexico. This UN-hosted Conference on key financial and development issues attracted 50 heads of state or government and over 200 ministers, as well as leaders from the private sector, civil society and all the major intergovernmental financial, trade, economic and monetary organizations.

The Monterrey Conference also marked the first quadripartite exchange of views between governments, civil society, the business community and the institutional stakeholders on global economic issues. These global discussions involved over 800 participants in 12 separate roundtables — co-chaired by heads of governments, the heads of the World Bank, International Monetary Fund, the World Trade Organization and the regional development banks, as well as ministers of finance, trade and foreign affairs. The outcome of the Conference, known as the Monterrey Consensus, provides a picture of the new global approach to financing development.

Subsequently, the General Assembly decided to reconstitute its high-level dialogue on strengthening international cooperation for development as the intergovernmental focal point for follow-up on the Conference and related issues — to be held during odd-numbered years beginning in 2003. It includes a policy dialogue, with the participation of the relevant stakeholders, on implementation of the results of the Conference, as well as on the coherence and consistency of the international monetary, financial and trading systems in support of development.

The Assembly also decided that interactions between representatives of the Economic and Social Council, the directors of the executive boards of the World Bank and the International Monetary Fund, and representatives of the appropriate intergovernmental body of the World Trade Organization would continue each spring. The April 2002 consultation was expanded to include roundtables with representatives from civil society and the business community.

The Fourth World Trade Organization (WTO) Ministerial Conference, held at Doha, Qatar, in 2001, also addressed the means of implementing sustainable development. Subsequent WTO Ministerial Conferences were held at Cancun in 2003, and in Hong Kong in 2005. A Follow-up International Conference on Financing for Development was to be held in Doha in the second half of 2008.

including the World Bank and the IMF. In addition, UNDP's country and regional programmes draw on the expertise of developing country nationals and NGOs. Seventy-five per cent of all UNDP-supported projects are implemented by local organizations.

At the country level, UNDP promotes an integrated approach to the provision of United Nations development assistance. In several developing countries, it has established a **United Nations Development Assistance Framework (UNDAF)** made up of United Nations teams under the leadership of the local United Nations resident coordinator, who is in many instances

34 countries. The Bank, which has a AAA credit rating, raises nearly all its money through the sale of its bonds in the world's financial markets.

The second type of loan goes to the poorest countries, which are usually not creditworthy in the international financial markets and are unable to pay near-market interest rates on the money they borrow. Lending to the poorest countries is done by a World Bank affiliate, the **International Development Association (IDA)**. Funded largely by contributions from 40 rich member countries, IDA helps the world's poorest countries by providing grant financing and credits. These "credits" are actually interest-free loans with a 10-year grace period and maturities of 35 to 40 years. In fiscal year 2007, IDA provided $11.9 billion in financing for 189 new projects in 64 low-income countries. It is the world's largest source of concessional assistance for the world's poorest countries.

Under its regulations, the Bank can lend only to governments, but it works closely with local communities, NGOs and private enterprise. Its projects are designed to assist the poorest sectors of the population. Successful development requires that governments and communities "own" their development projects. The Bank encourages governments to work closely with NGOs and civil society to strengthen participation by people affected by Bank-financed projects. NGOs based in borrowing countries collaborate in about half of these projects.

The Bank encourages the private sector by advocating stable economic policies, sound government finances, and open, honest and accountable governance. It supports many sectors in which private-sector development is making rapid inroads — finance, power, telecommunications, information technology, oil and gas and industry. The Bank's regulations prohibit it from lending directly to the private sector, but a Bank affiliate — the **International Finance Corporation (IFC)** — exists expressly to promote private sector investment by supporting high-risk sectors and countries. Another affiliate, the **Multilateral Investment Guarantee Agency (MIGA)**, provides political risk insurance (guarantees) to those who invest in or lend to developing countries.

But the World Bank does much more than lend money. It also routinely includes technical assistance in the projects it finances. This may include advice on such issues as the overall size of a country's budget and where the money should be allocated, or how to set up village health clinics, or what sort of equipment is needed to build a road. The Bank funds a few projects each year devoted exclusively to providing expert advice and training. It also trains people from borrowing countries on how to create and carry out development programmes.

The IBRD supports sustainable development projects in such areas as reforestation, pollution control and land management; water, sanitation and agriculture; and conservation of natural resources. It is the main funder of the **Global Environment Facility (GEF)**, as well as the world's largest long-term financier of HIV/AIDS programmes, having committed about $4 billion since 1988. It has also put significant resources into the **Heavily Indebted Poor Countries (HIPC)** Initiative, aimed at providing poor countries with debt relief amounting to $41 billion over time.

At their July 2005 summit, the leaders of the "Group of Eight" developed nations proposed 100 per cent cancellation of debt owed to the IDA, the IMF and the African Development Fund by some of the world's poorest countries, mostly in Africa and Latin America. Debt relief under the resulting **Multilateral Debt Relief Initiative (MDRI)** is estimated at about $50 billion, including $37 billion from IDA alone, which began implementing it at the start of fiscal year 2007.

Lending for stability

Many countries turn to the **International Monetary Fund (IMF)**, a United Nations specialized agency, when internal or external factors seriously undermine their balance-of-payments position, fiscal stability or capacity to meet debt-service commitments. The IMF offers advice and policy recommendations to overcome these problems, and often makes financial resources available to member countries in support of economic reform programmes.

Members with balance-of-payments problems generally avail themselves of the IMF's financial resources by "purchasing" reserve assets — in the form of other members' currencies and Special Drawing Rights — with an equivalent amount of their own currencies. The IMF levies charges on these loans, and requires that members repay the loans by repurchasing their own currencies from the IMF over a specified time.

The main IMF facilities are:

* *Stand-by arrangements*, designed to provide short-term balance-of-payments assistance for deficits of a temporary or cyclical nature; these must be repaid within 5 years.

* *Extended Fund Facility*, designed to support medium-term programmes aimed at overcoming balance-of-payments difficulties stemming from macroeconomic and structural problems; these must be repaid within 10 years.

* *Poverty Reduction and Growth Facility* (PRGF), a concessional facility designed for low-income member countries with the explicit goal of reducing poverty. Members qualifying for funding may borrow up to 140 per cent of their quota under a three-year arrangement (and up to 185 per cent under exceptional circumstances). Loans carry an annual interest rate of 0.5 per cent; repayments are made beginning 5 1/2 years and ending 10 years after disbursement. As of August 2006, 78 low-income countries were eligible for this assistance.

* *Exogenous Shocks Facility*, provides PRGF-type support for low-income countries that do not have PRGR programmes in place, when facing such exogenous shocks as commodity price changes (including oil), natural disasters, and crisis in neighbouring countries that disrupt trade.

* *Compensatory Financing Facility*, which provides timely financing for members experiencing temporary export shortfalls or excesses in cereal import costs.

The **Multilateral Investment Guarantee Agency (MIGA)** is an investment insurance affiliate of the Bank. Its goal is to facilitate the flow of private investment for productive purposes to developing member countries, by offering investors long-term political risk insurance — that is, coverage against the risks of expropriation, currency transfer, war and civil disturbance — and by providing advisory services. MIGA carries out promotional programmes, disseminates information on investment opportunities, and provides technical assistance that enhances the investment promotion capabilities of countries. Since its inception in 1988, MIGA has issued nearly 900 guarantees for projects in 96 developing countries, worth more than $17.4 billion and facilitated several times that amount in foreign direct investment.

The **United Nations Conference on Trade and Development (UNCTAD)** helps developing countries and economies in transition promote foreign direct investment and improve their investment climate — with a view to minimizing its negative impact and maximizing its benefits for development. UNCTAD helps governments understand the policy implications of FDI and to formulate and implement policies accordingly.

UNCTAD promotes understanding of the linkages between investment, trade, enterprise development and technological capacity-building, and conducts research on global FDI trends. These are presented in its annual *World Investment Report, Investment Policy Reviews, World Investment Directory* and other studies.

Trade and development

In 2007, for the fifth consecutive year, world trade was expected to maintain its momentum, with estimated overall output growth of 3.6 per cent, according to the 2007 *Trade and Development Report* of the United Nations Conference on Trade and Development (UNCTAD).

Developing countries in particular increased their per capita gross domestic product (GDP) by nearly 30 per cent between 2003 and 2007, UNCTAD reports, compared to 10 per cent in the highly industrialized countries. In East and South Asia, owing mainly to strong performances by China and India, economic growth allowed these subregions to more than double their per capita GDP in only 14 years.

Africa was set to continue expanding at around 6 per cent in 2007, while growth rates in Latin America and West Asia were expected to be close to 5 per cent — raising hopes of greater progress towards the United Nations Millennium Development Goals (MDGs). Nevertheless, imbalances in the world economy continue to increase; some see this as a matter of serious concern, while others view it as a natural and ultimately harmless consequence of an increasingly integrated global economy.

The **United Nations Conference on Trade and Development (UNCTAD)** is tasked with ensuring the integration of all countries in global trade. As the UN's focal point for dealing

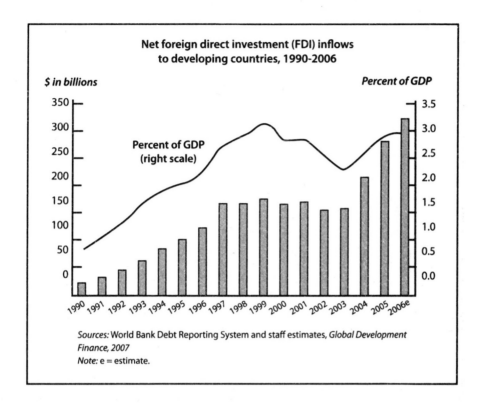

Net foreign direct investment (FDI) inflows to developing countries, 1990-2006

Sources: World Bank Debt Reporting System and staff estimates, *Global Development Finance, 2007*
Note: e = estimate.

UNCTAD's work helps clarify trends and shape thinking and policies regarding the trade-development nexus in the context of globalization. It also enables developing countries to participate effectively in international trade in goods, services and commodities. It was one of the main authors of the concept of special and differential treatment for developing countries, and a key actor in its incorporation into the General Agreement on Tariffs and Trade and, later, the World Trade Organization. UNCTAD is also the UN system's focal point on trade logistics. By providing institutional, legal and operational solutions to reduce transaction costs and increase transport connectivity, it helps improve developing countries' access to world markets.

Current UNCTAD research highlights the fact that a "second generation" of trade-driven globalization is emerging, characterized by economic multi-polarity, and with the emerging South and South-South trade playing a significant role. Nevertheless, UNCTAD has raised the question of how the international trading system might be reshaped so as to sustain the current expansion of trade and its changing geography — while dealing decisively with the continuing spectre of worsening poverty and underdevelopment in some countries.

UNCTAD also promotes enterprise development, particularly for small and medium-sized enterprises, through regular intergovernmental discussions and through technical cooperation. UNCTAD's technical cooperation activities involve nearly 300 projects in

Promoting equitable trade for inclusive development

Intergovernmental negotiations, research and technical assistance under UNCTAD auspices have resulted in the following:

- Agreement on a Generalized Systems of Preferences (1971), which facilitates the preferential treatment of over $70 billion of developing-country exports to industrialized countries annually.

- Agreement on a Global System of Trade Preferences among developing countries (1989).

- International commodity agreements, including those for cocoa, coffee, sugar, natural rubber, jute and jute products, tropical timber, tin, olive oil and wheat.

- The Common Fund for Commodities, which provides financial backing for the operation of international stocks and for R&D projects in the area of commodities.

- The General Assembly's 1980 adoption of the only universally applicable, voluntary code on competition — the Set of Multilaterally Agreed Equitable Principles and Rules for the Control of Restrictive Business Practices — which is reviewed every five years, most recently in 2005.

- The creation of the East African Organic Standard (EAOS) in 2007. The EAOS will become the second regional organic standard in the world after the European Union's.

- The Trade Analysis and Information System (TRAINS), the most comprehensive publicly available international database on trade, tariffs and non-tariff measures.

one of three roles: implementing its own programme; executing a programme on behalf of other agencies and donors; or providing advice and management assistance to national projects.

FAO's Investment Centre assists developing countries in formulating investment operations in agricultural and rural development, in partnership with international financing institutions. Each year, the Centre carries out more than 600 field missions for some 140 investment programmes and projects in around 100 countries. It spends some $25 million annually (of which FAO provides around $9 million) to help mobilize funding commitments of about $3 billion a year for approved investment proposals.

FAO is active in land and water development, plant and animal production, forestry, fisheries, economic, social and food security policy, investment, nutrition, food standards and food safety, and commodities and trade. For example:

Projects throughout Pakistan support sustainable crop production, diversification of crop production, management of revolving funds, and farm service centres. Farmers are actively involved in FAO projects, and training is provided to build capacities in rural community organizations, including village-based business support services.

FAO has provided important technical support to Brazil's Zero Hunger Programme since its inception — a programme which improved the lives and nutritional intake of more than 8 million families during the period 2003-2005. In addition, a Food Products Procurement

UNIDO designs and implements technical cooperation programmes to support the industrial development efforts of its clients. Its thematic priorities are:

- *Poverty reduction through productive activities*, by promoting industry, especially through small and medium enterprises, in less developed areas, with a focus on employment creation, income generation and institutional capacity-building;

- *Trade capacity-building*, by helping countries to develop both production and trade-related capacities, including the capacity to conform to the standards of international markets;

- *Environment and energy*, by promoting industrial energy efficiency and renewable sources of energy, particularly in rural areas, and supporting other activities for sustainable industrial development.

UNIDO assists governments, business associations and the private industrial sector with services which translate its core functions and thematic priorities into action: industrial governance and statistics; investment and technology promotion; industrial competitiveness and trade; private sector development; agro-industries; sustainable energy and climate change; the *Montreal Protocol* on substances that deplete the ozone layer; and environmental management.

UNIDO also serves as a global forum to generate and disseminate industry-related knowledge in its three thematic priority areas, and to provide a platform for all actors in the public and private sectors.

UNIDO's 13 investment and technology promotion offices, financed by the countries in which they are located, promote business contacts between industrialized countries and developing countries and countries with economies in transition. It has 5 investment promotion units, 35 national cleaner production centres and 10 international technology centres. Headquartered in Vienna, UNIDO is represented in 43 developing countries.

Labour

Concerned with both the economic and social aspects of development, the **International Labour Organization (ILO)** is one of the specialized agencies that predates the United Nations, as it was established in 1919. Its long and diverse work in the setting and monitoring of labour standards in the workplace has provided a framework of international labour standards and guidelines which have been adopted in national legislation by virtually all countries.

ILO is guided by the principle that social stability and integration can be sustained only if they are based on social justice — particularly the right to employment with fair compensation in a healthy workplace. Over the decades, ILO has helped to create such hallmarks as the eight-hour day, maternity protection, child-labour laws, and a whole range of policies that promote safety in the workplace and peaceful industrial relations.

International aviation

In 2006, more than 2.1 billion passengers flew on some 24 million flights, and 39 million tonnes of freight were shipped by air. The safe and orderly growth of international flight is overseen by a United Nations specialized agency, the **International Civil Aviation Organization (ICAO)**.

ICAO aims to meet the public's need for the safety, security, efficiency and continuity of international civil aviation and to minimize its adverse effects on the environment. It also works to strengthen the law governing civil aviation.

To meet these objectives, ICAO:

- adopts international standards and recommendations which are applied to the design and performance of aircraft and much of their equipment; the performance of airline pilots, flight crews, air traffic controllers, and ground and maintenance crews; and security requirements and procedures at international airports;

- formulates visual and instrument flight rules, as well as the aeronautical charts used for international navigation. Aircraft telecommunications systems, radio frequencies and security procedures are also its responsibility;

- works towards minimizing the impact of aviation on the environment through reductions in aircraft emissions and through noise limits; and

- facilitates the movement of aircraft, passengers, crews, baggage, cargo and mail across borders, by standardizing customs, immigration, public health and other formalities.

As acts of unlawful interference continue to pose a serious threat to the safety and security of international civil aviation, ICAO continues to pursue policies and programmes designed to prevent them. In the wake of the terrorist attacks on 11 September 2001 in the United States, ICAO developed an aviation security plan of action — including a universal audit programme to evaluate the implementation of security standards and recommend remedial action where necessary.

In addition, ICAO meets requests from developing countries for help in improving air transport systems and training for aviation personnel. It has helped to establish regional training centres in several developing countries. Each year, the agency is involved in more than 200 technical cooperation projects in about 100 countries. Projects may include the procurement of aviation goods and services ranging in value from $100,000 to more than $100 million. The criteria for ICAO assistance are based on what countries need to make civil aviation safe and efficient, in accordance with ICAO's Standards and Recommended Practices.

ICAO works in close cooperation with such UN specialized agencies as the IMO, the ITU and the WMO. The International Air Transport Association, the Airports Council International, the International Federation of Air Line Pilots' Associations and other international organizations also participate in many ICAO meetings.

Various IMO conventions address liability and compensation issues. The most significant include the 1992 *Protocol of the International Convention on Civil Liability for Oil Pollution Damage* (CLC Convention, 1969) and the 1992 *Protocol of the International Convention on the Establishment of an International Fund for Compensation for Oil Pollution Damage* (IOPC Fund, 1971), which together provide compensation to victims of oil pollution damage. The *Athens Convention relating to the Carriage of Passengers and their Luggage by Sea* (PAL, 1974) sets compensation limits for passengers on ships.

In December 2002, the IMO adopted an International Ship and Port Facility Security Code, which requires compliance with new measures aimed at protecting shipping against terrorist attacks. Adopted under amendments to the *International Convention for the Safety of Life at Sea* (SOLAS), the Code became mandatory on 1 July 2004. In 2005, IMO adopted amendments to the Convention for the Suppression of Unlawful Acts Against the Safety of Maritime Navigation, 1988 and its related Protocol, introducing the right of a state party to board a ship flying the flag of another state party when the requesting party has reasonable grounds to suspect that the ship or a person on board the ship is, has been, or is about to be involved in, the commission of an offence under the Convention.

IMO's technical cooperation programme aims to support the implementation of its international standards and regulations, particularly in developing countries, and to assist governments in operating a shipping industry successfully. The emphasis is on training, and IMO has under its auspices the **World Maritime University** in Malmö, Sweden, the International Maritime Law Institute in Malta and the International Maritime Academy in Trieste, Italy.

Telecommunications

Telecommunications have become a key to the global delivery of services. Banking, tourism, transportation and the information industry all depend on quick and reliable global telecommunications. The sector is being revolutionized by powerful trends, such as globalization, deregulation, restructuring, value-added network services, intelligent networks and regional arrangements. Such developments have transformed telecommunications from its earlier status as a public utility to one having strong links with commerce and trade. It has been projected that the $2.1 trillion global telecommunications market will grow to $2.5 trillion in 2008 and $3 trillion in 2010.

The **International Telecommunication Union (ITU)** is the world's oldest intergovernmental organization, dating back to 1865. It coordinates the public and private sectors to provide global telecommunications networks and services.

Specifically, ITU:

* develops standards which foster the interconnection of national communications infrastructures into global networks, allowing the seamless exchange of information — be it data, faxes or phone calls — around the world;

The UPU forms a single postal territory of countries for the reciprocal exchange of letter-post items. Every member state agrees to transmit the mail of all other members by the best means used for its own mail. As the primary vehicle of cooperation between national postal services, the UPU works to improve international postal services, provide postal customers in every country with harmonized and simplified procedures for their international mail, and make available a universal network of up-to-date products and services.

The UPU sets indicative rates, maximum and minimum weight and size limits, and the conditions of acceptance of letter-post items, including priority and non-priority items, letters, aerogrammes, postcards, printed matter and small packets. It prescribes the methods for calculating and collecting transit charges (for letter-post items passing through one or more countries) and terminal dues (for imbalance of mails). It also establishes regulations for registered and air mail, and for items requiring special precautions, such as infectious and radioactive substances.

Thanks to UPU, new products and services are integrated into the international postal network. In this way, such services as registered letters, postal money orders, international reply coupons, small packets, postal parcels and expedited mail services have been made available to most of the world's citizens.

The agency has taken a strong leadership role in certain activities, such as the application of electronic data interchange technology by the postal administrations of member countries and the monitoring of quality of postal services worldwide.

The UPU provides technical assistance through multi-year projects aimed at optimizing national postal services. It also conducts short projects which may include study cycles, training fellowships, and the expertise of development consultants who carry out on-the-spot studies on training, management or postal operations. The UPU has also made international financial institutions increasingly aware of the need for investment in the postal sector.

Around the world, postal services are making a determined effort to revitalize the postal business. As part of a communications market that is experiencing explosive growth, they have to adapt to a rapidly changing environment, becoming more independent, self-financing enterprises and providing a wider range of services. The UPU is playing a leadership role in promoting this revitalization.

Intellectual property

Intellectual property in various forms — including books, feature films, artistic performance media and computer software — has become a central issue in international trade relations. Millions of patent, trademark and industrial design registrations are currently in force worldwide. In today's knowledge-based economy, intellectual property is a tool for promoting wealth creation as well as economic, social and cultural development.

A United Nations specialized agency, the **World Intellectual Property Organization (WIPO)**, is responsible for promoting the protection of intellectual property all over the world through cooperation among states, and for administering various international

Global statistics

Governments, public institutions and the private sector rely heavily on relevant, accurate, comparable and timely statistics at national and global levels, and the United Nations has served as a global focal point for statistics since its founding.

The **Statistical Commission** is the United Nations intergovernmental body mandated to strengthen the harmonization of official statistics worldwide. Composed of 24 member states, it oversees the work of the UN **Statistics Division** in developing methodologies and standards for the collection, compilation and dissemination of statistics.

The Statistics Division offers a broad range of services for producers and users of statistics. Its yearbooks and compendiums — including the *Statistical Yearbook, Monthly Bulletin of Statistics, World Statistics Pocketbook,* the official *Millennium Development Goals Indicators* database, and the *UN-data* portal — present a broad cross-section of information, in print and online. Its specialized publications cover such matters as demographic, social and housing statistics, national accounts, economic and social classifications, energy, international trade, and the environment.

The Division also aims to improve national capabilities in developing countries by providing technical advisory services, training programmes and workshops organized throughout the world on various topics. (See *http://unstats.un.org/unsd*. For the *UN-data* portal, see *http://data.un.org*)

Public administration

A country's public sector is arguably the most important component in the successful implementation of its national development programmes. The new opportunities created by globalization, the information revolution and democratization have dramatically affected the state and how it functions. Managing the public sector in an environment of unremitting change has become a demanding challenge for national decision-makers, policy developers and public administrators.

The United Nations, through its Programme on Public Administration and Finance, assists countries in their efforts to strengthen, improve and reform their governance systems and administrative institutions. Managed by DESA's **Division for Public Administration and Development Management**, the Programme helps governments ensure that their governance — including their public economic, administrative and financial institutions — functions in an effective, responsive, pro-poor and democratic manner. The Division promotes sound public policies, effective and responsive public administration, efficient, engaging service delivery, and openness to change. (See *www.unpan.org/dpepa.asp*)

Activities include helping governments in developing countries design national programmes for improving ethics; transparency and accountability in public policies; strengthening capacities for local governments and decentralized governance; innovations in the delivery of public services; civil service reforms; reconstructing governance and public administration institutions after severe conflict; human resources development and management in the public sector;

The Organization has been in the forefront of supporting government efforts to extend social services relating to health, education, family planning, housing and sanitation to all people. In addition to developing models for social programmes, the United Nations has helped to integrate economic and social aspects of development. Its evolving policies and programmes have always stressed that the components of development — social, economic, environmental and cultural — are interconnected and cannot be pursued in isolation.

Globalization and liberalization are posing new challenges to social development. There is a growing desire to see a more equitable sharing of the benefits of globalization. There is a need to better direct the benefits of liberalized trade and investment towards reducing poverty, increasing employment and promoting social integration.

The United Nations takes a people-centred approach in the social area, placing individuals, families and communities at the centre of development strategies. It places great emphasis on social development — in part to offset the tendency of economic and political problems to dominate the international agenda at the expense of such social issues as health, education and population, or such groups as women, children and the elderly.

Many UN global conferences have focused on these issues. The World Summit for Social Development (Copenhagen, 1995) marked the first time the international community came together to advance the struggle against poverty, unemployment and social disintegration — to create a new awareness of social responsibility for the 21st century. The Summit's originality lay in its universality, its scope, its ethical basis, and its call for renewed forms of partnership within and among nations. The *Copenhagen Declaration for Social Development* and its 10 commitments represent a social contract at the global level.

The diverse issues of social development represent a challenge for developing and developed countries alike. To differing degrees, all societies are confronted by the problems of unemployment, social fragmentation and persistent poverty. And a growing number of social problems — from forced migration to drug abuse, organized crime and the spread of diseases — can be successfully tackled only through concerted international action.

The United Nations addresses the issues of social development through the General Assembly and the **Economic and Social Council (ECOSOC)**, where system-wide policies and priorities are set and programmes endorsed. One of the Assembly's six main committees, the **Social, Humanitarian and Cultural Committee**, takes up agenda items relating to the social sector. Under ECOSOC, the main intergovernmental body dealing with social concerns is the **Commission for Social Development**. Composed of 46 member states, the Commission advises ECOSOC and governments on social policies and on the social aspects of development. The theme for its 2007 session was "Promoting Full Employment and Decent Work for All".

Within the Secretariat, the **Division for Social Policy and Development** of the Department of Economic and Social Affairs services these intergovernmental bodies, providing research, analysis and expert guidance. Throughout the UN system, there are many specialized agencies, funds, programmes and offices that address different aspects of social development.

Major world conferences since 1990

- World Conference on Education for All, 1990, Jomtien, Thailand
- World Summit for Children, 1990, New York
- International Conference on Nutrition, 1992, Rome
- United Nations Conference on Environment and Development (UNCED), 1992, Rio de Janeiro
- World Conference on Human Rights, 1993, Vienna
- International Conference on Population and Development, 1994, Cairo
- Global Conference on the Sustainable Development of Small Island Developing States, 1994, Barbados
- World Summit for Social Development, 1995, Copenhagen
- Fourth World Conference on Women: Action for Equality, Development and Peace, 1995, Beijing
- Second United Nations Conference on Human Settlements (Habitat II), 1996, Istanbul
- World Food Summit, 1996, Rome
- World Education Forum, 2000, Dakar
- Third United Nations Conference on the Least Developed Countries, 2001, Brussels
- World Conference against Racism, 2001, Durban
- World Food Summit: five years after, 2002, Rome
- International Conference on Financing for Development, 2002, Monterrey
- Second World Assembly on Ageing, 2002, Madrid
- World Summit on Sustainable Development, 2002, Johannesburg
- International Ministerial Conference of Landlocked and Transit Developing Countries and Donor Countries and Representatives of International Financial and Development Institutions on Transit Transport Cooperation, 2003, Almaty, Kazakhstan
- World Conference on Disaster Reduction, 2005, Kobe, Japan
- World Summit on the Information Society, 2003 (Geneva) and 2005 (Tunis)

Special sessions of the General Assembly have reviewed progress made five years after the United Nations Conferences on Environment and Development (1997), Small Island Developing States (1999), Population and Development (1999), Women (2000), Social Development (2000), Human Settlements (2001), Children (2002), the *Millennium Declaration* (2005), Small Arms (2006). Another special session addressed the problems of HIV/AIDS (2001, reviewed in 2006).

of categories in nearly every country in the world. Designed as a tool for policy-makers, development practitioners, journalists, students and others, it can be used to track progress through interactive maps and country-specific progress, learn about countries' challenges and achievements and get the latest news, and support organizations working on the MDGs around the world. The MDG Monitor was compiled by UNDP, in close cooperation with various UN agencies and with private-sector support from Cisco and Google. It is located online at *www.mdgmonitor.org*.

The international financial institutions of the UN system play a central role in funding numerous programmes that focus on the social aspects of poverty eradication, in support of the Millennium Development Goals. The World Bank, comprising the International Bank for Reconstruction and Development (IBRD) and the International Development Association (IDA), provided some $24.7 billion for operations during fiscal year 2007. Its projects include support for water reforms in Morocco, poverty alleviation in Indonesia, helping curb HIV/AIDS in India, reducing emissions connected with climate change in Bolivia, building infrastructure in rural Senegal, dramatically improving access to primary school education in Afghanistan, rebuilding Timor-Leste's health system, and promoting growth in middle-income countries.

Reducing poverty

The United Nations system put poverty reduction at the top of the international agenda when it proclaimed 1997-2006 the **International Decade for the Eradication of Poverty**. In their 2000 *Millennium Declaration*, world leaders resolved to halve, by 2015, the number of people living on less than $1 a day, and also set targets in the fight against poverty and disease.

A key player in this effort is the **United Nations Development Programme (UNDP)**, which has made poverty alleviation its chief priority. UNDP works to strengthen the capacity of governments and civil society organizations to address the whole range of factors that contribute to poverty. These include increasing food security; generating employment opportunities; increasing people's access to land, credit, technology, training and markets; improving the availability of shelter and basic services; and enabling people to participate in the political processes that shape their lives. The heart of UNDP's anti-poverty work lies in empowering the poor.

Fighting hunger

Food production has increased at an unprecedented rate since the United Nations was founded in 1945, and during the period 1990-1997, the number of hungry people worldwide fell dramatically — from 959 million to 791 million. However, today that number has risen again, and some 854 million people do not have enough to eat — more than the populations of the United States, Canada and the European Union combined. This is despite the fact that there is enough food in the world today for every man, woman and child to lead a healthy and productive life. Of the chronically hungry, 820 million live in developing countries.

Millennium Declaration targets for poverty, disease and the environment

At the Millennium Summit in September 2000, world leaders committed themselves to the following targets:

- By 2015, cut in half the proportion of the world's people whose income is less than one dollar a day and the proportion of people unable to reach or afford safe drinking water.
- Also by 2015, ensure that both male and female children everywhere will be able to complete a full course of primary schooling and have equal access to all levels of education.
- Reduce maternal mortality by three quarters and under-five child mortality by two thirds.
- Halt and reverse the spread of HIV/AIDS, malaria and other major diseases.
- Provide special assistance to children orphaned by HIV/AIDS.
- By 2020, achieve significant improvement in the lives of at least 100 million slum dwellers.
- Promote gender equality and the empowerment of women as ways to combat poverty, hunger and disease and to stimulate sustainable development.
- Develop and implement strategies that give young people everywhere a chance to find decent and productive work.
- Encourage the pharmaceutical industry to make essential drugs more widely available and affordable for all who need them in developing countries.
- Develop partnerships with the private sector and civil society organizations in pursuit of development and poverty eradication.
- Ensure that the benefits of new technologies — especially information and communication technologies — are available to all.

In the *Millennium Declaration*, world leaders also resolved to take action on a number of environmental issues, namely:

- Ensure the entry into force of the Kyoto Protocol, preferably by 2002, and begin the required reduction in emissions of greenhouse gases.
- Press for full implementation of the Convention on Biological Diversity and the Convention to Combat Desertification, especially in Africa.
- Stop unsustainable exploitation of water resources by developing water management strategies at the regional, national and local levels.
- Intensify cooperation to reduce the number and effects of natural and man-made disasters.
- Ensure free access to information on the human genome sequence.

(See box, *2005 World Summit Outcome*, in chapter 1)

On the verge of a polio-free world

When the Global Polio Eradication Initiative was launched in 1988, there were 350,000 cases of the disease worldwide — paralysing more than 1,000 children in more than 125 countries on 5 continents every day. After a concerted campaign, including National Immunization Days to immunize millions of children under five, that figure has dropped to 1,951 reported cases in 2005 — more than a 99 per cent reduction. In 2006, only four countries in the world remained endemic for the disease — Afghanistan, India, Nigeria and Pakistan.

More than 5 million people in the developing world, who would otherwise have been paralysed, are walking today because they have been immunized against polio. Tens of thousands of public health workers and millions of volunteers have been trained. Transport and communications systems for immunization have been strengthened. Since 1988, more than 2 billion children worldwide have been immunized. In 2006, partners in the Global Polio Eradication Initiative vaccinated 375 million children during 187 immunization campaigns in 36 countries, with 2.1 billion doses of vaccine.

This success has been possible through an unprecedented partnership for health spearheaded by WHO, UNICEF, the United States Centers for Disease Control and Prevention, and Rotary International. As the largest private sector donor, Rotary has already contributed more than $600 million to the effort. Health ministries, donor governments, foundations, corporations, celebrities, philanthropists, health workers and volunteers have also been engaged. (See *www.polioeradication.org*)

The public health savings of polio eradication, once immunization stops, are estimated to be $1.5 billion a year.

programmes, such as food-for-training and food-for-work; programmes to address the generational hunger cycle, such as mother-and-child nutrition; and nutritional support to HIV/AIDS victims.

WFP relies entirely on voluntary contributions to finance its humanitarian and development projects. Despite having no independent source of funds, it has the largest budget of any major UN agency or programme — as well as the lowest overhead. Governments are its principal source of funding, but WFP's corporate partners are making an increasingly vital contribution to its mission. WFP also works with more than 3,200 NGOs, whose grass-roots and technical knowledge is invaluable in assessing how to deliver its food aid to the right people.

Health

In most parts of the world, people live longer, infant mortality is decreasing and illnesses are kept in check as more people have access to basic health services, immunization, clean water and sanitation. The United Nations has been deeply involved in many of these advances, particularly in developing countries, by supporting health services, delivering essential drugs,

---

The UN combats HIV/AIDS
(www.unaids.org)

The number of people dying from AIDS-related illnesses has declined in the past two years, due in part to the life-prolonging effects of antiretroviral therapy (ART), according to the *2007 AIDS Epidemic Update* — produced by the Joint United Nations Programme on HIV/AIDS (UNAIDS) and the World Health Organization (WHO).

Global HIV incidence — the number of new HIV infections per year — is estimated to have peaked in the 1990s at over 3 million. In 2007, it was 2.5 million — an average of more than 6,800 new infections each day. Nevertheless, AIDS is among the leading causes of death globally and remains the primary cause of death in Africa.

"Unquestionably, we are beginning to see a return on investment", UNAIDS Executive Director Dr. Peter Piot says. "But with more than 6,800 new infections and over 5,700 deaths each day due to AIDS we must expand our efforts in order to significantly reduce the impact of AIDS worldwide."

As the leading advocate for a worldwide response to AIDS, UNAIDS is on the ground in 75 countries. Its priorities include: leadership and advocacy; developing information; evaluating the effectiveness of policy commitments and national responses; mobilizing resources; and promoting global, regional and national partnerships among people living with HIV, civil society, and high-risk groups.

UNAIDS keeps AIDS on the international political agenda. It played a key role in sponsoring the General Assembly's 2001 special session on HIV/AIDS, which produced a unanimous *Declaration of Commitment on HIV/AIDS*. It manages the World AIDS Campaign, intended to hold governments accountable for the promises they have made, particularly in the *Declaration* (*http://worldaidscampaign.info*). It also initiated the Global Coalition on Women and AIDS (*http://womanandaids.unaids.org*).

Active since 1996, UNAIDS promotes the role of civil society, mobilizes the private sector, and engages media companies in the fight against AIDS. It has negotiated with pharmaceutical companies to reduce drug prices in developing countries, and works closely with those countries to help them achieve universal access to HIV prevention, care and treatment.

UNAIDS is a combined effort of 10 UN agencies: ILO, UNDP, UNESCO, UNFPA, UNHCR, UNICEF, UNODC, WHO, WFP and the World Bank. Its core budget for 2006-2007 was $320.5 million. AIDS funding is also provided by the Global Fund to Fight AIDS, Tuberculosis and Malaria (*www.theglobalfund.org*) and bilateral donors.

In their 2000 *Millennium Declaration*, world leaders resolved to halt and begin to reverse the spread of HIV/AIDS by 2015, and to provide assistance to children orphaned by the disease.

---

problems. The **United Nations Children's Fund (UNICEF)** focuses on child and maternal health, and the **United Nations Population Fund (UNFPA)** focuses on reproductive health and family planning. The specialized agency coordinating global action against disease is the **World Health Organization (WHO)**. WHO has set ambitious goals for achieving health middle-income countries to 1.3 million — up from 400,000 at the end of 2003. A WHO/ UNICEF strategy helped reduce the number of measles deaths worldwide from 871,000 in 1999 to 454,000 in 2004 — a 48 per cent decrease. During 2004-2005, WHO procured and distributed 1.3 million insecticide-treated nets, protecting some 2.5 million people from mosquitoes that transmit malaria; and tens of millions of nets were procured and distributed by other partners and countries.

A motor for health research. Working with its partners in health research, WHO gathers data on current conditions and needs, particularly in developing countries. These range from epidemiological research in remote tropical forests to monitoring the progress of genetic research. WHO's tropical disease research programme has focused on the resistance of the malaria parasite to the most commonly used drugs, and on fostering the development of new drugs and diagnostics against tropical infectious diseases. Its research also helps to improve national and international surveillance of epidemics, and to develop preventive strategies for new and emerging diseases.

Standard-setting. WHO establishes international standards on biological and pharmaceutical substances. It has developed the concept of "essential drugs" as a basic element of primary health care.

WHO works with countries to ensure the equitable supply of safe and effective drugs at the lowest possible cost and with the most effective use. To this end, it has developed a "model list" of several hundred drugs and vaccines considered essential to help prevent or treat over 80 per cent of all health problems. Nearly 160 countries have adapted the list to their own requirements, and the list is updated every two years. WHO also cooperates with member states, civil society and the pharmaceutical industry to develop new essential drugs for priority health problems in poor and middle-income countries, and to continue production of established essential drugs.

Through the international access afforded to the United Nations, WHO oversees the global collection of information on communicable diseases, compiles comparable health and disease statistics, and sets international standards for safe food, as well as for biological and pharmaceutical products. It also provides unmatched evaluation of the cancer-producing risks of pollutants, and has put into place the universally accepted guidance for global control of HIV/AIDS.

Human settlements

In 1950, New York City was the only metropolitan area with a population of over 10 million. By the year 2005, there were 20 such "mega-cities" — all but four in developing countries. In 1950, only 30 per cent of the world's population was urban. Today, more than half of its 6.5 billion people live in towns and cities. Nearly 1 billion of the world's people live in slums; in developing countries, nearly 42 per cent of the urban population live in slums.

The **United Nations Human Settlements Programme (UN-HABITAT)** — formerly known as the United Nations Centre for Human Settlements — is the lead agency within the United Nations system for addressing this situation (see *www.unhabitat.org*). It is mandated environment, local economic development, basic urban services, and cultural heritage. The studies aim at developing urban poverty reduction policies at local, national and regional levels.

- *Sustainable Cities Programme* — a joint UN-HABITAT/UNEP initiative that builds capacities in urban environmental planning and management, using participatory methods. With its sister programme, *Localizing Agenda 21*, it currently operates in over 30 cities worldwide.

- *Localizing Agenda 21* — promotes the global plan of action for sustainable development adopted at the 1992 "Earth Summit" (*Agenda 21*), by translating its human settlements components into action at the local level and stimulating joint venture initiatives in selected medium-sized cities.

- *Safer Cities Programme* — launched in 1996 at the request of African mayors, it seeks to promote the development of strategies at the city level to adequately address and ultimately prevent urban crime and violence.

- *Urban Management Programme* — a joint effort by UN-HABITAT, UNDP and external support agencies. This network of over 40 anchor and partner institutions, covering 140 cities in 58 countries, works to strengthen the contribution that cities and towns in developing countries make towards economic growth, social development and poverty alleviation.

- *Water and Sanitation Programme* —to improve access to safe water and help provide adequate sanitation to millions of low-income urban dwellers, and measuring that impact. It supports the MDG target to "reduce by half the proportion of people without sustainable access to safe drinking water by 2015", and the 2002 World Summit on Sustainable Development target "to halve by 2015, the proportion of people who do not have access to basic sanitation".

Education

Great strides have been made in education in recent years, marked by a significant increase in the number of children in schools. Nevertheless, some 77 million children have no access to primary education, and many who start attending are forced to leave because of poverty or family and social pressures. Despite enormous literacy efforts, 781 million adults remain illiterate, two thirds of them women. The United Nations Literacy Decade (2003-2012) seeks to draw greater attention to this pressing issue.

Research has shown the close relationship between access to education and improved social indicators. Schooling has a special multiplier effect for women. A woman who is educated will typically be healthier, have fewer children and have more opportunities to increase household income. Her children, in turn, will experience lower mortality rates, better nutrition and better overall health. For this reason, girls and women are the focus of the education programmes of many United Nations agencies.

Research and training

Academic work in the form of research and training is carried out by a number of specialized United Nations organizations. This work is aimed at enhancing understanding of the global problems we face, as well as fostering the human resources required for the more technical aspects of economic and social development and the maintenance of peace and security.

The mission of the **United Nations University (UNU)** is to contribute, through research and capacity-building, to efforts to resolve the pressing global problems of concern to the United Nations, its peoples and member states. An international community of scholars, UNU is a bridge between the UN and the international academic community — a think-tank for the United Nations system; a builder of capacities, particularly in developing countries; and a platform for dialogue and new creative ideas. UNU partners with over 40 United Nations entities and hundreds of cooperating research institutions around the world.

UNU's academic work addresses specific issues of concern to the United Nations. Its current thematic focus covers five areas: peace and security; good governance; economic and social development; science, technology and society; and environment and sustainability. Academic activities are carried out at the UNU Centre in Tokyo, and through research and training centres and programmes located in various parts of the world. These include:

- *UNU Food and Nutrition Programme for Human and Social Development,* Ithaca, New York, and Boston, Massachusetts, United States (1975) — focuses on food and nutrition capacity-building.

- *UNU Geothermal Training Programme,* Reykjavik, Iceland (1979) — geothermal research, exploration and development.

- *UNU World Institute for Development Economics Research* (UNU-WIDER), Helsinki, Finland (1985) — economic and social development.

- *UNU Programme for Biotechnology in Latin America and the Caribbean,* Caracas, Venezuela (1988) — biotechnology and society.

- *UNU - Maastricht Economic and Social Research and Training Centre on Innovation and Technology,* Maastricht, the Netherlands (1990) — social and economic impact of new technologies.

- *UNU Institute for Natural Resources in Africa,* Accra, Ghana (1990) — natural resources management.

- *UNU International Institute for Software Technology,* Macau, China (1992) — software technologies for development.

- *UNU Institute of Advanced Studies,* Yokohama, Japan (1995) — economic restructuring for sustainable development.

- *UNU International Leadership Academy,* Amman, Jordan (1995) — leadership development.

development policies and processes affect different social groups. It works to stimulate dialogue and contributes to policy debate within and outside the UN system. Its research themes during the first decade of the 21st century include social policy and development; markets, business and regulation; gender and development; civil society and social movements; democracy, governance and well-being; and identities, conflict and cohesion (see *www.unrisd.org*).

Population and development

The UN estimates that despite significant reductions in fertility as contraceptive use has increased in most countries, both developed and developing, population continues to increase globally by about 1.14 per cent per year. At this rate, assuming continued fertility declines, world population is expected to increase from 6.7 billion in July 2007, to 9.2 billion by the year 2050. Rapid population growth weighs heavily on the earth's resources and environment, often outstripping efforts towards development. The UN has addressed the relationship between population and development in many ways, placing special emphasis on advancing the rights and status of women, which is seen as key to social and economic progress.

Moreover, patterns are shifting, creating new needs. For example, the global number of persons aged 60 or over is expected to increase from 705 million in 2007 to nearly 2 billion in 2050, when the number of older persons will exceed the number of children for the first time in history. By 2008, half the world will be living in cities for the first time ever — with more than twice the number of urban dwellers living in the less developed regions. That ratio is expected to reach 10 to 1 by 2019.

Over the decades, the UN has been carrying out operational activities in many developing countries in response to population trends. Various parts of the Organization have worked together to build national statistical offices, take censuses, make projections and disseminate reliable data. The United Nations quantitative and methodological work, particularly its authoritative estimates and projections of population size and change, has been pioneering. This has led to a significant increase in national capacities to plan ahead, incorporate population policies into development planning, and take sound economic and social decisions.

The **Commission on Population and Development**, composed of 47 member states, is charged with studying and advising ECOSOC on population changes and their effects on economic and social conditions. It has primary responsibility for reviewing the implementation of the programme of action of the 1994 International Conference on Population and Development.

The **Population Division** of the United Nations Department of Economic and Social Affairs serves as the secretariat of the Commission. It also provides the international community with up-to-date and scientifically objective information on population and development. It undertakes studies on population levels, trends, estimates and projections, as well as on population policies and the link between population and development. The Division maintains major databases, including *The Population, Resources, Environment and Development Databank*, which is available to the public on CD-ROM. The Division

counselling were available, and if their husbands, extended families and communities were more supportive. UNFPA works with governments, the private sector and NGOs to meet people's family planning needs.

UNFPA is the lead United Nations organization for advancing the programme of action adopted at the 1994 International Conference on Population and Development (ICPD). In meeting the ICPD goals, UNFPA also brings its expertise in reproductive health and population issues to the worldwide collaborative effort to meet the Millennium Development Goals.

Gender equality and empowerment of women

Promotion of equality between women and men and the empowerment of women is central to the work of the United Nations. Gender equality is not only a goal in its own right, but is also recognized as a critical means for achieving all other development goals, including the Millennium Development Goals. Eradicating poverty and hunger, achieving universal primary education and health for all, combating HIV/AIDS and facilitating sustainable development all require systematic attention to the needs, priorities and contributions of women as well as men. The UN actively promotes women's human rights and works to eradicate the scourge of violence against women, including in armed conflict and through trafficking. The UN also adopts global norms and standards and supports follow-up and implementation at the national level, including through its development assistance activities. (See *www.un.org/womenwatch*)

The **Commission on the Status of Women**, under ECOSOC, monitors progress towards gender equality throughout the world by reviewing implementation of the platform for action that emerged from the Fourth World Conference on Women (Beijing, 1995). The Commission makes recommendations for further action to promote women's rights, and to address discrimination and inequality in all fields. The major contributions of the 45-member Commission during more than 60 years of activity include the preparation of and follow-up to four world conferences on women, including the Beijing Conference, and development of the treaty on women's human rights — the *Convention on the Elimination of All Forms of Discrimination against Women.*

The **Committee on the Elimination of Discrimination against Women (CEDAW)** monitors adherence to the *Convention on the Elimination of All Forms of Discrimination against Women.* The 23-member Committee holds constructive dialogues with states parties on their implementation of the Convention, based on reports they submit. Its recommendations have contributed to a better understanding of women's rights, and of the means to ensure the enjoyment of those rights and the elimination of discrimination against women.

The **Division for the Advancement of Women,** in the Department of Economic and Social Affairs, supports the efforts of the Commission on the Status of Women, the Economic and Social Council and the General Assembly to advance the global policy agenda for gender equality and strengthen the mainstreaming of gender perspectives in all areas of the United Nations.

World conferences on women

Building on the energy of national women's movements, United Nations conferences in Mexico City (1975), Copenhagen (1980) , Nairobi (1985) and Beijing (1995) have galvanized understanding, commitment and action concerning gender equality and the empowerment of women around the world.

At the Fourth World Conference on Women (Beijing, 1995), representatives of 189 governments adopted the *Beijing Declaration* and *Platform for Action,* to address discrimination and inequality and ensure the empowerment of women. in all spheres of public and private life. The *Platform* identifies 12 critical areas of concern:

- the persistent and increasing burden of poverty on women;
- unequal access to and inadequate educational opportunities;
- inequalities in health status, inadequate health-care services, and unequal access to health care;
- violence against women;
- effects of conflict on women;
- inequality in women's participation in the definition of economic structures and policies, and in the production process;
- inequality in the sharing of power and decision-making;
- insufficient mechanisms to promote the advancement of women;
- lack of awareness of, and commitment to, internationally and nationally recognized women's human rights;
- insufficient mobilization of mass media to promote women's contribution to society;
- lack of adequate recognition and support for women's contribution to managing natural resources and safeguarding the environment;
- the girl child.

At its twenty-third special session in 2000, the General Assembly conducted a five-year review of the *Beijing Declaration* and *Platform for Action.* Countries reaffirmed the commitments they made in Beijing and pledged additional initiatives, such as strengthening legislation against all forms of domestic violence, and enacting laws and policies to eradicate such harmful practices as early and forced marriage and female genital mutilation. Targets were set to ensure free compulsory primary education for both girls and boys, and to improve women's health through wider access to health care and prevention programmes.

In 2005, the Commission on the Status of Women conducted a 10-year review, in which member states reaffirmed the *Beijing Declaration* and *Platform for Action* and committed themselves to accelerated action to address the gap between global policies and implementation at the national level.

"A World Fit for Children"

From 8 to 10 May 2002, more than 7,000 people participated in the most important international conference on children in more than a decade — the special session of the United Nations General Assembly on children. It was convened to review progress since the World Summit for Children in 1990 and re-energize global commitment to children's rights. The special session was a landmark — the first one devoted exclusively to children and the first to include them as official delegates.

The special session culminated in the official adoption, by some 180 nations, of its outcome document, A World Fit for Children. The new agenda for and with the world's children comprised 21 specific goals and targets for the next decade, with a focus on four key priority areas: promoting healthy lives; providing quality education for all; protecting children against abuse, exploitation and violence; and combating HIV/AIDS.

The document's Declaration committed leaders to completing the unfinished agenda of the 1990 World Summit for Children, and to achieving other goals and objectives, in particular those of the UN *Millennium Declaration*. It also reaffirmed leaders' obligation to promote and protect the rights of each child, acknowledging the legal standards set by the Convention on the Rights of the Child and its Optional Protocols.

The Plan of Action sets out three necessary outcomes: the best possible start in life for children; access to a quality basic education, including free and compulsory primary education; and ample opportunity for children and adolescents to develop their individual capacities. It includes strong calls to support families, eliminate discrimination and tackle poverty. It also calls upon a wide range of actors and partners to play key roles, including: children, parents, families and other caregivers; local governments and parliamentarians; NGOs and the private sector; religious, spiritual, cultural and indigenous leaders; the mass media; regional and international organizations; and people who work with children.

To achieve these goals, the plan calls for the mobilization of resources at both national and international levels. It supports the development of local partnerships, as well as the pursuit of such global targets as the allocation by industrialized countries of 0.7 per cent of their gross national product for official development assistance (ODA). And it supports the 20/20 Initiative — a compact between developing and industrialized countries calling for 20 per cent of developing countries' budgets and 20 percent of ODA to be allocated to basic social services.

Social integration
(www.un.org/esa/socdev)

There are several social groups that the United Nations has come to recognize as deserving special attention, including youth, older persons, persons with disabilities, minorities and indigenous populations. Their concerns are addressed by the General Assembly, ECOSOC and the Commission for Social Development. Specific programmes for these groups are carried out within the United Nations Department of Economic and Social Affairs.

young people and increase opportunities for their participation in society. It also called for a World Conference of Ministers Responsible for Youth to meet regularly under the aegis of the United Nations. Its first session, held in Lisbon in 1998, adopted the ***Lisbon Declaration on Youth*** and recommended initiatives at the national, regional and global levels.

- In 1999, the General Assembly declared that 12 August be commemorated each year as International Youth Day. It recommended that public information activities be organized to support the Day as a way to promote better awareness of the *World Programme of Action for Youth*.

- Governments include youth delegates regularly in their official delegations to the General Assembly and other UN meetings.

- Various UN forums also consider the social and economic impact of globalization on young people, with particular attention to its policy implications.

In their *Millennium Declaration*, the heads of state or government at the Millennium Summit resolved to "develop and implement strategies that give young people everywhere a real chance to find decent and productive work". In 2001, the Secretary-General's Youth Employment Network was established as a joint initiative of the UN, the ILO and the World Bank to translate the Summit commitments into action (*www.ilo.org/yen*).

Older persons
(www.un.org/esa/socdev/ageing)

The world is in the midst of an historically unique and irreversible process of demographic transition that will result in older populations everywhere. Mainly as a result of declining fertility rates, the proportion of persons aged 60 and over is expected to double between 2007 and 2050, and their actual number will more than triple — reaching 2 billion by 2050. In most countries, the population aged 80 or over is growing faster than any other group and is likely to quadruple in coming years — from 94 million in 2007, to 394 million in 2050.

Europe and North America are already well advanced in the process of population ageing. But the less developed regions, where 64 per cent of all older persons live today — a number expected to be close to 80 per cent by 2050 — may benefit from a large, younger workforce. Even in those countries where this first "dividend" dissipates as the support ratio stops growing, continued ageing of the population may produce a *second* "dividend", as people, expecting to live longer, accumulate wealth to cover consumption needs after retirement.

The world community has come to recognize the need to integrate the emerging process of global ageing into the larger context of development, and to design policies within a broader "life course" and a society-wide perspective. In the light of recent global initiatives and the guiding principles emerging from major UN conferences, older persons are increasingly seen as contributors to development, whose abilities to act for the betterment of themselves and their societies should be woven into policies and programmes at all levels.

In response to the challenge and opportunities of global ageing, the United Nations has taken several initiatives:

In addition, the General Assembly has declared 2005-2015 as the Second International Decade on the World's Indigenous People. Its main objectives are:

- Promoting non-discrimination and the inclusion of indigenous peoples in the design, implementation and evaluation of laws, policies, resources, programmes and projects;

- Promoting the full and effective participation of indigenous peoples in decisions which affect their lifestyles, traditional lands and territories, cultural integrity, collective rights, or any other aspect of their lives;

- Re-evaluating development policies that depart from a vision of equity, including respect for the cultural and linguistic diversity of indigenous peoples;

- Adopting targeted policies, programmes, projects and budgets for the development of indigenous peoples, including concrete benchmarks, with particular emphasis of indigenous women, children and youth; and

- Developing strong monitoring mechanisms and enhancing accountability at all levels in the implementation of legal, policy and operational frameworks for the protection of indigenous peoples and the improvement of their lives.

On 13 September 2007, the General Assembly adopted the ***United Nations Declaration on the Rights on Indigenous Peoples***, setting out the individual and collective rights of indigenous peoples, including their rights to culture, identity, language, employment, health and education. The *Declaration* emphasizes the rights of indigenous peoples to maintain and strengthen their own institutions, cultures and traditions and to pursue their development in keeping with their own needs and aspirations. It prohibits discrimination against them, and promotes their full and effective participation in all matters that concern them, as well as their right to remain distinct and to pursue their own visions of economic and social development.

Persons with disabilities
(www.un.org/esa/socdev/enable)

Persons with disabilities are often excluded from the mainstream of society. Discrimination takes various forms, ranging from invidious discrimination, such as the denial of educational opportunities, to more subtle forms of discrimination, such as segregation and isolation because of the imposition of physical and social barriers. Society also suffers, since the loss of the enormous potentials of persons with disabilities impoverishes humankind. Changes in the perception and concepts of disability involve both changes in values and increased understanding at all levels of society.

Since its inception, the United Nations has sought to advance the status of persons with disabilities and to improve their lives. The concern of the United Nations for the well-being and rights of such persons is rooted in its founding principles, which are based on human rights, fundamental freedoms and the equality of all human beings.

In the 1970s, the concept of the human rights of persons with disabilities gained wider international acceptance. In 1971, the General Assembly adopted the *Declaration on the Rights*

terrorism — what have been called the "uncivil" elements of society. The Office — which has 21 field offices and liaison offices in New York — is composed of a crime programme, which also addresses terrorism and its prevention, and a drug programme. (See *www.unodc.org*)

Drug control

More than 110 million people worldwide use illicit drugs at least once a month, and some 25 million persons are addicts or "problem users". Drug abuse is responsible for lost wages, soaring health-care costs, broken families and deteriorating communities. In particular, drug use by injection is fuelling the rapid spread of HIV/AIDS and hepatitis in many parts of the world.

There is a direct link between drugs and an increase in crime and violence. Drug cartels undermine governments and corrupt legitimate businesses. Revenues from illicit drugs fund some of the most deadly armed conflicts.

The financial toll is staggering. Enormous sums are spent to strengthen police forces, judicial systems and treatment and rehabilitation programmes. The social costs are equally jarring: street violence, gang warfare, fear, urban decay and shattered lives.

The United Nations is addressing the global drug problem on many levels. The **Commission on Narcotic Drugs**, a functional commission of ECOSOC, is the main intergovernmental policy-making and coordination body on international drug control. Made up of 53 member states, it analyses the world drug abuse and trafficking problem and develops proposals to strengthen international drug control. It monitors implementation of the international drug control treaties and the guiding principles and measures adopted by the General Assembly. (See *www.unodc.org*)

The **International Narcotics Control Board (INCB)** is a 13-member, independent, quasi-judicial body that monitors governments' compliance with international drug control treaties and assists them in this effort. It strives to ensure that drugs are available for medical and scientific purposes and to prevent their diversion into illegal channels. It sends investigative missions and technical visits to drug-affected countries, and conducts training programmes for drug control administrators, particularly those from developing countries. (See *www.incb.org*)

A series of treaties, adopted under United Nations auspices, require that governments exercise control over the production and distribution of narcotic and psychotropic substances, combat drug abuse and illicit trafficking, and report to international organs on their actions. These treaties are:

- The *Single Convention on Narcotic Drugs* (1961), which seeks to limit the production, distribution, possession, use and trade in drugs exclusively to medical and scientific purposes, and obliges states parties to take special measures for particular drugs such as heroin. The 1972 *Protocol* to the Convention stresses the need for treatment and rehabilitation of drug addicts.

- The *Convention on Psychotropic Substances* (1971), which establishes an international control system for psychotropic substances. It responds to the diversification and expansion of the spectrum of drugs, and introduces controls over a number of synthetic drugs.

has opened up new forms of transnational crime. Multinational criminal syndicates have expanded the range of their operations from drug and arms trafficking to money laundering. Traffickers move millions of illegal migrants each year, generating gross earnings of up to $10 billion. A country plagued by corruption is likely to attract less investment than a relatively uncorrupt country, and to lose economic growth as a result.

The **Commission on Crime Prevention and Criminal Justice**, made up of 40 member states, is a functional body of ECOSOC. It formulates international policies and coordinates activities in crime prevention and criminal justice.

Through its crime programme, UNODC carries out the mandates established by the Commission, and is the United Nations office responsible for crime prevention, criminal justice and criminal law reform. It pays special attention to combating transnational organized crime, corruption, terrorism and trafficking in human beings. Its strategy is based on international cooperation and the provision of assistance for those efforts. It fosters a culture based on integrity and respect for the law, and promotes the participation of civil society in combating crime and corruption.

UNODC supports the development of new international legal instruments on global crime, including the *United Nations Convention against Transnational Organized Crime* and its three *Protocols*, which entered into forced in September 2003; and the *United Nations Convention against Corruption*, which entered into force in December 2005. It is now promoting their ratification and helping states put their provisions into effect.

UNODC also provides technical cooperation to strengthen the capacity of governments to modernize their criminal justice systems. In 1999, in cooperation with United Nations Interregional Crime and Justice Research Institute (UNICRI), it launched the *Global Programme against Corruption*, and the *Global Programme in Trafficking in Human Beings* and *Global Studies on Organized Crime*. And UNODC's Anti-Organized Crime and Law Enforcement Unit assists states in taking effective, practical steps, in line with the UN Convention against Corruption, to fight organized crime.

The UN Office on Drugs and Crime promotes and facilitates the application of United Nations standards and norms in crime prevention and criminal justice as cornerstones of humane and effective criminal justice systems — basic requisites for fighting national and international crime. More than 100 countries have relied on these standards for elaborating national legislation and policies. The Office also analyses emerging trends in crime and justice, develops databases, issues global surveys issued, gathers and disseminates information, and undertakes country-specific needs assessments and early warning measures — for example, on the escalation of terrorism.

A *Global Programme against Terrorism* was launched in 2002, with the provision of legal technical assistance to countries on becoming party to and implementing the 12 universal anti-terrorism instruments.

In January 2003, UNODC expanded its technical cooperation activities to strengthen the legal regime against terrorism, providing legal technical assistance to countries on becoming party to and implementing the universal anti-terrorism instruments. Between 2003 and 2006,

Programme; the International Hydrological Programme; the International Basic Sciences Programme; and the International Geoscience Programme. In addition, through science education and capacity-building initiatives, UNESCO helps to increase the scientific capacity of developing countries to enable their sustainable development.

In the wake of advances in cloning living beings, UNESCO member states in 1997 adopted the *Universal Declaration on the Human Genome and Human Rights* — the first international text on the ethics of genetic research. The *Declaration* sets universal ethical standards on human genetic research and practice, balancing the freedom of scientists to pursue their work with the need to safeguard human rights and protect humanity from potential abuses. In 2003, UNESCO's General Conference adopted the *International Declaration on Human Genetic Data*, and in 2005, it adopted the *Universal Declaration on Bioethics and Human Rights*.

In the social and human sciences, UNESCO focuses on promoting philosophy and social sciences research; promoting and teaching human rights and democracy; combating all forms of discrimination; improving the status of women; and addressing forms of discrimination arising from illnesses such as HIV/AIDS.

Culture and development

UNESCO's cultural activities are concentrated on protecting and safeguarding cultural heritage in all its forms, and promoting intercultural dialogue. Under the 1972 *Convention concerning the Protection of the World Cultural and Natural Heritage,* 184 states have pledged their cooperation to protect 851 outstanding sites in 141 countries — towns, monuments and natural environments that have been placed on the World Heritage List. A 1970 UNESCO convention prohibits the illicit import, export and transfer of cultural property.

In 2003, the UNESCO General Conference unanimously adopted the *UNESCO Declaration concerning the Intentional Destruction of Cultural Heritage* — mainly in response to the tragic destruction in March 2001 of the Buddhas of Bamiyan in Afghanistan. UNESCO's 2003 *Convention for the Safeguarding of the Intangible Cultural Heritage* encompasses oral traditions, customs, languages, performing arts, social practices, rituals, festive events, traditional knowledge, traditional crafts, the protection of endangered languages and the promotion of linguistic diversity. The 2005 *Convention on the Protection and Promotion of the Diversity of Cultural Expressions,* recognizing cultural goods and services as vehicles of identity and values, seeks to strengthen their creation, production, distribution and enjoyment, particularly by sustaining related industries in developing countries.

UNESCO's activities in all these areas focus on strengthening the contribution of culture to sustainable development and promoting its crucial role for building social cohesion, intercultural dialogue and peace.

Communication and information

UNESCO is a world leader in promoting press freedom and pluralistic, independent media. It works to promote the free flow of information and to strengthen the communication

An Alliance of Civilizations

On 14 July 2005, Secretary-General Kofi Annan announced the launch of a new initiative — an Alliance of Civilizations — in response to concerns that extremists had been exploiting the sense of a widening gap between Islamic and Western societies.

The Alliance was established as a coalition against such forces — to advance mutual respect for religious beliefs and traditions, and to reaffirm humanity's increasing interdependence in all areas. It represents a committed international effort to bridge divides and overcome prejudice, misconceptions, misperceptions and polarization which threaten world peace.

A high-level group of eminent persons was established to guide the Alliance, including such renowned theologians as Archbishop Desmond Tutu of South Africa, author Karen Armstrong of the United Kingdom, Rabbi Arthur Schneier of the United States, and Prof. Mehmet Aydin of Turkey, as well as administrators of cultural institutions, such as Ismail Serageldin of Egypt's Biblioteca Alexandria. It is co-chaired by Mr. Aydin and former UNESCO Director-General, Federico Mayor.

The high-level group's first report, issued in November 2006, analysed the state of relations between Muslim and Western societies and put forward a range of proposals in the areas of education, media, youth and migration, to build bridges and promote a culture of respect. It also recommended the appointment a high representative to help defuse crises that arise at the intersection of culture and politics, take steps to restart the Middle East peace process, and encourage political pluralism in Muslim countries.

On 26 April 2007, Secretary-General Ban Ki-moon appointed former Portuguese President Jorge Sampaio as the first UN High Representative for the Alliance of Civilizations. From 15 to 16 January 2008, in Madrid, the Alliance will hold its first Annual Forum — a high-level, action-driven event, aimed at developing partnerships to promote cross-cultural understanding at the global level.

The Alliance was originally proposed by Spanish Prime Minister José Luis Rodriguez Zapatero and co-sponsored by Turkish Prime Minister Recep Tayyip Erdogan, and both countries continue to act as its co-sponsors. (For additional information, see *www.unaoc.org*).

international organizations. By making extensive use of the latest web-based collaborative technologies, it aims to minimize the need for physical meetings. It also aims significantly to expand the circle of participants in policy and partnership debates by actively engaging non-governmental participants from developing countries, media, academia, youth and women's groups.

It held its inaugural meeting on 19 June 2006 in Kuala Lumpur.

Sustainable development summits

At the United Nations Conference on Environment and Development (UNCED) (Rio de Janeiro, 1992), also known as the Earth Summit, it was agreed that environmental protection and social and economic development are fundamental to sustainable development, based on the "Rio Principles". To achieve such development, world leaders adopted a global programme entitled Agenda 21.

In Agenda 21, governments outlined a blueprint for action to move the world away from an unsustainable model of economic growth towards one based on the protection and renewal of environmental resources. It also recommended ways to strengthen the role of women, trade unions, farmers, children and young people, indigenous peoples, the scientific community, local authorities, business, industry and NGOs in achieving sustainable development.

In 1997, the General Assembly held a special session (Earth Summit + 5) on the implementation of Agenda 21. While emphasizing the urgency of putting Agenda 21 into practice, states differed on how to finance sustainable development. The session's final document recommended the adoption of legally binding targets to reduce emission of greenhouse gases leading to climate change; moving more forcefully towards sustainable patterns of energy production, distribution and use; and focusing on poverty eradication as a prerequisite for sustainable development.

The World Summit on Sustainable Development (*Johannesburg, 2002*) reviewed progress since the Earth Summit. Its Johannesburg Declaration and 54-page Plan of Implementation included commitments on specific time-bound goals relating to sanitation; chemical use and production; the maintenance and restoration of fish stocks; and reducing the loss of biodiversity. The special needs of Africa and of the small island developing states were specifically addressed, as were such new issues as sustainable production and consumption patterns, energy and mining.

---

economic and social development activities. Development cannot be achieved unless the environment is protected.

Agenda 21

Governments took an historic step towards ensuring the future of the planet when the 1992 Earth Summit adopted *Agenda 21*, a comprehensive plan for global action in all areas of sustainable development.

In *Agenda 21*, governments outlined a detailed blueprint for action that could move the world away from its present unsustainable model of economic growth towards activities that will protect and renew the environmental resources on which growth and development depend. Areas for action include: protecting the atmosphere; combating deforestation, soil loss and desertification; preventing air and water pollution; halting the depletion of fish stocks; and promoting the safe management of toxic wastes.

Agenda 21 also addresses patterns of development which cause stress to the environment, including: poverty and external debt in developing countries; unsustainable patterns of

Changing human behaviour

Achieving sustainable development worldwide entails changing patterns of production and consumption — what we produce, how it is produced and how much we consume. Finding ways to do this, particularly in the industrialized countries, was first put on the international agenda at the Earth Summit. Since then, the Commission on Sustainable Development has spearheaded a work programme aimed at challenging the behaviour of individual consumers, households, industrial concerns, businesses and governments. Its actions have included expanding the UN Guidelines for Consumer Protection to include a section promoting sustainable consumption.

In 2002, the World Summit on Sustainable Development reaffirmed the importance of such efforts. It identified changing unsustainable patterns of consumption and production as crucial. It expressed a renewed commitment to accelerate such change, with developed countries taking the lead by developing and implementing relevant policies; promoting cleaner production; increasing awareness; and enhancing corporate responsibility. Discussions on these issues involved business and industry, governments, consumer organizations, international bodies, the academic community and NGOs.

Using fewer resources and reducing waste is simply better business. It saves money and generates higher profits. It protects the environment by conserving natural resources and creating less pollution, thus sustaining the planet for the enjoyment and well-being of future generations.

Member states agreed to the *Johannesburg Declaration on Sustainable Development* and a 54-page *Plan of Implementation* detailing the priorities for action. The Summit reaffirmed sustainable development as a central element of the international agenda. paved the way for sustained measures to address the world's most pressing challenges, and emphasized the links between economic and social development and the conservation of natural resources. A unique outcome of the Summit was that the internationally agreed commitments were complemented by a range of voluntary partnership initiatives for sustainable development. (See box, *Sustainable development summits*)

Financing sustainable development

At the Earth Summit, it was agreed that most financing for *Agenda 21* would come from within each country's public and private sectors. However, new and additional external funds were deemed necessary to support developing countries' efforts to implement sustainable development practices and protect the global environment.

The **Global Environment Facility (GEF)**, established in 1991, helps developing countries fund projects that protect the global environment and promote sustainable livelihoods in local communities. Over the years, it has provided $6.8 billion in grants and generated over $24 billion in cofinancing from recipient governments, international development agencies, a growing network of centres of excellence, including the UNEP Collaborating Centre on Water and the Environment (*www.ucc-water.org*), the UNEP Risoe Centre on Energy, Climate Change and Sustainable Development (*www.uneprisoe.org*), the Global Resource Information Database (GRID) centres (*www.unep.org/dewa/partnerships/grid*) and the UNEP World Conservation Monitoring Centre (*www.unep-wcmc.org*).

UNEP acts to protect oceans and seas and promote the environmentally sound use of marine resources under its *Regional Seas Programme,* which now covers more than 140 countries. This programme works towards the protection of shared marine and water resources through 13 conventions or action plans, the most recent one dealing with the Caspian Sea under the 2003 *Tehran Convention*; it entered into force on 12 August 2006. Regional conventions and action plans for which UNEP provides the secretariat cover eastern Africa, West and Central Africa, the Mediterranean, the Caribbean, the East Asian seas and the north-west Pacific. (See *www.unep.org/regionalseas*)

Coastal and marine areas cover some 70 per cent of the earth's surface and are vital to the planet's life-support system. Most pollution comes from industrial wastes, mining, agricultural activities and emissions from motor vehicles, some of which occurs thousands of miles inland. The *Global Programme of Action for the Protection of the Marine Environment from Land-based Activities,* adopted in 1995 under UNEP auspices, is considered a milestone in international efforts to protect oceans, estuaries and coastal waters from pollution caused by human activities on land. The programme, which has a coordination office in The Hague, addresses what might be the most serious threat to the marine environment: the flow of chemicals, pollutants and sewage into the sea. (See *www.gpa.unep.org*)

UNEP's Paris-based **Division of Technology, Industry and Economics** is active in UN efforts aimed at encouraging decision-makers in government, industry and business to adopt policies, strategies and practices that are cleaner and safer, use natural resources more efficiently, and reduce pollution risks to people and the environment. The Division facilitates the transfer of safer, cleaner and environmentally sound technologies, especially those which deal with urban and freshwater management; helps countries to build capacities for the sound management of chemicals and the improvement of chemical safety worldwide; supports the phase-out of ozone- depleting substances in developing countries and countries with economies in transition; assists decision-makers to make better, more informed energy choices which fully integrate environmental and social costs; and works with governments and the private sector to integrate environmental considerations in their activities, practices, products and services. (See *www.unep.org/resources/business/DTIE*)

UNEP Chemicals — the Division's chemicals branch — provides countries with access to information about toxic chemicals; assists countries in building their capacities to produce, use and dispose of chemicals safely; and supports international and regional actions needed to reduce or eliminate chemical risks. (See *www.chem.unep.ch*)

In collaboration with FAO, UNEP facilitated the negotiation of the *Rotterdam Convention on Prior Informed Consent Procedures for Certain Hazardous Chemicals and Pesticides in*

Heeding the warnings of scientists worldwide, the nations of the world came together in Rio de Janeiro to sign the 1992 *United Nations Framework Convention on Climate Change*. To date, 191 countries have joined in this international treaty, by which developed countries agreed to reduce emissions of carbon dioxide and other greenhouse gases they release into the atmosphere to 1990 levels by 2000. Those countries, which accounted for 60 per cent of annual carbon dioxide emissions, also agreed to transfer to developing countries the technology and information needed to help them respond to the challenges of climate change. (See *www.unfccc.int*)

However, in 1995, evidence presented by IPCC scientists made it clear that the 1992 target, even if reached on time, would not be enough to prevent global warming and its associated problems. So in 1997, countries that had ratified the Convention met in Kyoto, Japan, and agreed on a legally binding *Protocol* under which developed countries are to reduce their collective emissions of six greenhouse gases by 5.2 per cent between 2008 and 2012, taking 1990 levels as the baseline. To date, 175 states have become party to the *Protocol*, which also established several innovative "mechanisms" aimed at reducing the costs of curbing emission levels.

The *Kyoto Protocol* entered into force on 16 February 2005. Of the six gases it seeks to control, carbon dioxide, methane and nitrous oxide occur naturally in the atmosphere, but human activities have increased their levels dramatically. Sulfur hexafluoride is a synthetic gas with devastating impact on the atmosphere (1 kg is equal to 22,200 kg of carbon dioxide). Hydrofluorocarbons (HFCs) and perfluorocarbons (PFCs), also synthetic, are *classes* of chemicals, and 1 kg of each is equivalent in terms of greenhouse warming to many tonnes of carbon dioxide.

When the United Nations first began to mobilize world public opinion to address the threat posed by climate change, there were many who still considered it a theory and "unproven". Differences in scientific opinion, though minimal, were vocal, and the means required to make predictive models were still being perfected. But by 2006, all that had changed, and in early 2007, the IPCC issued its strongest report ever.

Making use of major advances in climate modelling and the collection and analysis of data, and based on a review of the most up-to-date, peer-reviewed scientific literature, the Panel reported with 90 per cent certainty that significant global warming was in process and increasing — to a degree that was directly attributable to human activity. What's more, the consequences were already visible and would worsen unless major corrective action was taken.

The report, a consensus agreement of climate scientists and experts from 40 countries and endorsed by 113 governments, indicated that the world faces an average temperature rise of around 3 degrees C by the end of this century if greenhouse gas emissions continue to rise at their current pace.

The result would include more extreme temperatures, heat waves, new wind patterns, worsening drought in some regions, heavier precipitation in others, melting glaciers and Arctic ice, and rising sea levels worldwide. And while the number of tropical cyclones (typhoons and

Synthesis Report on Climate Change

On 17 November 2007, the Intergovernmental Panel on Climate Change (IPCC) issued The Synthesis Report, integrating and distilling the wealth of information contained in three reports issued during the year. Among its observations:

- "Warming of the climate system is unequivocal, as is now evident from observations of increases in global average air and ocean temperatures, widespread melting of snow and ice, and rising global average sea level … The temperature increase is widespread over the globe, and is greater at higher northern latitudes."

- "Global GHG [greenhouse gas] emissions due to human activities have grown since pre-industrial times, with an increase of 70% between 1970 and 2004 … There is high agreement and much evidence that with the current climate change mitigation policies and related sustainable development practices, global GHG emissions will continue to grow over the next few decades."

- "Continued GHG emissions at or above current rates would cause further warming and induce many changes in the global climate system during the 21st century … Anthropogenic warming could lead to some impacts that are abrupt or irreversible."

- "There is new and stronger evidence of observed impacts of climate change on unique and vulnerable systems (such as polar and high mountain communities and ecosystems), with increasing levels of adverse impacts as temperatures increase further."

- "There is now higher confidence in the projected increases in droughts, heatwaves, and floods as well as their adverse impacts."

- "There is increasing evidence of greater vulnerability of specific groups such as the poor and elderly in not only developing but also developed countries. Moreover, there is increased evidence that low-latitude and less-developed areas generally face greater risk, for example in dry areas and mega-deltas … Sea level rise under warming is inevitable."

- "A wide variety of policies and instruments are available to governments to create the incentives for mitigation action … There is high agreement and much evidence that notable achievements of the UNFCCC and its Kyoto Protocol are the establishment of a global response to climate change, stimulation of an array of national policies, and the creation of an international carbon market and new institutional mechanisms that may provide the foundation fur future mitigation efforts."

(For the full report, see www.unfccc.int)

Foundation for Democracy and Development, which works for sustainable development; and Han Seeung-soo, former President of the General Assembly and current head of the Korea Water Forum.

The special envoys have been discussing the issue with the world's major political figures, especially national leaders. They also formulated proposals ahead of the Secretary-General's

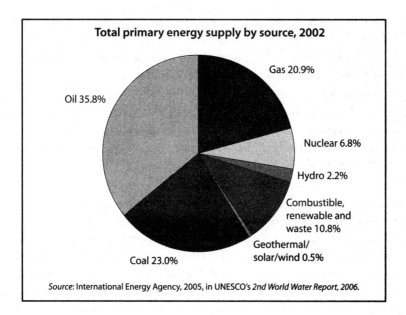

Total primary energy supply by source, 2002

Gas 20.9%

Oil 35.8%

Nuclear 6.8%

Hydro 2.2%

Combustible, renewable and waste 10.8%

Geothermal/ solar/wind 0.5%

Coal 23.0%

Source: International Energy Agency, 2005, in UNESCO's *2nd World Water Report, 2006.*

a unique challenge for the island states and the international community at large. Since the 1992 Earth Summit, these states and islands have been considered "a special case both for environment and development".

At the Global Conference on the Sustainable Development of Small Island Developing States (Barbados, 1994), a *Programme of Action* was adopted that set forth policies, actions and measures at all levels to promote sustainable development for these states. In January 2005, meeting at Mauritius to conduct a 10-year review of the *Barbados Programme*, the international community approved a wide-ranging set of specific recommendations for its further implementation.

The *Mauritius Strategy* addresses such issues as climate change and rising sea levels; natural and environmental disasters; management of wastes; coastal, marine, freshwater, land, energy, tourism and biodiversity resources; transportation and communication; science and technology; globalization and trade liberalization; sustainable production and consumption, capacity development, and education for sustainable development; health; culture; knowledge management and information for decision-making. (See *www.un.org/ohrlls*)

Sustainable forest management

With international trade in forest products totalling some $270 billion annually, more than 1.6 billion people depend on forests for their livelihoods. As the foundation for indigenous knowledge, forests provide profound socio-cultural benefits. And as ecosystems, forests play a critical role in mitigating the effects of climate change and protecting biodiversity. Yet every year, some 13 million hectares of the world's forests are lost to deforestation, which in turn accounts for up to 20 per cent of the global greenhouse gas emissions that contribute to global

The consequences of desertification and drought include food insecurity, famine and poverty. The ensuing social, economic and political tensions can create conflicts, cause more impoverishment and further increase land degradation. Growing desertification worldwide threatens to increase by millions the number of poor people forced to seek new homes and livelihoods.

The United Nations *Convention to Combat Desertification in those Countries Experiencing Serious Drought and/or Desertification, Particularly in Africa* (1994) seeks to address this problem. It focuses on rehabilitation of land, improving productivity, and the conservation and management of land and water resources. It emphasizes the establishment of an enabling environment for local people to help reverse land degradation. It also contains criteria for the preparation by affected countries of national action programmes, and gives an unprecedented role to NGOs in preparing and carrying out action programmes. The treaty, which entered into force in 1996, has 192 states parties. (See *www.unccd.int*)

Many UN bodies provide assistance to combat desertification. UNDP funds anti-desertification activities through its Nairobi-based Drylands Development Centre (*www.undp.org/drylands*). IFAD has committed more than $3.5 billion over 27 years to support dryland development. The World Bank organizes and funds programmes aimed at protecting fragile drylands and increasing their agricultural productivity. FAO provides practical help to governments for sustainable agricultural development. And UNEP supports regional action programmes, data assessment, capacity-building and public awareness of the problem.

To further mobilize public awareness of the problem, the General Assembly declared 2006 the **International Year of Deserts and Desertification**, inviting the active participation of countries, international organizations and civil society. (See *www.iydd.org*)

Biodiversity, pollution and overfishing

Biodiversity — the variety of plant and animal species — is essential for human survival. The protection and conservation of the diverse range of species of animal and plant life and their habitats is the aim of the *United Nations Convention on Biological Diversity* (1992), to which 190 states are party. The Convention obligates states to conserve biodiversity, ensure its sustainable development, and provide for the fair and equitable sharing of benefits from the use of genetic resources. Its *Cartagena Protocol on Biosafety*, which entered into force in 2003, aims to ensure the safe use of genetically modified organisms. It has 143 states parties. (See *www.cbd.int*)

Protection of endangered species is also enforced under the 1973 *Convention on International Trade in Endangered Species,* administered by UNEP. The 172 states parties meet periodically to update the list of which plant and animal species or products, such as ivory, should be protected by quotas or outright bans (*www.cites.org*). The 1979 *Bonn Convention on the Conservation of Migratory Species of Wild Animals,* and a series of associated agreements, aims to conserve terrestrial, marine and avian migratory species and their habitats. The treaty has 104 states parties. (See *www.cms.int*)

disposal of wastes, and partly to the tightening of controls through conventions. (See Global Marine Oil Pollution Information Gateway, *http://oils.gpa.unep.org*)

The pioneer *International Convention for the Prevention of Pollution of the Sea by Oil* was adopted in 1954, and IMO took over responsibility for it in 1959. In the late 1960s, a number of major tanker accidents led to further action. Since then, IMO has developed many measures to prevent accidents at sea and oil spills, to minimize their consequences, and to combat marine pollution — including that caused by the dumping into the seas of wastes generated by land-based activities.

The main treaties are: the *International Convention Relating to Intervention on the High Seas in Cases of Oil Pollution Casualties,* 1969; the *Convention on the Prevention of Marine Pollution by Dumping of Wastes and Other Matters,* 1972; and the *International Convention on Oil Pollution Preparedness, Response and Cooperation,* 1990.

IMO has also tackled the environmental threats caused by routine operations such as the cleaning of oil cargo tanks and the disposal of engine-room wastes — in tonnage terms a bigger menace than accidents. The most important of these measures is the *International Convention for the Prevention of Pollution from Ships, 1973, as modified by its 1978 Protocol* (MARPOL 73/78). It covers not only accidental and operational oil pollution, but also pollution by chemicals, packaged goods, sewage and garbage; and a new Annex adopted in 1997 covers the prevention of air pollution from ships. Amendments to the Convention adopted in 1992 oblige all new oil tankers to be fitted with double hulls, or a design that provides equivalent cargo protection in the event of a collision or grounding. The regulations phase out pre-existing single-hull tankers by 2010, with certain tankers exempted up to 2015.

Two IMO treaties — the *International Convention on Civil Liability for Oil Pollution Damage* (CLC) and the *International Convention on the Establishment of an International Fund for Oil Pollution Damage* (FUND) — establish a system for providing compensation to those who have suffered financially as a result of pollution. The treaties, adopted in 1969 and 1971 and revised in 1992, enable victims of oil pollution to obtain compensation much more simply and quickly than had been possible before.

Weather, climate and water

From weather prediction to climate-change research and early warnings on natural hazards, the **World Meteorological Organization (WMO)** coordinates global scientific efforts to provide timely and accurate information relating to weather, climate, and the hydrological and atmospheric environment. Its user community includes the general public, governments, and such industrial sectors as aviation, shipping and energy production. WMO's programmes and activities contribute to the safety of life and property, sustainable economic and social development, and the protection of the environment. (See *www.wmo.int*)

Within the United Nations system, WMO is the authoritative scientific voice on the earth's atmosphere and climate. It organizes and facilitates international cooperation in establishing of desertification; and improve agriculture and the management of water, energy and other resources. In agriculture, for instance, prompt meteorological advice can mean a substantial reduction in losses caused by droughts, pests and disease.

The *Hydrology and Water Resources Programme* helps to assess, manage and conserve global water resources. It promotes global cooperation in evaluating water resources and in developing hydrological networks and services, including data collection and processing, hydrological forecasting and warning, and the supply of meteorological and hydrological data for design purposes. The programme, for instance, facilitates cooperation with respect to water basins shared between countries, and provides specialized forecasting in flood-prone areas, thus helping to preserve life and property.

WMO's *Space Programme* was created to contribute to the development of the Global Observing System of the *World Weather Watch* programme, as well as to other WMO-supported programmes and associated observing systems. Its purpose is to provide improved data, products and services continuously, and to facilitate their wider availability and meaningful use worldwide. The *Education and Training Programme* encourages the exchange of scientific knowledge through courses, seminars and conferences, curriculum development, the introduction of new techniques and training materials, and support to training centres. It places several hundred specialists from all over the world in advanced courses each year.

The *Technical Cooperation Programme* helps developing countries obtain technical expertise and equipment to improve their national meteorological and hydrological services. It fosters the transfer of technology, as well as of meteorological and hydrological knowledge and information. The *Regional Programme* supports the implementation of programmes and activities having a regional focus, through four regional and six subregional WMO offices worldwide.

Natural resources and energy

The United Nations has long been assisting countries in managing their natural resources. As early as 1952, the General Assembly declared that developing countries have "the right to determine freely the use of their natural resources" and that they must use such resources towards realizing economic development plans in accordance with their national interests.

An ECOSOC body composed of government-nominated experts, the 24-member **Committee on Energy and Natural Resources for Development** develops guidelines on policies and strategies for ECOSOC and governments in cooperation with the **Commission on Sustainable Development**. Its Sub-group on Energy reviews trends and issues in energy development, as well as coordination of UN system activities in the field of energy. Its Sub-group on Water Resources considers issues relating to the integrated management of land and water resources.

Water resources. It is estimated that 1 billion people lack basic access to a sufficient water supply, defined as a source likely to provide 20 litres per person per day at a distance no greater than 1,000 metres. Such sources would include household connections, public standpipes, boreholes, protected dug wells, protected springs and rainwater collections.

To address this problem, the *Johannesburg Plan of Implementation*, adopted by the World Summit on Sustainable Development, set out the following goals: ensuring sanitation coverage in all rural areas by 2025; improving sanitation in public institutions, including schools; promoting safe hygiene practices; promoting affordable and socially and culturally acceptable technologies and practices; integrating sanitation into water resources management strategies; developing innovative partnerships and financing mechanisms; and strengthening existing information networks.

Although there has been significant progress in meeting the international community's goals relating to drinking water, progress with respect to sanitation has fallen short. According to the *World Water Development Report 2006*, much greater input and effort will be required to meet the Johannesburg goal "to halve, by the year 2015, the proportion of people … who do not have access to basic sanitation". To raise public awareness of the issue, encourage governments to implement effective policies, and mobilize communities to improve and change sanitation and hygiene practices through sanitation-health-education campaigns, the General Assembly has declared 2008 as the International Year of Sanitation.

Energy. Some 1.6 billion people currently lack access to electricity, and 2.4 billion people lack access to modern fuels for cooking and heating. Yet while energy, in adequate supply, is essential to economic advancement and poverty eradication, the environmental and health effects of conventional energy systems are a matter of serious concern. Moreover, the increasing demand for energy per capita, coupled with the rising global population, is resulting in consumption levels that cannot be sustained using current energy systems.

UN system activities on energy help developing countries in many ways — including through education, training and capacity-building, assistance on policy reforms, and the provision of energy services. However, while efforts are being made to move towards renewable sources of energy that are significantly less polluting, additional demand still outpaces the introduction of new capacity. Further efforts are needed to improve energy efficiency and move towards cleaner fossil fuel technologies in the transition towards sustainable development.

The United Nations system has mobilized to meet this challenge, with a particular view towards supporting achievement of the Millennium Development Goals. In 2004, the Chief Executives Board of the UN system established "UN-Energy", as the principal interagency mechanism in the field of energy. Its task is to help ensure coherence in the UN system's response to the World Summit on Sustainable Development, as well as the effective engagement of major actors from the private sector and the NGO community for implementing the Summit's energy-related decisions. (See *http://esa.un.org/un-energy* and *www.un.org/esa/progareas/sustdev.html*)

Technical cooperation. The United Nations maintains an active programme of technical cooperation in the field of water, minerals, energy and relating to small island developing states. Technical cooperation assistance and advisory services relating to water and mineral resources emphasize environmental protection, investment promotion, legislation and sustainable development. Technical cooperation relating to energy deals with access to energy, production. Examples include work related to mutation breeding, through which some 2,000 new beneficial varieties of crops have been developed using radiation-based technology — thereby improving food production. Another example is the use of isotope hydrology to map underground aquifers, manage ground and surface waters, detect and control pollution, and monitor dam leakage and safety — thus improving access to safe drinking water. Still another example concerns medical treatment, in which the Agency supplies radiotherapy equipment and trains staff to safely treat cancer patients in developing and middle-income countries.

The IAEA collects and disseminates information on virtually every aspect of nuclear science and technology through its *International Nuclear Information System* (INIS) in Vienna. With UNESCO, it operates the International Centre for Theoretical Physics in Trieste, Italy (*www.ictp.trieste.it*), and maintains several laboratories. The IAEA works with FAO in research on atomic energy in food and agriculture, and with WHO on radiation in medicine and biology. Its Marine Environment Laboratory in Monaco carries out worldwide marine pollution studies with UNEP and UNESCO (*www-naweb.iaea.org/naml*).

The **United Nations Scientific Committee on the Effects of Atomic Radiation (UNSCEAR)**, a separate body established in 1955, assesses and reports on the levels and effects of exposure to ionizing radiation. Governments and organizations worldwide rely on its estimates as the scientific basis for evaluating radiation risk, establishing radiation protection and safety standards, and regulating radiation sources.

HUMAN RIGHTS

One of the great achievements of the United Nations is the creation of a comprehensive body of human rights law — a universal and internationally protected code to which all nations can subscribe and to which all people can aspire. The Organization has defined a broad range of internationally accepted rights, including economic, social and cultural rights and political and civil rights. It has also established mechanisms to promote and protect these rights and to assist governments in carrying out their responsibilities.

The foundations of this body of law are the United Nations Charter and the Universal Declaration of Human Rights, adopted by the General Assembly in 1945 and 1948, respectively. Since then, the United Nations has gradually expanded human rights law to encompass specific standards for women, children, persons with disabilities, minorities, migrant workers and other vulnerable groups, who now possess rights that protect them from discriminatory practices that had long been common in many societies.

Rights have been extended through ground-breaking General Assembly decisions that have gradually established their universality, indivisibility and interrelatedness with development and democracy. Education campaigns have informed the world's public of their inalienable rights, while numerous national judicial and penal systems have been enhanced through UN training programmes and technical advice. The United Nations machinery to monitor compliance with human rights treaties has acquired a remarkable cohesiveness and weight among member states.

The United Nations High Commissioner for Human Rights works to strengthen and coordinate United Nations efforts for the protection and promotion of all human rights of all persons around the world. The Secretary-General has made human rights the central theme that unifies the Organization's work in the key areas of peace and security, development, humanitarian assistance, and economic and social affairs. Virtually every United Nations body and specialized agency is involved to some degree in the protection of human rights. (For the UN and human rights, see *www.un.org/rights*)

Human rights instruments

At the San Francisco Conference in 1945 at which the United Nations was established, some 40 non-governmental organizations (NGOs) representing women, trade unions, ethnic organizations and religious groups joined forces with government delegations, mostly from smaller countries, and pressed for more specific language on human rights than had been proposed by other states. Their determined lobbying resulted in the inclusion of some provisions on human rights in the United Nations Charter, laying the foundation for the post-1945 era of international lawmaking.

Thus, the Preamble to the Charter explicitly reaffirms "faith in fundamental human rights, in the dignity and worth of the human person, in the equal rights of men and women and of nations large and small". Article 1 establishes that one of the four principal tasks of the United

Defining universal rights

The Universal Declaration of Human Rights is the cornerstone of the wide-ranging body of human rights law created over the decades.

Its Articles 1 and 2 state that "all human beings are born equal in dignity and rights" and are entitled to all the rights and freedoms set forth in the Declaration "without distinction of any kind such as race, colour, sex, language, religion, political or other opinion, national or social origin, property, birth or other status".

Articles 3 to 21 set forth the civil and political rights to which all human beings are entitled, including:

- The right to life, liberty and security.
- Freedom from slavery and servitude.
- Freedom from torture or cruel, inhuman or degrading treatment or punishment.
- The right to recognition as a person before the law; the right to judicial remedy; freedom from arbitrary arrest, detention or exile; the right to a fair trial and public hearing by an independent and impartial tribunal; the right to be presumed innocent until proved guilty.
- Freedom from arbitrary interference with privacy, family, home or correspondence; freedom from attacks upon honour and reputation; the right to protection of the law against such attacks.
- Freedom of movement; the right to seek asylum; the right to a nationality.
- The right to marry and to found a family; the right to own property.
- Freedom of thought, conscience and religion; freedom of opinion and expression.
- The right to peaceful assembly and association.
- The right to take part in government and to equal access to public service.

Articles 22 to 27 set forth the economic, social and cultural rights to which all human beings are entitled, including:

- The right to social security.
- The right to work; the right to equal pay for equal work; the right to form and join trade unions.
- The right to rest and leisure.
- The right to a standard of living adequate for health and well-being.
- The right to education.
- The right to participate in the cultural life of the community.

Finally, Articles 28 to 30 recognize that everyone is entitled to a social and international order in which the human rights set forth in the Declaration may be fully realized; that these rights may only be limited for the sole purpose of securing recognition and respect of the rights and freedoms of others and of meeting the requirements of morality, public order and the general welfare in a democratic society; and that each person has duties to the community in which she or he lives.

The United Nations Democracy Fund

The Charter of the United Nations highlights the importance of democracy and democratic values. The Universal Declaration of Human Rights and many subsequent UN declarations, conventions and covenants express the United Nations vision and commitment to these values. In the International Covenant on Civil and Political Rights, in particular, states parties take on binding obligations with respect to elections, the freedoms of expression, association and assembly, and other democratic principles.

During the 1990s, changes in various parts of the world made democracy a key theme of the decade. The UN system increased its operational activities in support of the democratization process, and in 1992 the Electoral Assistance Division was established. In 2000, UNDP placed democratic governance at the heart of its development cooperation programme.

Continuing this process, Secretary-General Kofi Annan, in July 2005, established the **UN Democracy Fund (UNDEF)**. Its aim is to promote democracy throughout the world by providing assistance for projects that consolidate and strengthen democratic institutions and facilitate democratic governance — complementing existing UN efforts on elections, human rights, support to civil society, pluralistic media and the rule of law.

UNDEF does not promote any single model of democracy. Rather, it reflects the view expressed in the outcome document of the 2005 World Summit, that "democracy is a universal value based on the freely expressed will of people to determine their own political, economic, social and cultural system and their full participation in all aspects of their lives".

The Fund officially began its work on 6 March 2006, with the first meeting of its Advisory Board. (For additional information, see *www.un.org/democracyfund*)

makes provisions for various aspects of their everyday lives, including their right to work, education, public assistance and social security, and their right to travel documents. It has 144 states parties. The *Protocol relating to the Status of Refugees* (1967) ensures the universal application of the Convention, which was originally designed for refugees from the Second World War. The Protocol also has 144 states parties.

Including the two covenants already mentioned, seven core international human rights treaties are monitored for compliance by states parties (see *www.ohchr.org/english/bodies/hrc*). When states become party to these conventions, they agree to have their human rights legislation and practices reviewed by independent expert bodies:

- The *International Convention on the Elimination of All Forms of Racial Discrimination* (1966) is accepted by 173 states parties. Beginning with the premise that any policy of superiority based on racial differences is unjustifiable, scientifically false and morally and legally condemnable, it defines "racial discrimination" and commits states parties to take measures to abolish it in both law and practice. The Convention established a monitoring body, the **Committee on the Elimination of Racial Discrimination**, to consider reports from their families to know the circumstances of such disappearances and the fate of the disappeared person, as well as to claim reparations. The Convention will enter into force when it has received 20 ratifications. Opened for signature on 6 February 2007, it currently has 61 signatures and is awaiting its first ratification. A **Committee on Enforced Disappearances** will be established as its monitoring body.

- The *Convention on the Rights of Persons with Disabilities* (2006) will outlaw discrimination against the world's 650 million persons with disabilities in all areas of life, including employment, education, health services, transportation and access to justice. Opened for signature on 30 March 2007, it currently has 101 signatures and 2 states parties, of the 20 needed to enter into force. A **Committee on Rights of Persons with Disabilities** will be established as its monitoring body. An *Optional Protocol* to the Convention will give individuals recourse to that Committee when all national options have been exhausted. It currently has 55 signatures and 1 state party, of the 10 needed to enter into force.

The Universal Declaration and other United Nations instruments have also formed part of the background to several regional agreements, such as the *European Convention on Human Rights,* the *American Convention on Human Rights* and the *African Charter of Human and Peoples' Rights.*

Other standards

In addition, the United Nations has adopted many other standards and rules on the protection of human rights. These "declarations", "codes of conduct" and "principles" are not treaties to which states become party. Nevertheless, they have a profound influence, not least because they are carefully drafted by states and adopted by consensus. Among the most important of these:

- The *Declaration on the Elimination of All Forms of Intolerance and of Discrimination Based on Religion and Belief* (1981) affirms the right of everyone to freedom of thought, conscience and religion and the right not to be subject to discrimination on the grounds of religion or other beliefs.

- The *Declaration on the Right to Development* (1986) established that right as "an inalienable human right by virtue of which each person and all peoples are entitled to participate in, contribute to and enjoy economic, social, cultural and political development in which all human rights and fundamental freedoms can be fully realized". It adds that "equality of opportunity for development is a prerogative both of nations and of individuals".

- The *Declaration on the Rights of Persons Belonging to National or Ethnic, Religious and Linguistic Minorities* (1992) proclaims the right of minorities to enjoy their own culture; to profess and practise their own religion; to use their own language; and to leave any country, including their own, and to return to their country. The Declaration calls for action by states to promote and protect these rights.

- The *Declaration on Human Rights Defenders* (1998) seeks to recognize, promote and protect the work of human rights activists all over the world. It enshrines the right of

Special rapporteurs and working groups

The special rapporteurs and working groups on human rights are on the front lines in the protection of human rights. They investigate violations and intervene in individual cases and emergency situations, in what are referred to as "special procedures". Human rights experts are independent. They serve in their personal capacity for a maximum of six years and are not remunerated. The number of such experts has grown steadily over the years. There are currently 38 such special procedure mandates.

In preparing their reports to the Human Rights Council and the General Assembly, these experts use all reliable resources, including individual complaints and information from NGOs. They may also activate "urgent-action procedures", to intercede with governments at the highest level. A significant portion of their research is done in the field, where they meet both with authorities and victims, and gather on-site evidence. Their reports are made public, thus helping to publicize violations and to emphasize the responsibility of governments for the protection of human rights.

These experts examine, monitor and publicly report on human rights situations in specific countries, or on major human rights violations worldwide.

- Country-specific special rapporteurs, independent experts and representatives — currently report on Burundi, Cambodia, the Democratic People's Republic of Korea, the Democratic Republic of the Congo, Haiti, Liberia, Myanmar, the occupied Palestinian territories, Somalia and the Sudan.

- Thematic special rapporteurs, representatives and working groups — currently report on adequate housing, people of African descent, arbitrary detention, the sale of children, education, enforced or involuntary disappearances, summary executions, extreme poverty, the right to food, freedom of opinion and expression, freedom of religion or belief, physical and mental health, human rights defenders, independence of the judiciary, indigenous people, internally displaced persons, mercenaries, migrants, minority issues, racism and racial discrimination, economic reform policies and foreign debt, terrorism, torture, the illicit movement and dumping of toxic and dangerous products and wastes, trafficking in persons, transnational corporations, and violence against women.

designate experts or fact-finding groups, organize on-the-spot visits, pursue discussions with governments, provide assistance, and condemn violations it has uncovered.

If a particular situation is deemed sufficiently serious, the Council may order an investigation by either a group of independent experts (working group) or an individual (special rapporteur or representative). Based on information received from these experts, the Council then calls upon the government concerned to bring about needed changes. (See *box, Special rapporteurs and working groups*.)

World Conference on Human Rights

The Second World Conference on Human Rights (Vienna, 1993) reaffirmed the universality and central role of human rights.

The Conference revealed tensions around many issues — such as national sovereignty, universality, the role of NGOs, and the question of impartiality and non-selectivity in the application of international human rights standards. In the Vienna Declaration and Programme of Action, 171 states proclaimed that human rights had become the "legitimate concern of the international community" and that "all human rights are universal, indivisible, interdependent and interrelated".

The Declaration states that "while the significance of national and regional particularities and various historical, cultural and religious backgrounds must be borne in mind, it is the duty of states, regardless of their political, economic and cultural systems, to promote and protect all human rights and fundamental freedoms."

"Democracy, development and respect for human rights and fundamental freedoms are interdependent and mutually reinforcing", the Declaration states. It thus reaffirms both the universal right to development and the inextricable relationship between development and human rights.

The **Office of the High Commissioner for Human Rights (OHCHR)** is the focal point for United Nations human rights activities. It serves as the secretariat for the Human Rights Council, the treaty bodies (expert committees that monitor treaty compliance) and other UN human rights organs. It also undertakes human rights field activities, and provides advisory services and technical assistance. In addition to its regular budget, some of the Office's activities are financed through extrabudgetary resources. (See *www.ohchr.org*)

The High Commissioner has taken specific steps to institutionalize cooperation and coordination with other UN bodies involved in human rights, such as the United Nations Children's Fund (UNICEF), the United Nations Educational, Scientific and Cultural Organization (UNESCO), the United Nations Development Programme (UNDP), the Office of the United Nations High Commissioner for Refugees (UNHCR) and the United Nations Volunteers (UNV). Similarly, the Office works in the area of peace and security in close cooperation with the departments of the United Nations Secretariat. The Office is also part of the Inter-Agency Standing Committee (IASC), which oversees the international response to humanitarian emergencies.

Education and information. For the United Nations, education is a fundamental human right and one of the most effective instruments for the promotion of human rights. Human rights education, whether in formal or non-formal settings, seeks to advance a universal culture of human rights through innovative teaching methods, the spreading of knowledge and the modification of attitudes. During the **United Nations Decade for Human Rights Education (1995-2004),** particular efforts were made to increase global awareness and foster a universal culture of human rights. It led many countries to promote human rights education by including it in their school curriculums and adopting national action plans.

- As forum of appeal — Under the First Optional Protocol to the International Covenant on Civil and Political Rights, as well as the International Convention on the Elimination of All Forms of Racial Discrimination, the Convention Against Torture and the Optional Protocol to the Convention on the Elimination of All Forms of Discrimination against Women, individuals can bring complaints against states that have accepted the relevant appeal procedure, once all domestic remedies have been exhausted. In addition, the Human Rights Council hears numerous complaints annually, submitted by NGOs or individuals.

- As fact-finder — The Human Rights Council has mechanisms to monitor and report on the incidence of certain kinds of abuses, as well as on violations in a specific country. The special rapporteurs or representatives and working groups are entrusted with this politically sensitive, humanitarian and sometimes dangerous task. They gather facts, keep contact with local groups and government authorities, conduct on-site visits when governments permit, and make recommendations on how respect for human rights might be strengthened.

- As discreet diplomat — The Secretary-General and the UN High Commissioner for Human Rights raise human rights concerns with member states on a confidential basis, on such issues as the release of prisoners and the commutation of death sentences. The Human Rights Council may ask the Secretary-General to intervene or send an expert to examine a specific human rights situation, with a view to preventing flagrant violations. The Secretary-General may also undertake quiet diplomacy in the exercise of his "good offices", to communicate the United Nations legitimate concern and curb abuses.

The right to development

The principle of equality of opportunity for development is deeply embedded in the United Nations Charter and the Universal Declaration on Human Rights. The *Declaration on the Right to Development,* adopted by the General Assembly in 1986, marked a turning point, by proclaiming this as an inalienable human right, by which each person and all peoples are entitled to participate in, contribute to and enjoy economic, social, cultural and political development.

The right to development is given prominence in the 1993 Vienna declaration of the Second World Conference on Human Rights, and is cited in the outcomes of other major UN summits and conferences as well, including the 2000 *Millennium Declaration.* In 1998, the Commission on Human Rights established a dual mechanism to address this issue, namely: a working group to monitor progress, analyse obstacles and develop strategies for implementing the right to development; and an independent expert on the right to development, who reports on the current state of progress in implementing the right to development.

The rights of labour

The **International Labour Organization (ILO)** is the UN specialized agency entrusted with defining and protecting the rights of labour. Its tripartite **International Labour Conference** — made up of government, employer and worker representatives — has adopted 187 conventions and 198 recommendations on all aspects of work life, comprising a system of international labour. While its recommendations provide guidance on policy, legislation and practice, its conventions create binding obligations for those states which ratify them (see *www.ilo.org/ilolex*).

Conventions and recommendations have been adopted on such matters as labour administration, industrial relations, employment policy, working conditions, social security, occupational safety and health. Some seek to ensure basic human rights in the workplace, while others address such issues as the employment of women and children, and such special categories as migrant workers and the disabled. (For information on the ILO's international labour standards, by subject, see *www.ilo.org/public/english/standards/norm/subject*).

ILO's supervisory procedure to ensure that its conventions are applied both in law and in practice is based on objective evaluations by independent experts, and on the examination of cases by the ILO's tripartite bodies. There is also a special procedure for investigating complaints of infringement of the freedom of association. (See *www.ilo.org/public/english/standards/norm/applying*)

The ILO has brought about many landmark conventions:

- On forced labour (1930) — requires the suppression of forced or compulsory labour in all its forms.

- *On freedom of association and protection of the right to organize* (1948) — establishes the right of workers and employers to form and join organizations without prior authorization, and lays down guarantees for the free functioning of such organizations.

- *On the right to organize and collective bargaining* (1949) — provides for protection against anti-union discrimination, for protection of workers' and employers' organizations, and for measures to promote collective bargaining.

- *On equal remuneration* (1951) — calls for equal pay and benefits for work of equal value.

- *On discrimination* (1958) — calls for national policies to promote equality of opportunity and treatment, and to eliminate discrimination in the workplace on grounds of race, colour, sex, religion, political opinion, extraction or social origin.

- *On minimum age* (1973) — aims at the abolition of child labour, stipulating that the minimum age for employment shall not be less than the age of completion of compulsory schooling.

- *On the worst forms of child labour* (1999) — prohibits child slavery, debt bondage, prostitution and pornography, dangerous work, and forcible recruitment for armed conflict.

The General Assembly has also taken a number of measures to protect the rights of migrant workers.

- Also in 1985, when the South African government proclaimed a state of emergency and escalated repression, the Security Council, for the first time, called on governments to take significant economic measures against South Africa under Chapter VII of the Charter.

The transition from the apartheid government to a non-racial democracy was facilitated by a 1990 national peace accord between the government and major political parties, with the full support of the United Nations. Two Security Council resolutions in 1992 emphasized the involvement of the international community in facilitating that transition.

To strengthen the structures of the peace accord, the Security Council in 1992 deployed the **United Nations Observer Mission in South Africa (UNOMSA)**, which observed the 1994 elections that led to the establishment of a non-racial and democratic government. With the installation of a new government and adoption of the country's first non-racial, democratic constitution, apartheid had come to an end.

Racism

In 1963, the General Assembly adopted the *United Nations Declaration on the Elimination of All Forms of Racial Discrimination*. The Declaration affirms the fundamental equality of all persons and confirms that discrimination between human beings on the grounds of race, colour or ethnic origin is a violation of the human rights proclaimed in the Universal Declaration and an obstacle to friendly and peaceful relations among nations and peoples.

Two years later, the General Assembly adopted the *International Convention on the Elimination of All Forms of Racial Discrimination*, which obliges states parties to adopt legislative, judicial, administrative and other measures to prevent and punish racial discrimination.

In 1993, the General Assembly proclaimed the **Third Decade to Combat Racism and Racial Discrimination (1993-2003)** and called on all states to take measures to combat new forms of racism, especially through laws, administrative measures, education and information.

Also in 1993, the Commission on Human Rights appointed a special rapporteur on contemporary forms of racism, racial discrimination, xenophobia and related intolerance. The special rapporteur's continuing mandate is to examine incidents of contemporary forms of racism worldwide; racial discrimination; any form of discrimination against blacks, Arabs and Muslims; xenophobia; anti-Semitism; and related expressions of intolerance, as well as governmental measures to overcome them.

As decided by the General Assembly, the third **World Conference against Racism, Racial Discrimination, Xenophobia and Related Intolerance** was held in South Africa in 2001. It focused on practical measures to eradicate racism, including measures of prevention, education and protection, and adopted the Durban declaration and programme of action. Previous such conferences had been held in Geneva in 1978 and 1983. The Durban Review Conference to follow up on the Durban Plan of Action will be held in 2009.

The rights of children

Millions of children die every year from malnutrition and disease. Countless others become victims of war, natural disaster, HIV/AIDS and extreme forms of violence, exploitation and abuse. Millions of children, especially girls, do not have access to quality education. The **United Nations Children's Fund** (UNICEF), the only UN agency mandated to advocate for children's rights, strives to sustain global commitment to the *Convention on the Rights of the Child*, which embodies universal ethical principles and international legal standards of behaviour towards children.

The General Assembly in 2000 adopted two *Optional Protocols* to the Convention: one prohibits the recruitment of children under 18 into armed forces or their participation in hostilities; the other strengthens prohibitions and penalties concerning the sale of children, child prostitution and child pornography.

The **Committee on the Rights of the Child**, established under the Convention, meets regularly to monitor the progress made by states parties in fulfilling their obligations. The Committee makes suggestions and recommendations to governments and to the General Assembly on ways in which children's rights under the Convention may be met.

On child labour, the United Nations seeks to protect working children from exploitation and hazardous conditions that endanger their physical and mental development; to ensure children's access to quality education, nutrition and health care; and, in the long term, to achieve the progressive elimination of child labour.

- The International Programme on the Elimination of Child Labour, an initiative of the **International Labour Organization (ILO)**, seeks to raise awareness and mobilize action through the provision of technical cooperation. Direct interventions focus on the prevention of child labour; the search for alternatives, including decent employment for parents; and rehabilitation, education and vocational training for children.

- UNICEF supports programmes providing education, counselling and care to children working in very hazardous conditions — whether as sex slaves or even as domestic workers — and vigorously advocates against the violation of their rights.

- The General Assembly has urged governments to take action on the problem of street children, who are increasingly involved in and affected by crime, drug abuse, violence and prostitution.

- The Subcommission on the Promotion and Protection of Human Rights has called for steps to halt the recruitment or conscription of children into armed forces. The Secretary-General's special representative for children and armed conflict works to enhance child protection during conflicts.

- The Human Rights Council also receives reports from a special rapporteur on the sale of children, child prostitution and child pornography.

- A 2006 study by the Secretary-General painted a detailed picture of the nature, extent and causes of violence against children, recommending actions to prevent and respond to it. The study was developed under the leadership of Prof. Paulo Sérgio Pinheiro, an independent expert appointed by the Secretary-General, with the support of OHCHR, UNICEF and WHO.

and to combat degradation of their ancestral lands and territories. Subsequently, the General Assembly proclaimed 1993 as the **International Year of the World's Indigenous People**, followed by the **International Decade of the World's Indigenous People (1995-2004)**.

This increased focus on indigenous issues led, in 2000, to the establishment of the **Permanent Forum on Indigenous Issues** as a subsidiary organ of ECOSOC. This 16-expert forum, composed of an equal number of governmental and indigenous experts, advises ECOSOC; helps coordinate related UN activities; and considers indigenous concerns relating to economic and social development, culture, education, the environment, health and human rights. In addition, an Inter-Agency Support Group on Indigenous Issues promotes indigenous-related mandates throughout the intergovernmental system. (See *www.un.org/esa/socdev/unpfii*)

As the International Decade was drawing to a close, the General Assembly proclaimed a **Second International Decade of the World's Indigenous People (2005-2015)**. It has five key aims:

- To promote non-discrimination and the inclusion of indigenous peoples in the design, implementation and evaluation of laws, policies, resources, programmes and projects at all levels.

- To promote their full participation in decisions which directly or indirectly affect their lifestyles, traditional lands, cultural integrity, or any other aspect of their lives.

- To redefine development priorities in support of a vision of equity, including respect for the cultural and linguistic diversity of indigenous populations.

- To adopt targeted programmes, policies, projects and budgets for the development of indigenous peoples, including specific benchmarks, with a particular emphasis on women, children and youth.

- To promote strong monitoring mechanisms and enhance accountability at all levels with respect to the implementation of legal, policy and operational frameworks for the protection of indigenous peoples and the improvement of their lives.

On 29 June 2006, the Human Rights Council adopted the *Declaration on the Rights of Indigenous Peoples* and recommended it to the General Assembly, which adopted it on 13 September 2007.

The new *United Nations Declaration on the Rights on Indigenous Peoples* sets out the individual and collective rights of indigenous peoples, including their rights to culture, identity, language, employment, health and education. It emphasizes the rights of indigenous peoples to maintain and strengthen their own institutions, cultures and traditions, and to pursue their development in keeping with their own needs and aspirations. It also prohibits discrimination against them, and promotes their full and effective participation in all matters that concern them — including their right to remain distinct and to pursue their own visions of economic and social development.

Persons with Disabilities. The Convention was opened for signature on 30 March 2007. (For description, see section on "Other conventions", earlier in this chapter.)

United Nations activities. A growing body of data suggests the need to address disability issues in the context of national development, within the broad framework of human rights. The United Nations works with governments, NGOs, academic institutions and professional societies to promote awareness and build national capacities for broad human rights approaches to persons with disabilities. In doing so, it links disability issues with the international development agenda, including the Millennium Development Goals (MDGs).

Growing public support for disability action has focused on the need to improve information services, outreach and institutional mechanisms to promote equal opportunity. The UN has been increasingly involved in helping countries strengthen their national capacities to promote such action in their overall development plans. (See also *www.un.org/ disabilities* and *www.ohchr.org/english/issues/disability*)

Migrant workers

With increasing movement of people across international frontiers in search of work, a new human rights convention was approved to curb discrimination against migrant workers. In 1990, following 10 years of negotiations, the *International Convention on the Protection of the Rights of All Migrant Workers and Members of Their Families* was adopted by the General Assembly. The Convention:

- covers the rights of both documented and undocumented migrant workers and their families;

- makes it illegal to expel migrant workers on a collective basis or to destroy their identity documents, work permits or passports;

- entitles migrant workers to receive the same remuneration, social benefits and medical care as nationals; to join or take part in trade unions; and, upon ending their employment, to transfer earnings, savings and personal belongings;

- grants children of migrant workers the right to registration of birth and nationality, as well as access to education.

The Convention entered into force on 1 July 2003. States parties monitor its implementation through the **Committee on Migrant Workers**.

Administration of justice

The United Nations is committed to strengthening the protection of human rights in the judicial process. When individuals are under investigation by state authorities, when they are arrested, detained, charged, tried or imprisoned, there is always a need to ensure that the law is applied with due regard for the protection of human rights.

HUMANITARIAN ACTION

Since it first coordinated humanitarian relief operations in Europe following the devastation and massive displacement of people in the Second World War, the United Nations has been relied upon by the international community to respond to natural and man-made disasters that are beyond the capacity of national authorities alone. Today, the Organization is a major provider of emergency relief and longer-term assistance, a catalyst for action by governments and relief agencies, and an advocate on behalf of people struck by emergencies.

Conflicts and natural disasters continue to drive civilians from their homes. By the end of 2006, some 12.8 million people were displaced within their own countries and another 9.9 million people had become refugees by fleeing across international borders.

Natural disasters, mostly weather-related, affect more than 200 million people every year. UNDP reports that 94 per cent of natural disasters are caused by cyclones, floods, earthquakes and drought, with heat waves and forest fires also taking a toll in human suffering. An overwhelming 98.2 per cent of those killed in natural disasters* are in developing countries — indicating how poverty, population pressures and environmental degradation exacerbate human suffering.

Confronted with conflict and the escalating human and financial costs of natural disasters, the United Nations engages on two fronts. On one hand, it brings immediate relief to the victims, primarily through its operational agencies; on the other hand, it seeks more effective strategies to prevent emergencies from arising in the first place.

When disaster strikes, the UN and its agencies rush to deliver humanitarian assistance. For example, in 2006, the World Food Programme (WFP) fed nearly 88 million people in 78 countries, including most of the world's refugees and internally displaced persons (IDPs). The Office of the United Nations High Commissioner for Refugees (UNHCR) provided international protection and assistance to millions of refugees and IDPs. To fund emergency operations, the Office for the Coordination of Humanitarian Affairs (OCHA) launched inter-agency appeals that raised $3 billion for humanitarian aid.

Through such means as the humanitarian early warning system (HEWS) and the United Nations International Strategy for Disaster Reduction (ISDR), the UN works to prevent such occurrences and mitigate their effects. (For HEWS, see *www.hewsweb.org*; for ISDR, see *www.unisdr.org*)

---

* Reducing Disaster Risks: A Challenge for Development", UNDP Bureau for Crisis Prevention and Recovery, 2004.

UN family at work:
Pulling together for tsunami aid and recovery

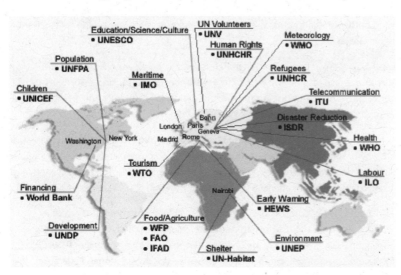

Source: UN News Service.

coordinates assistance in humanitarian crises that go beyond the capacity and mandate of any single agency. (See *www.ochaonline.un.org*)

Many actors — including governments, non-governmental organizations (NGOs) and United Nations agencies — seek to respond simultaneously to complex emergencies. OCHA works with them to ensure that there is a coherent framework within which everyone can contribute promptly and effectively to the overall effort.

When an emergency strikes, OCHA coordinates the international response. It undertakes consultations with member states and with members of the Inter-Agency Standing Committee (IASC) at Headquarters and in the field, to determine priorities for action. OCHA then provides support for the coordination of activities in the affected country.

For example, OCHA maintains an in-house emergency response capacity, supported by a 24-hour monitoring and alert system. UN disaster assessment and coordination teams can be dispatched within 12 to 24 hours of a natural disaster or sudden-onset emergency to gather information, assess needs and coordinate international assistance. OCHA ensures that military resources — when available and appropriate — are effectively used to respond to humanitarian emergencies.

OCHA also operates through a network of regional offices and of field offices, UN humanitarian coordinators and country teams. The humanitarian coordinator has overall responsibility for ensuring coherence of relief efforts in the field. By coordinating needs assessments, contingency planning and the formulation of programmes, OCHA supports the humanitarian coordinator and the operational agencies that deliver assistance.

OCHA also works with its partners in the humanitarian community to build consensus around policies and to identify specific humanitarian issues arising from operational experiences in the field. It tries to ensure that major humanitarian issues are addressed, including those that fall between the mandates of existing humanitarian bodies.

By advocating on humanitarian issues, OCHA gives voice to the silent victims of crises, and ensures that the views and concerns of the humanitarian community are reflected in overall efforts towards recovery and peacebuilding. OCHA promotes greater respect for humanitarian norms and principles, and draws attention to such specific issues as access to affected populations, the humanitarian impact of sanctions, anti-personnel landmines, and the unchecked proliferation of small arms.

To support humanitarian advocacy, policy making and emergency coordination, OCHA has developed a robust set of online tools. OCHA manages ReliefWeb — the world's foremost humanitarian website — providing the latest information on emergencies worldwide (see *www.reliefweb.int*). Its also hosts IRIN — a news service that offers accurate and impartial reporting and analysis about sub-Saharan Africa, the Middle East and Central Asia for the humanitarian community (*www.irinnews.org*).

Providing assistance and protection

Three United Nations entities — UNICEF, WFP and UNHCR — have primary roles in providing protection and assistance in humanitarian crises.

Children and women constitute the majority of refugees and displaced persons. In acute emergencies, the **United Nations Children's Fund (UNICEF)** works alongside other relief agencies to help re-establish basic services such as water and sanitation, set up schools, and provide immunization services, medicines and other supplies to uprooted populations.

UNICEF also consistently urges governments and warring parties to act more effectively to protect children. Its programmes in conflict zones have included the negotiation of ceasefires to facilitate the provision of such services as child immunization. To this end, UNICEF has pioneered the concept of "children as zones of peace" and created "days of tranquillity" and "corridors of peace" in war-affected regions. Special programmes assist traumatized children and help reunite unaccompanied children with parents or extended families. In 2006, UNICEF provided more than $513 million in humanitarian assistance relating to 53 emergencies.

The **World Food Programme (WFP)** provides fast, efficient relief to millions of people who are victims of natural or man-made disasters, including most of the world's refugees and internally displaced persons. Such crises consume the largest part of WFP's financial and human resources. A decade ago, two out of three tons of food aid provided by WFP was used to help people become self-reliant. Today, the picture is reversed, with more than 72 per cent of WFP resources going to victims of humanitarian crises. In 2006, that meant assistance to 63.4 million people — including IDPs, refugees, children orphaned by AIDS, and victims of conflict and such natural disasters as floods and drought — through 37 short-term emergency operations, 53 long-term relief and recovery operations and 35 special operations.

Protecting UN staff and humanitarian workers

United Nations personnel and other humanitarian workers in the field continue to be subject to attacks. Over the years, scores have been killed, taken hostage or detained while working in conflict areas. Violent incidents against UN staff have included armed robbery, assault and rape.

The heightened visibility of UN personnel as representatives of the international community places them at substantial risk of being targeted. This was strikingly brought home on 19 August 2003, when the bombing of UN headquarters in Baghdad left 22 dead and 150 injured. Among those killed was UN High Commissioner for Human Rights Sergio Vieira de Mello, on assignment as head of the UN mission there. It was the most deliberate and devastating single attack on UN civilian staff in the Organization's 62-year history.

In his annual report to the General Assembly on the protection of UN staff and the security of humanitarian personnel*, Secretary-General Ban Ki-moon said in September 2007 that he was deeply concerned by the "disturbing trends of unabated targeting of humanitarian workers in hostage incidents and deliberate threats" against UN personnel in conflict areas, particularly in areas of UN peacekeeping and peacebuilding operations, as well as the vulnerability of locally recruited personnel of the UN and humanitarian organizations.

Noting that "primary responsibility for the security and protection of the United Nations and associated personnel rests with the host governments", the Secretary-General stressed the importance of security collaboration between the UN and the host country on contingency planning, information exchange, risk assessment and combating impunity.

Observing that not all countries have fully investigated attacks or other threats against international and locally recruited UN and associated staff, or held perpetrators accountable under international and national law, he commended those governments and national and local authorities and officials "who continue to observe the internationally agreed principles on the protection of humanitarian and United Nations personnel".

The 1994 Convention on the Safety of United Nations and Associated Personnel obliges the governments of countries where the UN is at work to safeguard its staff, and to take preventive measures against murders and abductions.

---

* The Secretary-General's report can be viewed online by visiting the UN Official Document System (ODS) — http://documents.un.org — and searching for document A/62/324.

When war or disaster strikes, WFP responds quickly with emergency relief, then mounts programmes to facilitate smooth and effective recovery aimed at rebuilding lives and livelihoods. WFP is also responsible for mobilizing food and funds for all large-scale refugee-feeding operations managed by UNHCR. (For UNHCR's role in humanitarian crises, see section below on "International protection and assistance to refugees".)

Rural populations in the developing world are often the most vulnerable to disasters, with most of these communities dependent on agriculture for their food security and livelihoods. The

Refugees in their own country

Internally displaced persons (IDPs) are those who have been forced to flee their homes to escape war, generalized violence, human rights violations or natural and man-made disasters, but who have not crossed an international border. Civil wars have created large groups of such persons all over the world. Today, there are an estimated 12.8 million of them — more than the number of refugees.

While refugees often find safety, food and shelter in a second country and are protected by a well-defined body of international laws, the internally displaced may be trapped in an ongoing internal conflict at the mercy of warring parties, making the provision of relief hazardous or impossible. Primary responsibility for such persons lies with the national government, which is often unable — or unwilling — to help, and may even view them as "enemies of the state".

Yet like refugees, internally displaced persons need immediate protection and assistance, as well as long-term solutions, such as return or resettlement. UNHCR has increasingly been called on to aid such persons in various regions and countries — including Colombia, Cote d'Ivoire, the Democratic Republic of the Congo, Iraq, Lebanon, Sri Lanka, Timor-Leste, Uganda and elsewhere — providing assistance on the basis of humanitarian need rather than refugee status. But the task has been daunting.

Recognizing that no UN agency had the mandate and resources to protect and assist IDPs single-handedly, the Inter-Agency Standing Committee (IASC) in 2005 developed a collaborative model by which agencies pool their resources in responding to humanitarian crises. (See *www.humanitarianreform.org*)

Under this new "cluster approach", UNHCR, on 1 January 2006, accepted leadership responsibility and accountability for the clusters relating to protection; emergency shelter; and camp coordination and management.

With respect to situations resulting from natural disasters, it shares the lead: on shelter, with the International Federation of Red Cross and Red Crescent Societies (IFRC); on camps, with the International Organization for Migration (IOM); and on protection, with the Office of the United Nations High Commissioner for Human Rights (OHCHR) and the United Nations Children's Fund (UNICEF).

International protection and assistance to refugees

At the end of 2006, the Office of the **United Nations High Commissioner for Refugees (UNHCR)** was providing international protection and assistance to approximately 33 million people who had fled war or persecution — of whom 9.9 million were refugees, 12.8 million were internally displaced persons, 5.8 million were stateless persons, 2.6 million were returnees, and nearly 2 million were asylum-seekers and others of concern to the agency.

UNHCR has been one of the lead humanitarian agencies for some of the major emergencies in post-war history — in the Balkans, which produced the largest refugee flows in Europe since

- voluntary repatriation;
- resettlement in third countries for refugees who cannot return to their homes and who face protection problems in the country where they first sought asylum.

Although UNHCR's mandate is to protect and assist refugees, it has been called upon more and more to come to the aid of a wider range of people living in refugee-like situations. These include people displaced within their own countries; former refugees who may need UNHCR monitoring and assistance once they have returned home; stateless persons; and those who receive temporary protection outside their home countries but do not receive the full legal status of refugees. Today, refugees comprise the second largest group of people of concern to UNHCR.

Asylum-seekers are persons who have left their countries of origin and have applied for recognition as refugees in other countries, and whose applications are still pending. At the end of 2006, UNHCR was assisting 738,000 people in this category. South Africa was the main destination for asylum-seekers, followed by the United States, Kenya, France, the United Kingdom, Sweden and Canada. Some 34,200 Iraqi citizens claimed asylum in more than 70 countries during 2006, the number exceeded only by Somalia, with 45,600 Somali asylum claims.

Most refugees want to return home as soon as circumstances permit. At the end of 2006, UNHCR was assisting some 2.6 million returnees, and there were more than 700,000 refugee returns. The three main durable solutions for refugees are (a) voluntary repatriation to their home country in safety and dignity; (b) local integration in the country of asylum, where feasible; or (c) resettlement in a third country. Voluntary repatriation is generally considered the preferred option.

However, the sudden return of large numbers of people can quickly overwhelm fragile economic and social infrastructures. To ensure that returnees can rebuild their lives after they return home, UNHCR works with a range of organizations to facilitate reintegration. This requires emergency assistance for those in need, development programmes for the areas that have been devastated, and job-creation schemes.

The development of effective links between peace, stability, security, respect for human rights and sustainable development is increasingly seen as crucial for the achievement of durable solutions to the refugee problem.

Palestine refugees

The **United Nations Relief and Works Agency for Palestine Refugees in the Near East (UNRWA)** has been providing education, health, relief and social services to Palestine refugees since 1950. The General Assembly created UNRWA to provide emergency relief to some 750,000 Palestine refugees who had lost their homes and livelihoods as a result of the 1948 Arab-Israeli conflict. By the end of 2006, UNRWA was providing essential basic services to assist more than 4.5 million registered Palestine refugees in Jordan, Lebanon, Syria, and the occupied Palestinian territory (comprised of the West Bank and the Gaza Strip).

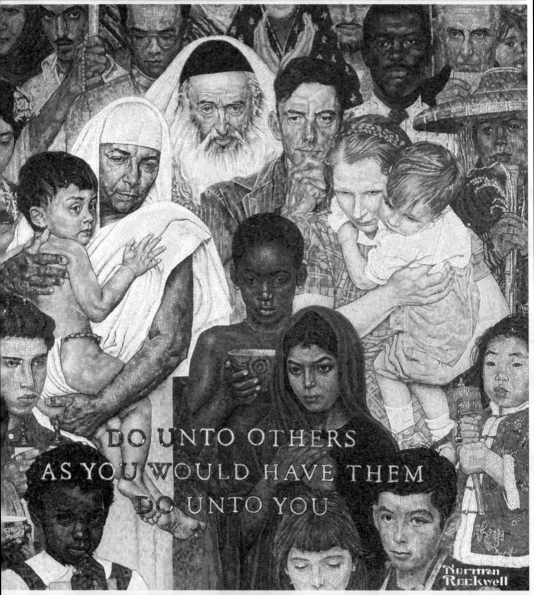

Chapter 6

DO UNTO OTHERS
AS YOU WOULD HAVE THEM
DO UNTO YOU

Norman
Rockwell

INTERNATIONAL LAW

Among the United Nations most pervasive achievements has been the development of a body of international law — conventions, treaties and standards — that play a central role in promoting economic and social development, as well as international peace and security. Many of the treaties brought about by the United Nations form the basis of the law that governs relations among nations. While the United Nations work in this area does not always receive attention, it has a daily impact on the lives of people everywhere.

The United Nations Charter specifically calls on the Organization to help in the settlement of international disputes by peaceful means, including arbitration and judicial settlement (Article 33), and to encourage the progressive development of international law and its codification (Article 13). Over the years, the United Nations has sponsored over 500 multilateral agreements, which address a broad range of common concerns among states and are legally binding for the countries that ratify them.

In many areas, the United Nations legal work has been pioneering, addressing problems as they take on an international dimension. It has been in the forefront of efforts to provide a legal framework in such areas as protecting the environment, regulating migrant labour, curbing drug trafficking and combating terrorism. This work continues today, as international law assumes a more central role across a wider spectrum of issues, including human rights law and international humanitarian law. (For the UN and international law, see *www.un.org/law*. For the UN Office of Legal Affairs, see *http://untreaty.un.org/ola*)

Judicial settlement of disputes

The primary United Nations organ for the settlement of disputes is the **International Court of Justice**. Popularly known as the World Court, it was founded in 1946. As of October 2007, it had delivered 93 judgments on disputes brought to it by states and issued 25 advisory opinions in response to requests by duly authorized United Nations organizations. Most cases have been dealt with by the full Court, but since 1981 six cases have been referred to special chambers at the request of the parties (see the Court's site at *www.icj-cij.org*).

In its judgments, the Court has addressed international disputes involving economic rights, rights of passage, the non-use of force, non-interference in the internal affairs of states, diplomatic relations, hostage-taking, the right of asylum and nationality. States bring such disputes before the Court in search of an impartial solution to their differences, on the basis of law. By achieving peaceful settlement on such questions as land frontiers, maritime boundaries and territorial sovereignty, the Court has often helped to prevent the escalation of disputes.

In a typical case of territorial rights, the Court in 2002 settled a sovereignty dispute between Cameroon and Nigeria over the oil-rich Bakassi peninsula, and then over the whole land and sea boundary between the two states. Earlier that year, it resolved a sovereignty dispute between Indonesia and Malaysia over two islands in the Celebes Sea, granting them

this, "the Respondent did nothing to prevent the Srebrenica massacres, claiming that they were powerless to do so, which hardly tallies with their known influence over the VRS". It was therefore in breach of its obligation under the Convention to take whatever action it could to prevent the genocide.

The Court in 1996 rejected objections by the United States to its jurisdiction in a 1992 case concerning the destruction of Iranian oil platforms by United States warships. In November 2003, the Court held that the United States actions could not be justified as necessary to protect its national security interests. However, as those actions did not constitute a breach of its obligations regarding freedom of commerce, Iran's claim for reparation could not be upheld. It also refused to uphold a United States counterclaim.

States often submit questions relating to economic rights. In 1995, in the midst of a dispute over fisheries jurisdiction between Canada and the European Union, Spain instituted a case against Canada after that country seized a Spanish fishing trawler on the high seas. A case involving environmental protection was brought by Hungary and Slovakia concerning the validity of a 1997 treaty they had concluded on the building of a barrage system on the Danube River. In 1997, the Court found both states in breach of their legal obligations, and called on them to carry out that treaty.

On 8 October 2007, the Court rendered its judgment in a case instituted in 1999 by Nicaragua against Honduras with regard to legal issues between the two states concerning maritime delimitations in the Caribbean Sea. The Court found that Honduras had sovereignty over certain disputed islands (Bobel Cay, Savanna Cay, Port Royal Cay and South Cay) and decided on the starting point and delimitation line of a single maritime boundary. The Court instructed the parties to negotiate in good faith with a view to agreeing on the course of a line between the present endpoint of the land boundary between Honduras and Nicaragua and the starting point of the maritime boundary between them as now determined by the Court.

The number of judicial cases submitted to the Court has increased significantly since the 1970s, when it had only one or two cases on its docket at any one time. During the past decade, that number has even exceeded 20 cases. At the end of 2006, there were 14 pending cases on the Court's docket, including two under active consideration.

The Court's advisory opinions have dealt with, among other things, admission to United Nations membership, reparation for injuries suffered in the service of the United Nations, the territorial status of Western Sahara, the expenses of certain peacekeeping operations and, more recently, the status of UN human rights rapporteurs. Two opinions, rendered in 1996 at the request of the General Assembly and the World Health Organization, concerned the legality of the threat or use of nuclear weapons.

In a 1971 advisory opinion requested by the Security Council, the Court stated that the continued presence of South Africa in Namibia was illegal and that South Africa was under obligation to withdraw its administration and end its occupation — clearing the way for the independence of Namibia in March 1990.

creating legal obligations. It adopted, on first reading, a set of draft articles on the law of transboundary aquifers. And it concluded its consideration of the topic, "Fragmentation of international law: difficulties arising from the diversification and expansion of international law" — taking note of the report and conclusions of its study group on this item.

Other topics currently being considered by the Commission include: reservations to treaties; effects of armed conflicts on treaties; responsibility of international organizations; expulsion of aliens; obligation to extradite or prosecute (*aut dedere aut judicare*); and shared natural resources.

International trade law

The **United Nations Commission on International Trade Law (UNCITRAL)** facilitates world trade by developing conventions, model laws, rules and legal guides designed to harmonize international trade law. Established by the General Assembly in 1966, this 60-nation body brings together representatives of the world's geographic regions and principal economic and legal systems. Over the years, UNCITRAL has become the core legal body of the UN system in the field of international trade law. The international trade law division of the United Nations Office of Legal Affairs serves as its secretariat. (See *www.uncitral.org*)

Over its 41-year history, the Commission has developed widely accepted texts that are viewed as landmarks in various fields of law. These include the UNCITRAL Arbitration Rules (1976); the *UNCITRAL Conciliation Rules* (1980); the *United Nations Convention on Contracts for the International Sale of Goods* (1980); the *UNCITRAL Model Law on International Commercial Arbitration* (1985); the *UNCITRAL Model Law on Procurement of Goods, Construction and Services* (1994); the *UNCITRAL Notes on Organizing Arbitral Proceedings* (1996); the *Model Law on Electronic Commerce* (1996); and the *UNCITRAL Model Law on Cross-Border Insolvency* (1997).

Other notable texts include: the *Convention on the Limitation Period in the International Sale of Goods* (1974); the *United Nations Convention on the Carriage of Goods by Sea (Hamburg Rules)* (1978); the *United Nations Convention on International Bills of Exchange and International Promissory Notes* (1988); the *UNCITRAL Legal Guide on Drawing Up International Contracts for the Construction of Industrial Works* (1988); the *United Nations Convention on the Liability of Operators of Transport Terminals in International Trade* (1991); the *UNCITRAL Legal Guide on International Countertrade Transactions* (1992); the *United Nations Convention on Independent Guarantees and Standby Letters of Credit* (1995); the *UNCITRAL Legislative Guide on Privately Financed Infrastructure Projects* (2000); the *United Nations Convention on the Assignment of Receivables in International Trade* (2001); the *UNCITRAL Model Law on Electronic Signatures* (2001); the *UNCITRAL Model Law on International Commercial Conciliation* (2002); and the *UNCITRAL Model Legislative Provisions on Privately Financed Infrastructure Projects* (2003).

More recently adopted texts include the *UNCITRAL Legislative Guide on Insolvency Law* (2004); the *United Nations Convention on the Use of Electronic Communications in International Contracts* (2005); the revised *UNCITRAL Model Law on International*

- The *Basel Convention on the Control of Transboundary Movement of Hazardous Wastes and their Disposal* (1989) and its amendment obligates states parties to reduce shipping and dumping of dangerous wastes across borders; to minimize the amount and toxicity generated by hazardous waste; and to ensure their environmentally sound management as close as possible to the source of generation. In 1999, states parties adopted a protocol on liability and compensation resulting from cross-border movement of hazardous wastes.

- The *Multilateral Fund for the Implementation of the Montreal Protocol* (1991) was established to assist developing country parties to the *Montreal Protocol* whose annual per capita consumption and production of ozone-depleting substances (ODS) is less than 0.3kg — referred to as Article 5 countries — to comply with its control measures. Contributions to the Multilateral Fund from non-Article 5 countries are determined according to the United Nations scale of assessments.

- The *Agreement on the Conservation of Small Cetaceans of the Baltic and North Seas* (1991), concluded under the auspices of the *Convention on Migratory Species,* aims to promote close cooperation among parties with a view to achieving and maintaining a favourable conservation status for small cetaceans. States parties are obligated to engage in habitat conservation and management, surveys and research, pollution mitigation and public information.

- The *Convention on Biological Diversity* (1992) seeks to conserve biological diversity, promote the sustainable use of its components, and encourage equitable sharing of the benefits arising from the use of genetic resources. Its *Cartagena Protocol on Biosafety* (2000) seeks to protect biological diversity from potential risks that might be posed by living modified organisms (LMOs) resulting from modern biotechnology. It establishes an advance inform agreement procedure for ensuring that countries are provided with prior written notification and information necessary to make informed decisions before agreeing to the first import of LMOs that are to be intentionally introduced into the environment.

- The *Framework Convention on Climate Change* (1992) obligates states parties to reduce emissions of greenhouse gases that cause global warming and related atmospheric problems. The Convention's *Kyoto Protocol* (1997) strengthens the international response to climate change by calling on industrialized countries to meet legally binding emission targets during the period 2008-2012. The protocol also establishes several mechanisms that allow some flexibility in how the industrialized countries make and measure their emissions reductions.

- The *International Convention to Combat Desertification in Those Countries Experiencing Serious Drought and/or Desertification, Particularly in Africa* (1994) seeks to promote international cooperation for action to combat desertification and to mitigate the effects of drought.

It is now universally accepted that all activities in the oceans and the seas must be carried out in conformity with the provisions of the Convention, whose authority is based on its near-universal acceptance. As of September 2007, the Convention had 155 states parties, including the European Community; and other states are in the process of becoming party to it. Nearly all states recognize and adhere to its provisions.

Impact of the Convention

Through national and international legislation and related decision-making, states have consistently upheld the Convention as the pre-eminent international legal instrument in the field. Its implicit authority has resulted in the near-universal acceptance of some of its key provisions, including: 12 nautical miles as the limit of the territorial sea; coastal states' sovereign rights and jurisdiction in an "exclusive economic zone" up to the limit of 200 nautical miles; and their sovereign rights over the continental shelf extending up to a distance of 200 nautical miles or, under certain circumstances, beyond that limit. It has also brought stability in the area of navigation — establishing the rights of innocent passage through the territorial sea, transit passage through narrow straits used for international navigation, sea lanes passage through archipelagic waters, and freedom of navigation in the exclusive economic zone.

The near-universal acceptance of the Convention was facilitated in 1994 by the General Assembly's adoption of the *Agreement Relating to the Implementation of Part XI of the Convention*, which removed certain obstacles relating to the seabed area that had prevented mainly industrialized countries from signing the Convention. The Part XI Agreement is now widely accepted, having 130 states parties, as of September 2007.

The Convention has also been acknowledged for its provisions on the rights of coastal States, in the exercise of their jurisdicadtion, to regulate, authorize and conduct marine scientific research, as well as their duties relating to the prevention, reduction and control of pollution of the marine environment, and on the rights of landlocked states to participate in the exploitation of the living marine resources of the exclusive economic zones of coastal states. Moreover, the Convention is recognized as the framework and foundation for any future instruments that seek to further clarify the rights and obligations of states in the oceans.

In this respect, the 1995 *Agreement on Straddling Fish Stocks and Highly Migratory Fish Stocks* implements provisions in the Convention relating to these fish stocks, setting out the legal regime for their conservation and management. It requires states to cooperate in adopting measures to ensure their long-term sustainability and to promote their optimum utilization. It provides for the application of a precautionary and ecosystem approach to fisheries management, and for the adoption of conservation and management measures based on the best scientific evidence available. States are also required to cooperate to achieve compatability of measures with respect to these stocks for areas under national jurisdiction and the adjacent high seas. As of September 2007, the Agreement had 67 parties.

Ireland v. United Kingdom, dealt with the prevention of land-based pollution from a plant designed to reprocess spent nuclear fuel into a new fuel known as "mixed oxide fuel". Of these 15 cases, the only one still on the court's docket is *Chile v. the European Union*, which concerns swordfish stocks in the south-eastern Pacific Ocean.

The purpose of the **Commission on the Limits of the Continental Shelf** is to facilitate implementation of the Convention with respect to delineation of the outer limits of the continental shelf when that submerged portion of the land territory of a coastal state extends *beyond* the 200 nautical miles from its coastline — established as the minimal legal distance under the Convention. Under its article 76, the coastal state may establish the outer limits of its *juridical* continental shelf in such cases through the application of specified scientific and technical formulas.

The Commission held its first session at United Nations Headquarters in 1997. Its 21 members, elected by the states parties to the Convention, serve in their personal capacity. They are experts in the fields of geology, geophysics, hydrography and geodesy. The Commission received its first submission by a state party, the Russian Federation, in December 2001. Since then (as of September 2007), submissions have been made by Brazil, Australia, Ireland, New Zealand, Norway, France, and jointly by France, Ireland, Spain and the United Kingdom. (See *www.un.org/Depts/los/clcs_new/clcs_home.htm*)

Meetings of states parties and General Assembly processes

Although the Convention does not provide for a periodic conference of states parties, the annual meeting of states parties, which is convened by the Secretary-General, has served as a forum where issues of concern have been discussed. This is in addition to its assigned administrative functions, such as election of members of the Tribunal and the Commission, as well as other budgetary and administrative actions. Similarly, the Secretary-General has convened annual informal consultations of the states parties to the UN Fish Stocks Agreement since its entry into force in 2001, to monitor its implementation, as well as a Review Conference in May 2006 to assess the effectiveness of the Agreement.

The General Assembly performs an oversight function with respect to ocean affairs and the law of the sea. In 2000, it established an open-ended, informal, consultative process to facilitate its own annual review of developments in the field. That process, convened annually, makes suggestions to the Assembly on particular issues, with an emphasis on identifying areas where coordination and cooperation among governments and agencies should be enhanced. Such topics have included safety of navigation and the protection of vulnerable marine ecosystems. The consultative process, originally instituted for three years, has twice been extended for additional three-year periods because of the positive results it has achieved.

In 2004, the Assembly also established an open-ended, informal, ad hoc working group to study issues relating to the conservation and sustainable use of marine biological diversity *beyond* areas of national jurisdiction. That working group met in 2006, and will meet again in 2008.

crimes against humanity. The Tribunal is located at The Hague, in the Netherlands. (See www.un.org/icty).

- The International Criminal Tribunal for Rwanda, established in 1994, is composed of four chambers (three trial chambers and an appeals chamber), a prosecutor and the registry. In 1998, the Tribunal handed down the first-ever conviction of genocide by an international court. The Tribunal is located in Arusha, Tanzania; the Office of the Prosecutor is in Kigali, Rwanda. (See www.ictr.org)

The **Special Court for Sierra Leone**, an independent judicial body, was established in January 2002 pursuant to an agreement between the government of Sierra Leone and the United Nations to prosecute persons who bear the greatest responsibility for the commission of crimes against humanity, war crimes and other serious violations of international humanitarian law, as well as crimes committed under relevant Sierra Leonean law within the territory of Sierra Leone since 30 November 1996. The Court is located in Freetown, Sierra Leone. The Secretary-General of the United Nations appoints the prosecutor and the registrar. The Secretary-General and the government of Sierra Leone each get to appoint judges of both the trial and appeals chambers of the Court. (See *www.sc-sl.org*)

The **Extraordinary Chambers in the Courts of Cambodia** is attached to the country's current judiciary system. It was established to prosecute former Khmer Rouge leaders for their alleged role in genocide and crimes against humanity, including the deaths of some 1.7 million people, between 17 April 1975 and 6 January 1979. With 17 national and 12 international judges and prosecutors, the Extraordinary Chambers is also mandated to try those responsible for grave breaches of the 1949 Geneva Conventions and other crimes defined by the Cambodian law instituting the Chambers, including murder, torture, religious persecutions, destruction of cultural property in armed conflict, and violations of the Vienna Convention on the protection of diplomats. It issued its first charges on 31 July 2007. (See *www.eccc.gov.kh*)

International terrorism

The United Nations has consistently addressed the problem of terrorism, at both the legal and political level.

In the legal sphere, the UN and its related bodies — such as the International Civil Aviation Organization (ICAO), the International Maritime Organization (IMO) and the International Atomic Energy Agency (IAEA) — have developed a network of international agreements that constitute the basic legal instruments against terrorism. These are the:

- Convention on Offences and Certain Other Acts Committed on Board Aircraft (Tokyo, 1963).
- Convention for the Suppression of Unlawful Seizure of Aircraft (The Hague, 1970).

The International Criminal Court
(www.icc-cpi.int)

The idea of a permanent international court to prosecute crimes against humanity was first considered at the United Nations in the context of the adoption of the Genocide Convention of 1948. For many years, differences of opinions forestalled further developments. In 1992, the General Assembly directed the International Law Commission to prepare a draft statute for such a court. The massacres in Cambodia, the former Yugoslavia and Rwanda made the need for it even more urgent.

Established by the Rome Statute of the International Criminal Court (*www.un.org/law/icc*), and adopted at a plenipotentiary conference in Rome on 17 July 1998, the International Criminal Court has jurisdiction to prosecute individuals who commit genocide, war crimes and crimes against humanity. It will also have jurisdiction over the crime of aggression when agreement is reached on the definition of such a crime. The Statute entered into force on 1 July 2002. As of 1 January 2007, it had 104 states parties.

The Court has 18 judges, elected by the states parties for a term limited to nine years, except that a judge shall remain in office to complete any trial or appeal which has already begun. No two judges can be from the same country. The President of the Court is Judge Philippe Kirsch (Canada); its Prosecutor is Luis Moreno Ocampo (Argentina); and its Registrar is Bruno Cathala (France).

The International Criminal Court is located at The Hague, in the Netherlands. Its budgetary expenditure in 2006 was Euros 64.7 million. As of August 2007, it had four cases on its docket, including the prosecution of alleged war crimes and crimes against humanity in the Darfur region of the Sudan.

whomever committed. It also urged states to take measures at the national and international levels to eliminate international terrorism.

An ad hoc committee established by the Assembly in 1996 is currently negotiating a comprehensive convention against international terrorism, to fill in gaps left by existing treaties.

On 28 September 2001, following the 11 September terrorist attack on the United States, the Security Council established its **Counter-Terrorism Committee**. Among its functions, the Committee monitors implementation of the Council's resolution 1373 (2001), which imposed certain obligations on member states. These include: criminalization of terrorism-related activities, including the provision of assistance to carry them out; denial of funding and safe haven to terrorists; and the exchange of information on terrorist groups. (See *www.un.org/sc/ctc*)

On 19 September 2006, the **United Nations Global Counter-Terrorism Strategy** was launched, following its unanimous adoption on 8 September by the General Assembly. Based on the fundamental conviction that terrorism in all its forms is unacceptable and can never be justified, the Strategy outlines a range of specific measures to address terrorism in all its aspects, at the national, regional and international levels. (See *www.un.org/terrorism*)

DECOLONIZATION

Nearly 100 nations whose peoples were formerly under colonial rule or a trusteeship arrangement have joined the United Nations as sovereign independent states since the world Organization was founded in 1945. Additionally, many other Territories have achieved self-determination through political association or integration with an independent state. The United Nations has played a crucial role in that historic change by encouraging the aspirations of dependent peoples and by setting goals and standards to accelerate their attainment of independence. United Nations missions have supervised elections leading to independence — in Togoland (1956 and 1968), Western Samoa (1961), Namibia (1989) and, most recently, in Timor-Leste (formerly East Timor).

The decolonization efforts of the United Nations derive from the Charter principle of "equal rights and self-determination of peoples", as well as from three specific chapters in the Charter (XI, XII and XIII) which are devoted to the interests of dependent peoples. Since 1960, the United Nations has also been guided by the General Assembly's *Declaration on the Granting of Independence to Colonial Countries and Peoples,* also known as the Declaration on decolonization, by which member states proclaimed the necessity of bringing colonialism to a speedy end. The United Nations has also been guided by General Assembly resolution 1541 (XV) of 15 December 1960, which defined the three options offering full self-government for Non-Self-Governing Territories.

Despite the great progress made against colonialism, more than 1 million people still live under colonial rule, and the United Nations continues its efforts to help achieve self-determination in the remaining Non-Self-Governing Territories. (See *www.un.org/Depts/dpi/decolonization*)

International trusteeship system

Under Chapter XII of the Charter, the United Nations established the international trusteeship system for the supervision of Trust Territories placed under it by individual agreements with the states administering them.

The system applied to: (a) Territories held under mandates established by the League of Nations after the First World War; (b) Territories detached from "enemy states" as a result of the Second World War; and (c) Territories voluntarily placed under the system by states responsible for their administration. The goal of the system was to promote the political, economic and social advancement of the Territories and their development towards self-government and self-determination.

The **Trusteeship Council** was established under Chapter XIII of the Charter to supervise the administration of Trust Territories and to ensure that governments responsible for their administration took adequate steps to prepare them for the achievement of the Charter goals.

In the early years of the United Nations, 11 Territories were placed under the trusteeship system *(see tables in Part Three)*. Over the years, all 11 Territories either became independent states or voluntarily associated themselves with a state.

The last one to do so was the Trust Territory of the Pacific Islands (Palau), administered by the United States. The Security Council in 1994 terminated the United Nations Trusteeship Agreement for that Territory, after it chose free association with the United States in a 1993 plebiscite. Palau became independent in 1994, joining the United Nations as its 185th member state. With no Territories left on its agenda, the trusteeship system had completed its historic task.

Non-Self-Governing Territories

The United Nations Charter also addresses the issue of other Non-Self-Governing Territories not brought into the trusteeship system.

Chapter XI of the Charter — the Declaration regarding Non-Self-Governing Territories — provides that member states administering Territories which have not attained self-government recognize "that the interests of the inhabitants of these Territories is paramount" and accept as a "sacred trust" the obligation to promote their well-being.

To this end, administering powers, in addition to ensuring the political, economic, social and educational advancement of the peoples, undertake to assist them in developing self-government and democratic political institutions. Administering powers have an obligation to transmit regularly to the Secretary-General information on the economic, social and educational conditions in the Territories under their administration.

In 1946, eight member states — Australia, Belgium, Denmark, France, the Netherlands, New Zealand, the United Kingdom and the United States — enumerated the Territories under their administration that they considered to be non-self-governing. In all, 72 Territories were enumerated, of which eight became independent before 1959. In 1963, the Assembly approved a revised list of 64 Territories to which the 1960 Declaration on decolonization applied. Today, only 16 such Territories remain, with France, New Zealand, the United Kingdom and the United States as administering powers *(see table on facing page)*.

In August 2005, Tokelau's national representative body, the General Fono, approved a draft treaty of free association between Tokelau and New Zealand, and by November it had approved a draft constitution. In February 2006, a referendum was held on self-government, in which 60 per cent of registered Tokelauans voted in favour of free association, falling just short of the required two-thirds majority. A second referendum, held in Tokelau from 20 to 24 October 2007, also failed to produce the required two-thirds majority for Tokelau to enter into self-governance in free association with New Zealand. Of 692 votes cast, 446 were in favour of self-governance — 16 votes short of the required majority.

States has maintained that it remains conscious of its role as an administering power and will continue to meet its responsibilities under the Charter. The United Kingdom has stated that while most of the Territories under its administration chose independence, a small number have preferred to remain associated with it.

At the end of the **International Decade for the Eradication of Colonialism (1991-2000)**, the General Assembly declared the **Second International Decade for the Eradication of Colonialism (2001-2010)**, calling on member states to redouble their effort to achieve complete decolonization.

In the case of certain Territories, such as Western Sahara, the Assembly has entrusted the Secretary-General with specific tasks to facilitate the process of decolonization, in accordance with the UN Charter and the objectives of the Declaration.

Namibia

The United Nations helped bring about the independence of Namibia in 1990 — a case history that reveals the complexity of the efforts required to ensure a peaceful transition.

Formerly known as South West Africa, Namibia was an African Territory once held under the League of Nations mandate system. The General Assembly in 1946 asked South Africa to administer the Territory under the trusteeship system. South Africa refused, and in 1949 informed the United Nations that it would no longer transmit information on the Territory, maintaining that the mandate had ended with the demise of the League.

The General Assembly in 1966, stating that South Africa had not fulfilled its obligations, terminated that mandate and placed the Territory under the responsibility of the United Nations Council for South West Africa, which was renamed the Council for Namibia in 1968.

In 1976, the Security Council demanded that South Africa accept elections for the Territory under United Nations supervision. The General Assembly stated that independence talks must involve the South West Africa People's Organization (SWAPO) — the sole representative of the Namibian people.

In 1978, Canada, France, the Federal Republic of Germany, the United Kingdom and the United States submitted to the Security Council a settlement proposal providing for elections for a constituent assembly under United Nations auspices. The Council endorsed the Secretary-General's recommendations for implementing the proposal, asked him to appoint a special representative for Namibia, and established the **United Nations Transition Assistance Group (UNTAG).**

Years of negotiations by the Secretary-General and his special representative, as well as United States mediation, led to the 1988 agreements for the achievement of peace in southern Africa, by which South Africa agreed to cooperate with the Secretary-General to ensure Namibia's independence through elections.

when 78.5 per cent of 450,000 registered voters rejected autonomy within Indonesia, militias opposing independence unleashed a campaign of systematic destruction and violence, killing many and forcing more than 200,000 East Timorese to flee their homes.

After intensive talks, Indonesia accepted the deployment of a UN-authorized multinational force. And in September 1999, acting under Chapter VII of the Charter, the Security Council authorized the dispatch of the **International Force in East Timor (INTERFET)**, which helped restore peace and security.

Immediately following that action, the Council, in October 1999, established the **United Nations Transitional Administration in East Timor (UNTAET)**, giving it full executive and legislative authority during the country's transition to independence. On 30 August 2001, more than 91 per cent of East Timor's eligible voters went to the polls to elect an 88-member constituent assembly, tasked with writing and adopting a new constitution and establishing the framework for future elections and the transition to full independence.

On 22 March 2002, the constituent assembly signed into force the Territory's first Constitution; on 14 April, after winning 82.7 per cent of the vote, Xanana Gusmão was appointed president-elect; and on 20 May 2002, the Territory attained independence. The constituent assembly was transformed into the national parliament, and the new country adopted the name Timor-Leste. On 27 September, it became the 191st member state of the United Nations.

Following the successful decolonization of East Timor, the UN has remained fully committed in supporting the independent country of Timor-Leste in its efforts to consolidate democratic institutions and advance socio-economic development. (For information on subsequent UN action in Timor-Leste, see the section on "UN Action for Peace" in Chapter 2.)

Western Sahara

The United Nations has been dealing since 1963 with an ongoing dispute concerning Western Sahara — a Territory on the north-west coast of Africa bordering Morocco, Mauritania and Algeria.

Western Sahara became a Spanish colony in 1884. In 1963, both Morocco and Mauritania laid claim to it. The International Court of Justice, in a 1975 opinion requested by the General Assembly, rejected the claims of territorial sovereignty by Morocco or Mauritania.

The United Nations has been seeking a settlement in Western Sahara since the withdrawal of Spain in 1976 and the ensuing fighting between Morocco — which had "reintegrated" the Territory — and the Popular Front for the Liberation of Saguia el-Hamra and Río de Oro (Frente POLISARIO), which was supported by Algeria *(see footnote to table in this chapter)*.

In 1979, the Organization of African Unity (OAU) called for a referendum to enable the people of the Territory to exercise their right to self-determination. By 1982, 26 OAU

UNITED NATIONS MEMBER STATES
(as of December 2006)

Member state	Date of admission	Scale of assessments for 2006 (per cent)	Population (est.)
Afghanistan	19 November 1946	0.001	22,576,000
Albania	14 December 1955	0.006	3,142,000
Algeria	8 October 1962	0.085	32,906,000
Andorra	28 July 1993	0.008	75,000
Angola	1 December 1976	0.003	12,768,000
Antigua and Barbuda	11 November 1981	0.002	83,000
Argentina	24 October 1945	0.325	38,971,000
Armenia	2 March 1992	0.002	3,220,000
Australia	1 November 1945	1.787	20,701,000
Austria	4 December 1955	0.887	8,233,000
Azerbaijan	2 March 1992	0.005	8,485,000
Bahamas	18 September 1973	0.016	307,000
Bahrain	21 September 1971	0.033	743,000
Bangladesh	17 September 1974	0.010	141,800,000
Barbados	9 December 1966	0.009	273,000
Belarus [a]	24 October 1945	0.020	9,825,000
Belgium	27 December 1945	1.102	10,479,000
Belize	25 September 1981	0.001	301,000
Benin	20 September 1960	0.001	6,770,000
Bhutan	21 September 1971	0.001	635,000
Bolivia	14 November 1945	0.006	9,627,000
Bosnia and Herzegovina	22 May 1992	0.006	3,843,000
Botswana	17 October 1966	0.014	1,740,000
Brazil	24 October 1945	0.876	186,771,000
Brunei Darussalam	21 September 1984	0.026	383,000
Bulgaria	14 December 1955	0.020	7,740,000
Burkina Faso	20 September 1960	0.002	12,802,000
Burundi	18 September 1962	0.001	6,412,000
Cambodia	14 December 1955	0.001	13,661,000
Cameroon	20 September 1960	0.009	15,429,000

Member state	Date of admission	Scale of assessments for 2006 (per cent)	Population (est.)
France	24 October 1945	6.301	60,873,000
Gabon	20 September 1960	0.008	1,269,000
Gambia	21 September 1965	0.001	1,509,000
Georgia	31 July 1992	0.003	4,400,000
Germany	18 September 1973	8.577	82,464,000
Ghana	8 March 1957	0.004	20,028,000
Greece	25 October 1945	0.596	11,104,000
Grenada	17 September 1974	0.001	103,000
Guatemala	21 November 1945	0.032	13,019,000
Guinea	12 December 1958	0.001	8,242,000
Guinea-Bissau	17 September 1974	0.001	1,296,000
Guyana	20 September 1966	0.001	760,000
Haiti	24 October 1945	0.002	8,374,000
Honduras	17 December 1945	0.005	7,028,000
Hungary	14 December 1955	0.244	10,087,000
Iceland	19 November 1946	0.037	296,000
India	30 October 1945	0.450	1,117,734,000
Indonesia [d]	28 September 1950	0.161	212,051,000
Iran (Islamic Republic of)	24 October 1945	0.180	70,603,000
Iraq	21 December 1945	0.015	28,810,000
Ireland	14 December 1955	0.445	4,131,000
Israel	11 May 1949	0.419	7,048,000
Italy	14 December 1955	5.079	58,607,000
Jamaica	18 September 1962	0.010	2,667,000
Japan	18 December 1956	16.624	127,757,000
Jordan	14 December 1955	0.012	5,104,000
Kazakhstan	2 March 1992	0.029	15,301,000
Kenya	16 December 1963	0.010	36,433,000
Kiribati	14 September 1999	0.001	85,000
Kuwait	14 May 1963	0.182	2,213,000
Kyrgyzstan	2 March 1992	0.001	5,192,000
Lao People's Democratic Republic	14 December 1955	0.001	5,622,000

Member state	Date of admission	Scale of assessments for 2006 (per cent)	Population (est.)
New Zealand	24 October 1945	0.256	4,140,000
Nicaragua	24 October 1945	0.002	5,145,000
Niger	20 September 1960	0.001	13,045,000
Nigeria	7 October 1960	0.048	140,004,000
Norway	27 November 1945	0.782	4,623,000
Oman	7 October 1971	0.073	2,577,000
Pakistan	30 September 1947	0.059	150,360,000
Palau	15 December 1994	0.001	20,000
Panama	13 November 1945	0.023	3,284,000
Papua New Guinea	10 October 1975	0.002	2,499,000
Paraguay	24 October 1945	0.005	5,899,000
Peru	31 October 1945	0.078	26,152,000
Philippines	24 October 1945	0.078	86,973,000
Poland	24 October 1945	0.501	38,161,000
Portugal	14 December 1955	0.527	10,549,000
Qatar	21 September 1971	0.085	744,000
Republic of Korea	17 September 1991	2.173	48,297,000
Romania	14 December 1955	0.070	21,583,000
Russian Federation [f]	24 October 1945	1.200	143,150,000
Rwanda	18 September 1962	0.001	8,129,000
Saint Kitts and Nevis	23 September 1983	0.001	46,000
Saint Lucia	18 September 1979	0.001	165,000
Saint Vincent and the Grenadines	16 September 1980	0.001	109,000
Samoa	15 December 1976	0.001	175,000
San Marino	2 March 1992	0.003	32,000
Sao Tome and Principe	16 September 1975	0.001	149,000
Saudi Arabia	24 October 1945	0.748	22,678,000
Senegal	28 September 1960	0.004	10,848,000
Senegal	28 September 1960	0.004	10,848,000
Serbia [g]	1 November 2000	0.021	7,441,000
Seychelles	21 September 1976	0.002	85,000
Sierra Leone	27 September 1961	0.001	4,963,000

Member state	Date of admission	Scale of assessments for 2006 (per cent)	Population (est.)
United States of America	24 October 1945	22.000	296,410,000
Uruguay	18 December 1945	0.027	3,241,000
Uzbekistan	2 March 1992	0.008	25,368,000
Vanuatu	15 September 1981	0.001	202,000
Venezuela	15 November 1945	0.200	27,031,000
Viet Nam	20 September 1977	0.024	80,670,000
Yemen	30 September 1947	0.007	19,495,000
Zambia	1 December 1964	0.001	11,799,000
Zimbabwe	25 August 1980	0.008	12,104,000

States which are not Members of the United Nations but which participate in certain of its activities, shall be called upon to contribute towards the expenses of the Organization on the basis of the following percentage rates:

Holy See		0.001	1,000

---

[a] On 19 September 1991, Byelorussia informed the United Nations that it had changed its name to Belarus.

[b] The Republic of Zaire informed the United Nations that, effective 17 May 1997, it had changed its name to Democratic Republic of the Congo.

[c] Egypt and Syria were original members of the United Nations from 24 October 1945. Following a plebiscite on 21 February 1958, the United Arab Republic was established by a union of Egypt and Syria and continued as a single member. On 13 October 1961, Syria, having resumed its status as an independent state, resumed its separate membership in the United Nations. On 2 September 1971, the United Arab Republic changed its name to the Arab Republic of Egypt.

[d] By letter of 20 January 1965, Indonesia announced its decision to withdraw from the United Nations "at this stage and under the present circumstances". By a telegram of 19 September 1966, it announced its decision "to resume full cooperation with the United Nations and to resume participation in its activities". On 28 September 1966, the General Assembly took note of this decision and the President invited representatives of Indonesia to take seats in the Assembly.

GROWTH IN UNITED NATIONS MEMBERSHIP, 1945-2006

Year	Number	Member States
1945	Original 51	Argentina, Australia, Belgium, Bolivia. Brazil, Belarus, Canada, Chile, China, Colombia, Costa Rica, Cuba, Czechoslovakia, Denmark, Dominican Republic, Ecuador, Egypt, El Salvador, Ethiopia, France, Greece, Guatemala, Haiti, Honduras, India, Iran, Iraq, Lebanon, Liberia, Luxembourg, Mexico, Netherlands, New Zealand, Nicaragua, Norway, Panama, Paraguay, Peru, Philippines, Poland, Russian Federation [1], Saudi Arabia, South Africa, Syrian Arab Republic, Turkey, Ukraine, United Kingdom of Great Britain and Northern Ireland, United States of America, Uruguay, Venezuela, Yugoslavia
1946	55	Afghanistan, Iceland, Sweden, Thailand
1947	57	Pakistan, Yemen [2]
1948	58	Myanmar
1949	59	Israel
1950	60	Indonesia
1955	76	Albania, Austria, Bulgaria, Cambodia, Finland, Hungary, Ireland, Italy, Jordan, Lao People's Democratic Republic, Libyan Arab Jamahiriya, Nepal, Portugal, Romania, Spain, Sri Lanka
1956	80	Japan, Morocco, Sudan, Tunisia
1957	82	Ghana, Malaysia
1958	82 [3]	Guinea
1960	99	Benin, Burkina Faso, Cameroon, Central African Republic, Chad, Congo, Côte d'Ivoire, Cyprus, Gabon, Madagascar, Mali, Niger, Nigeria, Senegal, Somalia, Togo, Democratic Republic of the Congo
1961	104 [4]	Mauritania, Mongolia, Sierra Leone, United Republic of Tanzania
1962	110	Algeria, Burundi, Jamaica, Rwanda, Trinidad and Tobago, Uganda
1963	112	Kenya, Kuwait
1964	115	Malawi, Malta, Zambia
1965	117 [5]	Gambia, Maldives, Singapore
1966	122 [6]	Barbados, Botswana, Guyana, Lesotho
1967	123	Democratic Yemen [2]
1968	126	Equatorial Guinea, Mauritius, Swaziland
1970	127	Fiji
1971	132	Bahrain, Bhutan, Oman, Qatar, United Arab Emirates

[3] The total remains the same because from 21 January 1958 Syria and Egypt continued as a single member (United Arab Republic)

[4] Syria resumed its status as an independent state.

[5] Indonesia withdrew as of 20 January 1965.

[6] Indonesia resumed its membership as of 28 September 1966.

[7] The Federal Republic of Germany and the German Democratic Republic were admitted to membership in the United Nations on 18 September 1973. Through the accession of the German Democratic Republic to the Federal Republic of Germany, effective from 3 October 1990, the two German states have united to form one sovereign state.

[8] The Socialist Federal Republic of Yugoslavia was an original member of the United Nations, the Charter having been signed on its behalf on 26 June 1945 and ratified 19 October 1945, until its dissolution following the establishment and subsequent admission as new members of Bosnia and Herzegovina, the Republic of Croatia, the Republic of Slovenia, The former Yugoslav Republic of Macedonia, and the Federal Republic of Yugoslavia. The Republic of Bosnia and Herzegovina, the Republic of Croatia and the Republic of Slovenia were admitted as members of the United Nations on 22 May 1992. On 8 April 1993, the General Assembly decided to admit as a member of the United Nations the state being provisionally referred to for all purposes within the United Nations as "The former Yugoslav Republic of Macedonia" pending settlement of the difference that had arisen over its name. The Federal Republic of Yugoslavia was admitted as a member of the United Nations on 1 November 2000. On 12 February 2003, it informed the United Nations that it had changed its name to Serbia and Montenegro, effective 4 February 2003. In a letter dated 3 June 2006, the President of the Republic of Serbia informed the Secretary-General that the membership of Serbia and Montenegro was being continued by the Republic of Serbia following Montenegro's declaration of independence from Serbia on 3 June 2006. On 28 June 2006 Montenegro was accepted as a United Nations member state by the General Assembly.

[9] Czechoslovakia was an original member of the United Nations from 24 October 1945. In a letter dated 10 December 1992, its Permanent Representative informed the Secretary-General that the Czech and Slovak Federal Republic would cease to exist on 31 December 1992 and that the Czech Republic and the Slovak Republic, as successor states, would apply for membership in the United Nations. Following the receipt of such applications, the Security Council, on 8 January 1993, recommended to the General Assembly that the Czech Republic and the Slovak Republic be admitted to United Nations membership. They were thus admitted on 19 January 1993 as member states.

UNIPOM
United Nations India-Pakistan Observation Mission
September 1965–March 1966

UNEF II
Second United Nations Emergency Force (Suez Canal and later Sinai Peninsula)
October 1973–July 1979

*UNDOF
United Nations Disengagement Observer Force (Syrian Golan Heights)
May 1974–

*UNIFIL
United Nations Interim Force in Lebanon
March 1978–

UNGOMAP
United Nations Good Offices Mission in Afghanistan and Pakistan
May 1988–March 1990

UNIIMOG
United Nations Iran-Iraq Military Observer Group
August 1988–February 1991

UNAVEM I
United Nations Angola Verification Mission I
December 1988–June 1991

UNTAG
United Nations Transition Assistance Group (Namibia and Angola)
April 1989–March 1990

ONUCA
United Nations Observer Group in Central America
November 1989–January 1992

*MINURSO
United Nations Mission for the Referendum in Western Sahara
April 1991–

*UNOMIG
United Nations Observer Mission in Georgia
August 1993–

UNOMIL
United Nations Observer Mission in Liberia
September 1993–September 1997

UNMIH
United Nations Mission in Haiti
September 1993–June 1996

UNAMIR
United Nations Assistance Mission for Rwanda
October 1993–March 1996

UNASOG
United Nations Aouzou Strip Observer Group (Chad/Lybia)
May–June 1994

UNMOT
United Nations Mission of Observers in Tajikistan
December 1994–May 2000

UNAVEM III
United Nations Angola Verification Mission III
February 1995–June 1997

UNCRO
United Nations Confidence Restoration Operation in Croatia
March 1995–January 1996

UNPREDEP
United Nations Preventive Deployment Force (former Yugoslav Republic of Macedonia)
March 1995–February 1999

UNMIBH
United Nations Mission in Bosnia and Herzegovina
December 1995–December 2002

*UNMIK
United Nations Interim Administration Mission in Kosovo
June 1999–

*UNAMSIL
United Nations Mission in Sierra Leone
October 1999–December 2005

UNTAET
United Nations Transitional Administration in East Timor
October 1999–May 2002

*MONUC
United Nations Observer Mission in the Democratic Republic of the Congo
December 1999–

*UNMEE
United Nations Mission in Ethiopia and Eritrea
July 2000–

UNMISET
United Nations Mission of Support in East Timor
May 2002–May 2005

*UNMIL
United Nations Mission in Liberia
September 2003–

*UNOCI
United Nations Operation in Côte d'Ivoire
April 2004–

*MINUSTAH
United Nations Stabilization Mission in Haiti
April 2004–

*UNMIS
United Nations Mission in the Sudan
March 2005–

DECOLONIZATION

Trust and Non-Self-Governing Territories that have achieved independence since the adoption of the 1960 Declaration*

State or entity	Date of admission to the United Nations
Africa	
Algeria	8 October 1962
Angola	1 December 1976
Botswana	17 October 1966
Burundi	18 September 1962
Cape Verde	16 September 1975
Comoros	12 November 1975
Djibouti	20 September 1977
Equatorial Guinea	12 November 1968
Gambia	21 September 1965
Guinea-Bissau	17 September 1974
Kenya	16 December 1963
Lesotho	17 October 1966
Malawi	1 December 1964
Mauritius	24 April 1968
Mozambique	16 September 1975
Namibia	23 April 1990
Rwanda	18 September 1962
Sao Tome and Principe	26 September 1975
Seychelles	21 September 1976
Sierra Leone	27 September 1961
Swaziland	24 September 1968
Uganda	25 October 1962
United Republic of Tanzania[1]	14 December 1961
Zambia	1 December 1964
Zimbabwe	18 April 1980
Asia	
Brunei Darussalam	21 September 1984
Democratic Yemen	14 December 1967
Oman	7 October 1971
Singapore	21 September 1965

* Declaration on the Granting of Independence to Colonial Countries and Peoples, adopted by the General Assembly on 14 December 1960.

DECOLONIZATION

Dependent Territories that have become integrated or associated
with independent states since the adoption of the 1960 Declaration*

Territory	Remarks
Cameroons under British administration	The northern part of the Trust Territory joined the Federation of Nigeria on 1 June 1961 and the southern part joined the Republic of Cameroon on 1 October 1961
Cook Islands	Fully self-governing in free association with New Zealand since August 1965
Ifni	Returned to Morocco in June 1969
Niue	Fully self-governing in free association with New Zealand since August 1974
North Borneo	North Borneo and Sarawak joined the Federation of Malaya in 1963 to form the Federation of Malaysia
São Joao Batista de Ajuda	Nationally united with Dahomey (now Benin) in August 1961
Sarawak	Sarawak and North Borneo joined the Federation of Malaya in 1963 to form the Federation of Malaysia
West New Guinea (West Irian)	United with Indonesia in 1963
Cocos (Keeling) Islands	Integrated with Australia in 1984

* Declaration on the Granting of Independence to Colonial Countries and Peoples, adopted by the General Assembly on 14 December 1960.

BUDGET OF THE UNITED NATIONS

For the 2006-2007 biennium, the appropriation for the regular budget of the United Nations (i.e. excluding the bulk of offices and programmes, as well as the specialized agencies and other associated bodies), as initially approved in 2005, totalled $3,829,916,200, divided into 14 main categories of expenditures, as follows (in United States dollars):

1.	Overall policy-making, direction and coordination	661,735,300
2.	Political affairs	571,471,500
3.	International justice and law	77,246,300
4.	International cooperation for development	372,156,400
5.	Regional cooperation for development	425,715,500
6.	Human rights and humanitarian affairs	209,058,900
7.	Public information	177,302,500
8.	Common support services	515,239,300
9.	Internal oversight	31,330,100
10.	Jointly financed activities and special expenses	104,400,800
11.	Capital expenditures	74,841,300
12.	Safety and security	190,954,100
13.	Development account	13,954,100
14.	Staff assessment*	405,332, 800

The main source of funds for the regular budget is the contributions of member states, who are assessed on a scale specified by the Assembly on the recommendation of the 18-member Committee on Contributions. The fundamental criterion on which the scale of assessments is based is the real capacity of member states to pay. The Assembly has fixed a maximum of 22 per cent of the budget for any one contributor and a minimum of 0.001 per cent. (For scale of assessments of member states, see pages 000-000.)

Initial income estimates for the biennium 2006-2007, other than assessments on member states, totalled $434,860,100.

1.	Income from staff assessment*	409,239,700
2.	General income	20,867,000
3.	Services to the public	4,753,400

---

*To equalize the net pay of all United Nations staff members, whatever their national tax obligations, the Organization deducts from their salaries a sum of money designated as "staff assessment". The rate of withholding is roughly equivalent to the amount paid by United States citizens for federal, state and local taxes calculated at the standard rate. The money collected by the United Nations from the staff assessment is then credited towards the United Nations membership "dues" of the staff member's home country.

UNITED NATIONS SPECIAL OBSERVANCES

INTERNATIONAL DECADES AND YEARS

2001-2010	Decade to Roll Back Malaria in Developing Countries, Particularly in Africa
2001-2010	Second International Decade for the Eradication of Colonialism
2001-2010	International Decade for a Culture of Peace and Non-violence for the Children of the World
2003-2012	United Nations Literacy Decade: Education for All
2005-2014	Second International Decade of the World's Indigenous People
2005-2014	United Nations Decade of Education for Sustainable Development
2005-2015	International Decade for Action, "Water for Life" (from 22 March 2005)
2008	International Year of the Potato
2008	International Year of Planet Earth
2008	International Year of Sanitation
2009	International Year of Reconciliation
2009	International Year of Natural Fibres
2010	International Year of Biodiversity
2011	International Year of Forests

ANNUAL DAYS AND WEEKS

27 January	International Day of Commemoration in memory of the victims of the Holocaust
21 February	International Mother Language Day
8 March	United Nations Day for Women's Rights and International Peace
21 March	International Day for the Elimination of Racial Discrimination
Beginning 21 March	Week of Solidarity with the Peoples Struggling against Racism and Racial Discrimination
22 March	World Day for Water
23 March	World Meteorological Day
4 April	International Day for Mine Awareness and Assistance in Mine Action
7 April	World Health Day
23 April	World Book and Copyright Day
3 May	World Press Freedom Day
8 and 9 May	Time of Remembrance and Reconciliation for those who lost Their Lives during the Second World War
15 May	International Day of Families
17 May	World Telecommunication Day

ANNUAL DAYS AND WEEKS

24 October	World Development Information Day
24-30 October	Disarmament Week
6 November	International Day for Preventing the Exploitation of the Environment in War and Armed Conflict
14 November	World Diabetes Day
16 November	International Day for Tolerance
20 November	Africa Industrialization Day
20 November	Universal Children's Day
21 November	World Television Day
Third Sunday of November	World Day of Remembrance for Road Traffic Victims
25 November	International Day for the Elimination of Violence against Women
29 November	International Day of Solidarity with the Palestinian People
1 December	World AIDS Day
2 December	International Day for the Abolition of Slavery
3 December	International Day of Disabled Persons
5 December	International Volunteer Day for Economic and Social Development
7 December	International Civil Aviation Day
10 December	Human Rights Day
11 December	International Mountain Day
18 December	International Migrants Day
19 December	United Nations Day for South-South Cooperation
20 December	International Human Solidarity Day

UNITED NATIONS INFORMATION CENTRES, SERVICES AND OFFICES

AFRICA

Accra

United Nations Information Centre, Gamal Abdel Nasser/Liberia Roads
(P.O. Box 2339), Accra, Ghana
Telephone: (233 21) 665 511 • Fax: (233 21) 665 578
E-mail: info@unic-ghana.org
Services to: Ghana, Sierra Leone

Algiers

United Nations Information Centre, 9A, rue Emile Payen, Hydra (Boite postale 444)
Algiers, Algeria
Telephone: (213 21) 48 08 71 • Fax: (213 21) 69 23 15
E-mail: unic.dz@undp.org (Internet: *www.unic.org.dz*)
Services to: Algeria

Antananarivo

United Nations Information Centre, 22 rue Rainitovo, (Boîte postale 1348)
Antananarivo, Madagascar
Telephone: (261 20) 22 241 15/22 375 06 • Fax: (261 20) 22 375 06
E-mail: unic.ant@dts.mg (Internet:*htpp://antananarivo.unic.org*)
Services to: Madagascar

Brazzaville

United Nations Information Centre, Avenue Foch, Case Ortf 15 (P.O. Box 13210 or 1018)
Brazzaville, Congo
Telephone: (242) 81 44 47/81 46 81/61 20 68 • Fax: (242) 81 27 44
E-mail: unic.cg@undp.org (Internet : *http://brazzaville.unic.org*)
Services to: Congo

Bujumbura

United Nations Information Centre, 117, Avenue de la Révolution (P.O. Box 2160)
Bujumbura, Burundi
Telephone: (257) 22 50 18/24 6743 • Fax: (257) 241 798
E-mail:unicbuj@undp.org (Internet: *http://bujumbura.unic.org*)
Services to: Burundi

Lomé

United Nations Information Centre, 107 Boulevard du 13 Janvier (P.O. Box 911)
Lomé, Togo
Telephone: (228) 221 2306 • Fax: (228) 221 2306 (same as telephone no.)
E-mail: cinutogo@cafe.tg
Services to: Togo, Benin

Lusaka

United Nations Information Centre, Revenue House, Ground floor, Cairo Road,
(P.O. Box 32905), Lusaka 10101, Republic of Zambia
Telephone: (260 1) 228 478 • Fax: (260 1) 222 958
E-mail: unic@zamtel.zm   (Internet: *http://lusaka.unic.org*)
Services to: Zambia, Botswana, Malawi, Swaziland

Maseru

United Nations Information Centre, UN Road, UN House (P.O. Box 301),
Maseru 100, Lesotho
Telephone: (266-22) 312 496/326 897 • Fax: (266-22) 310 042 (UNDP)
E-mail: mimosa.ramakatane@undp.org (Internet: *http://maseru.unic.org*)
Services to: Lesotho

Nairobi

United Nations Information Centre, United Nations Office, Gigiri (P.O. Box 30552),
Nairobi, Kenya
Telephone: (254 20) 762 3798/4560 • Fax: (254 20) 762 4349
E-mail: Nairobi.UNIC@unon.org (Internet: *www.unicnairobi.org*)
Services to: Kenya, Seychelles, Uganda

Ouagadougou

United Nations Information Centre, 14 Avenue de la Grande Chancellerie, Secteur No. 4
(P.O. Box 135), Ouagadougou 01, Burkina Faso
Telephone: (226) 50 30 60 76/50 33 65 03 • Fax: (226) 50 31 13 22
E-mail: cinu.oui@fasonet.bf (Internet: *http://ouagadougou.unic.org*)
Services to: Burkina Faso, Chad, Mali, Niger

Pretoria

United Nations Information Centre, Metro Park Building, 351 Schoeman Street
(P.O. Box 12677), Pretoria, South Africa
Telephone: (27 12) 354 8506 • Fax: (27 12) 354 8501
E-mail: unic@un.org.za (Internet: *http://pretoria.unic.org*)
Services to: South Africa

THE AMERICAS

Asunción

United Nations Information Centre, Avda. Mariscal López esq. Guillermo Saraví, Edificio Naciones Unidas,
(Casilla de Correo 1107), Asunción, Paraguay
Telephone: (595 21) 614 443 • Fax: (595 21) 611 988
E-mail: unic.py@undp.org
Services to: Paraguay

Bogotá

United Nations Information Centre, Calle 100 No. 8A-55, Piso 10 (P.O. Box 058964), Bogotá 2, Colombia
Telephone: (57 1) 257 6044 • Fax: (57 1) 257 7936
E-mail: cinucol@colomsat.net.co (Internet: *www.onucolombia.org*)
Services to: Colombia, Ecuador, Venezuela

Buenos Aires

United Nations Information Centre, Junín 1940, 1er piso, 1113 Buenos Aires, Argentina
Telephone: (54 11) 4803 7671/7672/0738 • Fax: (54 11) 4804 7545
E-mail: buenosaires@unic.org.ar (Internet: *www.unic.org.ar*)
Services to: Argentina, Uruguay

La Paz

United Nations Information Centre, Calle 14 esq. S. Bustamante, Edificio Metrobol 11, Calacoto,
(P.O. Box 9072), La Paz, Bolivia
Telephone: (591 2) 279 5544 Ext.511/2 • Fax: (591 2) 279 5820
E-mail: unicbol@un.org.bo (Internet: *www.nu.org.bo/cinu*)
Services to: Bolivia

Lima

United Nations Information Centre, Lord Cochrane 130, San Isidro (L-27)
(P.O. Box 14 0199), Lima, Perú
Telephone: (511) 441 8745/422 4149/422 0879 • Fax: (511) 441 8735
E-mail: informes@uniclima.org.pe (Internet: *www.uniclima.org.pe*)
Services to: Peru

Mexico City

United Nations Information Centre, Presidente Masaryk 29-2do. piso, Col. Chapultepec Morales, 11570 México, D.F.
Telephone: (52-55) 52 63 97 18 • Fax: (52-55) 52 03 86 38
E-mail: infounic@un.org.mx (Internet: *www.nacionesunidas.org.mx*)
Services to: Mexico, Cuba, Dominican Republic

ASIA AND THE PACIFIC
Bangkok
United Nations Information Service, United Nations Economic and Social Commission for Asia and the Pacific (ESCAP), United Nations Building, Rajdamnern Nok, Avenue, Bangkok 10200, Thailand
Telephone: 66 (0) 2 288 1866 • Fax: 66 (0) 2 288 1052
E-mail: unisbkk.unescap@un.org (Internet: *www.unescap.org/unis*)
Services to: Thailand, Cambodia, Lao People's Democratic Republic, Malaysia, Singapore, Socialist Republic of Vietnam, ESCAP

Beirut
United Nations Information Centre, United Nations Economic and Social Commission for Western Asia (ESCWA), Riad El Solh Square (P.O. Box 11-8575-4656), Beirut, Lebanon
Telephone: (961 1) 981 301/311/401 ext. 1533/34/35 • Fax: (961 1) 97 04 24 (UNIC)
E-mail: unic.beirut@un.org (Internet: *www.escwa.org.lb*)
Services to: Lebanon, Jordan, Kuwait, Syrian Arab Republic, ESCWA

Canberra
United Nations Information Centre, 7 National Circuit, Level 1, Barton, Canberra ACT 2600, (P.O. Box 5366 Kingston, ACT 2604) Australia
Telephone: (61 2) 627 38200 • Fax: (61 2) 627 38206
E-mail: unic@un.org.au (Internet: *www.un.org.au*)
Services to: Australia, Fiji, Kiribati, Nauru, New Zealand, Tonga, Tuvalu, Vanuatu, Samoa

Colombo
United Nations Information Centre, 202-204 Bauddhaloka Mawatha (P.O. Box 1505), Colombo 7, Sri Lanka
Telephone: (94 112) 580 691 ext. 207 or 274 • Fax: (94 112) 501 396
E-mail: mohan.samaranayakc@undp.org
Services to: Sri Lanka

Dhaka
United Nations Information Centre, IDB Bhaban (8th floor) Sher-e-Bangla Nagar, (P.O. Box 3658, Dhaka 1000), Dhaka 1207 Bangladesh
Telephone: (880 2) 8117 868 • Fax: (880 2) 8112 343
E-mail: unic.dhaka@undp.org (Internet: *www.unicdhaka.org*)
Services to: Bangladesh

Islamabad
United Nations Information Centre, House No. 26, Street 88, G-6/3 (P.O. Box 1107), Islamabad, Pakistan
Telephone: (92 51) 2270 610 • Fax: (92 51) 2271 856
E-mail: unic@dsl.net.pk (Internet: *www.un.org.pk/unic/unic.htm*)
Services to: Pakistan

Tehran

United Nations Information Centre, No. 39, Shahrzad Blvd., Darrous
(P.O. Box 15875-4557, Tehran), Islamic Republic of Iran
Telephone: (98 21) 2-287 3837 • Fax: (98 21) 2-287 3395
E-mail: unic@unic.un.org.ir (Internet: *www.unic-ir.org*)
Services to: Iran

Tokyo

United Nations Information Centre, UNU Building, 8th Floor, 53-70, Jingumae 5-chome,
Shibuya-ku, Tokyo 150-0001, Japan
Telephone: (81 3) 5467 4451 • Fax: (81 3) 5467 4455
E-mail: unic@untokyo.jp (Internet: *www.unic.or.jp*)
Services to: Japan

Yangon

United Nations Information Centre, 6 Natmauk Road, Tamwe Township (P.O. Box 230)
Yangon, Myanmar
Telephone: (95 1) 542-910 • Fax: (95 1) 542 634
E-mail: unic.myanmar@undp.org
Services to: Myanmar

EUROPE

Ankara

United Nations Information Centre, 2 Cadde No. 11, (P.K. 407), 06610 Cankaya,
Ankara, Turkey
Telephone: (90 312) 454 1052 • Fax: (90 312) 496 1499
E-mail: unic@un.org.tr (Internet: *www.un.org.tr/unic.html*)
Services to: Turkey

Brussels

United Nations Information Regional Centre, Résidence Palace, rue de la Loi/Wetstraat
155, Quartier Rubens, Block C2, 1040 Brussels, Belgium
Telephone: (32 2) 788 8484 • Fax: (32 2) 788 8485
E-mail: info@unric.org (Internet: *www.unric.org*)
Services to: Belgium, Cyprus, Denmark, Finland, France, Germany, Greece, Holy See,
Iceland, Ireland, Italy, Luxembourg, Malta, Monaco, Norway, Portugal, San Marino, Spain,
Sweden, the Netherlands, United Kingdom, European Union

OFFICES IN THE COMMONWEALTH OF
INDEPENDENT STATES AND ERITREA

Almaty

United Nations Office, 67 Tole Bi, Almaty 480091, Kazakhstan
Telephone: (7 3272) 582 643/695-327 • Fax: (7 3272) 582 645
E-mail: registry.kz@undp.org (Internet: *htpp://Kazakhstan.unic.org*)
Services to: Kazakhstan

Asmara

United Nations Office, Andinet Street, Zone 4 Admin. 07, Airport Road, (near Expo)
Asmara, Eritrea
Telephone: (291 1) 15 11 66 • Fax: (291 1) 15 10 81
E-mail: mohammed.salih@undp.org (Internet: *http://asmara.unic.org*)
Services to: Eritrea

Baku

United Nations Office, 3 UN 50th Anniversary Street, Baku 1001, Azerbaijan
Telephone: (99412) 498 98 88 • Fax: (99412) 498 32 35
E-mail: dpi@un-az.org (Internet: *www.un-az.org/dpi*)
Services to: Azerbaijan

Kiev

United Nations Office, 1 Klovskiy Uzviz, Kiev 01021, Ukraine
Telephone: (380 44) 253 93 63 • Fax: (380 44) 253 26 07
E-mail: registry@un.kiev.ua (Internet: *www.un.org.ua*)
Services to: Ukraine

Minsk

United Nations Office, 17 Kirov Street, 6th Floor 220050 Minsk, Belarus
Telephone: (375 17) 227 38 17 • Fax: (375 17) 226 03 40
E-mail: dpi.staff.by@undp.org (Internet: *www.un.by*)
Services to: Belarus

Tashkent

United Nations Office, 4 Taras Shevchenko St., Tashkent 700029, Uzbekistan
Telephone: (998 71) 133 0977 • Fax: (998 71) 120 3450
E-mail: infocentre.uz@undp.org (Internet: *htpp://unagencies.undp.uz/unic*)
Services to: Uzbekistan

FOR FURTHER READING

This selection of United Nations publications and products can be obtained from the Organization, some at no charge and other as sales items. The letters in parentheses at the end of each entry refer to where the publications can be obtained (see Where to Order, page 354).

Periodicals

Africa Recovery. Department of Public Information. E/F. Annual subscription: $20.00 (a)
Quarterly magazine covering issues of economic and social reform in Africa and international cooperation for development.

Development Update. Department of Public Information. Free
Bi-monthly newsletter with updates on the development activities of the UN system.

UN Chronicle. Department of Public Information. E/F/S/A/C/R. Annual subscription $25.00 (a)
Quarterly magazine providing coverage of the work of the UN and its agencies.

United Nations Development Business. Department of Public Information. Annual subscription $590.00 (b)
Bi-monthly newsletter providing information on opportunities to supply goods and services for projects financed by the United Nations, governments and the world's leading development banks. Also available as an online subscription.

General

60 Ways the United Nations Makes a Difference. Department of Public Information. Book: 48 pp. Sales No. E.05.I.91. ISBN: 9789211009866. E/F. $10.00; DVD: Sales No. E.05.I.100. ISBN: 9789211011302. E. $10.00 (a)
This DVD/Book presents, through the voices of young people from around the world, a sampling of what the United Nations and its component bodies have accomplished since 1945, when the world organization was founded.

Charter of the United Nations. Department of Public Information. DPI/511. E/F/S/A/ C/R. $3.50 (a)

Delivering as One: Report of the Secretary-General's High-level Panel on UN System-wide Coherence in the Areas of Development, Humanitarian Assistance and the Environment. Department of Public Information. 2007. 84 pp. Sales No. E.07.I.8. ISBN: 9789211011463. E. $18.00 (a)

Universal Declaration of Human Rights: 60th Anniversary Special Edition 1948 – 2008. Department of Public Information. DPI/876/Rev.4. E/F/S/A/C/R. $1.50 (a)

Human Development Report 2007/2008. United Nations Development Programme. 400 pp. Sales No. E.07.III.B.1. ISBN: 978023054709. E/F/S/A/C/R. $29.95 (a)
A comprehensive guide to global human development: it contains thought-provoking analyses of major issues, updated Human Development Indicators that compare the relative levels of human development of over 175 countries, and agendas to help transform development priorities.

The State of the World's Children 2008. United Nations Children's Fund. Sales No. E.08. XX.1. ISBN: 9789280641912. E/F/S. $25.00   Free summary available from UNICEF (a)
Draws international attention to the challenges facing children and presses for action to promote their well-being.

The State of the World Population 2007. United Nations Population Fund. 104 pp. Sales No. E.07.III.H.1. ISBN: 9780897148078. E/F/S/A/R. $17.50 (a)
Annual report on population issues and their impact on world development.

Demographic Yearbook 2004. Department of Economic and Social Affairs. 868 pp. Sales No. B.07.XIII.1.H. ISBN: 9789210510981. E/F. $120.00 (a)
A series which collects, compiles and disseminates official demographic statistics on a wide range of topics.

Energy Statistics Yearbook 2005. Department of Economic and Social Affairs. Sales No. B.08.XVII.4.H. ISBN: 9789210612296. E/F. $120.00 (a)
An internationally comparable series of commercial energy statistics summarizing world energy trends and presents annual data for 215 countries.

Industrial Commodity Statistics Yearbook 2004. Department of Economic and Social Affairs. 328 pp. Sales No. B.06.XVII.14.H. ISBN: 9789210612265. E/F. $160.00 (a)
This annual compilation provides statistics on the production, in physical quantities, of about 530 industrial commodities by country, geographical region, economic grouping and for the world.

International Trade Statistics Yearbook 2005. Department of Economic and Social Affairs. Sales No. B.07.XVII.7.H. ISBN: 9789210612272. E/F. $160.00 (a)
Provides the basic information for individual countries external trade performances in terms of value as well as in volume and price, the importance of trading partners and the significance of individual commodities imported and exported.

Report on the World Social Situation 2007. Department of Economic and Social Affairs. 192 pp. Sales No. E.07.IV.9. ISBN: 9789211302622. E. $20.00 (a)
The 2007 issue of the Report on the World Social Situation focuses on the key role of productive employment and decent work in reducing poverty and promoting social development.

United Nations Disarmament Yearbook 2006. Department for Disarmament Affairs. 556 pp. Sales No. E.07.IX.1. ISBN: 9789211422573. E/F/S/A/R/C. $65.00 (a)
Annual publication reviewing the main developments and negotiations during the year in all areas of disarmament.

War in Our Time: Reflections on Iraq, Terrorism and Weapons of Mass Destruction. United Nations University Press. 2007. 216 pp. Sales No. E.07.III.A.10. ISBN: 9789280811452. E. $20.00 (a)
The book's three topics — the Iraq war, the war on terror, and weapons of mass destruction — are among the most critical issues of our times.

Economic and Social

The World's Women 2005: Progress in Statistics. Department of Economic and Social Affairs. 184 pp. Sales No. E. 05.XVII.7. ISBN: 9789211614824. E/F/S/A/C/R. $25.00 (a)
A unique compilation of the latest data documenting progress for women worldwide in six areas: health, human rights and political decision-making, and families.

Indigenous Women and the United Nations System: Good Practices and Lessons Learned. Department of Economic and Social Affairs. 2007. 126 pp. Sales No. E.06.IV.9. ISBN: 9789211302547. E/F/S. $23.00 (a)
The publication contains cases submitted by the different UN agencies about their work with indigenous women in Africa, Asia and Latin America.

Progress of the World's Women 2005: Women, Work and Poverty. United Nations Development Fund for Women. 112 pp. Sales No. E.05.III.F.1. ISBN: 9781932827262. E/F/S. $17.95 (a)
This report marks the fifth anniversary of the UN Millennium Declaration and the tenth anniversary of the Beijing Platform for Action. It argues that unless governments and policymakers pay more attention to employment, and its links to poverty, the campaign to make poverty history will not succeed.

The Millennium Development Goals Report 2007. Department of Economic and Social Affairs. 36 pp. Sales No.E.07.I.15. ISBN: 9789211011531. E/F. $10.00 (a)
The report shows what can be achieved and how much still needs to be done.

The International Development Agenda and the Climate Change Challenge. Department of Economic and Social Affairs. 2007. 32 pp. Sales No. E.07.II.A.7.
ISBN: 9789211045710. E. $10.00 (a)
This publication examines the severity of the problem and its implications for the international development agenda.

Participatory Dialogue: Towards a Stable, Safe and Just Society for All. Department of Economic and Social Affairs. 2007. 188 pp. Sales No: E.07.IV.3. ISBN: 9789211302592. E/F/S. $39.00 (a)
The present publication offers an overview of social integration and related concepts, explores the role and principles of participatory dialogue in creating more socially cohesive societies, and provides practical examples of dialogue use and dialogic tools.

Women, Girls, Boys and Men: Different Needs - Equal Opportunities. United Nations Office for the Coordination of Humanitarian Affairs. 2007. 122 pp. Sales No. E.08. III.M.1. ISBN: 9789211320268. E. $25.00 (a)

The Handbook aims to help promote the ultimate goal of protecting and promoting the human rights of women, girls, boys and men in humanitarian action and advancing the goal of gender equality.

WHERE TO ORDER

(a) For North America, Latin America and the Caribbean and Asia and the Pacific: United Nations Publications, Room DC2-853, 2 UN Plaza, New York, NY 10017, USA. Tel.: (212) 963-8302. Toll Free: (800) 253-9646 (North America only). Fax: (212) 963-3489. E-mail: publications@un.org. Internet: *unp.un.org*

For Europe, Africa and the Middle East: United Nations Publications, UN Bookshop, Door 40, Palais des Nations, 1211 Geneva 10, Switzerland. Tel.: (41-22) 917-4872, Fax: (41-22) 917-0610, E-mail: unpubli@unog.ch. Internet: *unp.un.org*

(b) For subscriptions to Development Business:

UN Development Business
Subscription Department
PO Box 5850/ Grand Central Station
New York, NY 10163-5850 USA.

Tel.: (212) 963-1516
Fax: (212) 963-1381
E-mail: dbsubscribe@un.org
Internet: *www.devbusiness.com*

(c) World Health Organization (WHO):
Distribution and Sales
20 Avenue Appia, CH 1211 Geneva 27, Switzerland

Tel.: (41-22) 791-2476
Fax: (41-22) 791-4857
E-mail: publications@who.ch.

In the USA:

WHO Publications, 49 Sheridan Ave., Albany, NY 12210
Tel.: (518) 436-9686
E-mail: QCORP@compuserve.com

INDEX